BEYOND BELIEF

Journey To A Miracle

D1510954

Jeff Scislow

Beyond Belief—Journey to a Miracle

Copyright 2008 Jeff Scislow

www.JourneyToAMiracle.com
Jeff@JourneyToAMiracle.com

Published by Lifebushido and Best Agent Business
www.lifebushido.com – www.bestagentbusiness.com

Printed in the United States of America.

3rd Edition – June 2008

ISBN 978-0-9788854-6-5

Praise for
Beyond Belief—Journey to a Miracle

"I remember visiting Jeff in the hospital. I went to offer him some company, comfort and encouragement. Instead, I was the one who left encouraged by him! Jeff's optimism was contagious, his faith never wavered—the outcome was a miraculous healing."

David Linger
Exec. VP, Regional Director, RE/MAX North Central, Inc.
Bloomington, MN

"I have followed Jeff's business success for years. Year after year he performs at the top of his game. When faced with a life-threatening disease, he rose to the occasion and never gave up. His example of determination, perseverance and unwavering faith in God is one we can all gain strength from."

Gary Keller
Founder & Chairman, Keller Williams Realty International
Austin, TX

"With such a powerful and compelling story set forth in this book, the greatest tragedy would be to read it and decide 'it could not happen to me' or someone you love. Jeff Scislow is a man who dares to believe in God's timeless truths and his life shines as a beacon. Take his story as proof that God can and will prove Himself strong to those who believe."

Jane Park Smith
Ms. America 2008
Los Angeles, CA

"Do miracles happen? Does God answer prayers? Can faith heal? My spiritual upbringing engrained a 'Yes' to all three questions. However, when faced with a life threatening illness, I witnessed Jeff Scislow, by what seemed like an iron will of faith, receive a personal 'Yes' to each of those questions."

"I'd witnessed determination; focus, persistence, inquisitiveness and a charming personality serve him well in his business and then admired his ability to apply those same qualities in his battle for life. His greatest partner, faith in the Almighty, coupled with those qualities that make Jeff Scislow what he is... allows us to enjoy him and his powerful spirit today."

Howard Brinton
Founder and CEO, STAR POWER Systems
Boulder, CO

"Beyond Belief—Journey to a Miracle is one of those books that gives a pure injection of love, hope and faith. I truly believe that as some read this book, miracles of healing will take place. One thing for sure, all who read it will come away refreshed and in awe of the goodness of God."

Patricia King
Extreme Prophetic
Phoenix, AZ

"This book is a 'profile in courage'. I was with Jeff when he received the diagnosis and can say without reservation that without his bold reaction, he would not be alive today. Many of my friends bailed on Jeff when he took this radical direction, but I stuck with him, even though it stretched my faith to places it had not been before. I have used his story countless times to encourage others to choose life in the face of devastating diagnoses."

Dave Housholder
Pastor RobinwoodChurch.com   (formerly of Hosanna, Lakeville, MN)
Huntington Beach, CA

"While serving in the Marine Corps in the latter 1970's, Jeff consistently performed as one of the most outstanding Marines under my supervision. His determination and 'fight' that he displayed at that time is evident throughout this book as he overcame obstacles, most importantly, the fight for his life."

Sergeant Major John M. Roberson
USMC, Retired
Kalispell, MT

"I've personally known Jeff for many years. His drive and determination not only set him apart as a person, but have made him one of the most successful sales associates within the worldwide RE/MAX organization. After receiving a medical 'death sentence,' Jeff rose to the occasion and met the challenge head on with a unique sense of optimism. As one of thousands who witnessed the events unfold during Jeff's period of illness, I can say without hesitation that his strong faith, fighting attitude and expectation of a miracle are the reasons he is alive today."

"'BEYOND BELIEF—Journey to a Miracle' explores the depths of Jeff's experience, the choices he made and the miracle he received. Prepare yourself for victory, as you allow this book to inspire and impact your life."

Margaret Kelly
CEO, RE/MAX International
Denver, CO

"I believe the Lord initially led Jeff to the medical clinic where I practice and entrusted me to care for His servant. Despite the life threatening diagnosis and 'medicine's' inability to find a cure, Jeff was steadfast in his belief that the Lord would see him through. His faith in the Lord would be the 'shining star' leading him through his darkest hour. His is a story to inspire us all!"

Scott Podratz, PA-C
Family Practice/Urgent Care Medicine
Eagan, Minnesota

"When I arrived at the intensive care unit of the hospital I was warned to wash my hands and be careful around Jeff, as he could die from common germs. While with Jeff, the doctor came in with the test results. The doctor hesitated with the weight of the news he was about to deliver. In short the doctor told Jeff, 'You're the man who got hit by lightning,' – as there was no reason 'why Jeff', but the fact was 'Jeff' received the deadly diagnosis."

"What amazed me was Jeff's response! After being told he would die from the disease, Jeff somehow became excited by the details of the bad news as he sat up in bed, as weak as he was, got a sparkle in his eye and said, 'Wow, won't this make a great testimony when God heals me!'"

"Jeff's unnatural response began this amazing journey of faith. Others would be overwhelmed by the report. Jeff was fascinated by every detail and became excited by the news. He believed and expected that the hand of God would perform a miracle in his life and began right then telling everyone about it!"

"As a minister that has had miracles in and around my life, I am deeply touched by the miraculous healing that Jeff is now testifying to. This is not just a book on a miracle happening to Jeff, but a book that will open the door to a miracle happening in your life and in the life of those that you love!"

Doug Stanton
Doug Stanton Ministries International
Minneapolis, MN

Table of Contents

Introduction

About the Author

I've often wondered what it would be like to write a book—to tell the story of some interesting event that I have had the good pleasure of experiencing. I often felt that I would write someday, but which part of my life would draw enough interest to make such a book worth writing? What kind of a story would captivate and inspire others?

Many have suggested that I tell the story about how I met and married my wife: how we met as pen pals from opposite sides of the globe and wrote letters for seven years, how through persistence I overcame all odds of us ever being together and how we've now been married for over 20 years with four wonderful children.

Others believed a book on determination and perseverance would inspire others. Such a book could, in part, describe the time when at the age of 14 I watched a story of a young girl my age (Nancy) who had been swimming at a public beach in a suburb of St. Paul, Minnesota, across town from where I lived in Bloomington. A small aircraft had lost power and crashed into the water where many people were swimming. Nancy nearly lost her life. Although her life was spared, her legs were not; they required amputation. The medical bills were astronomical. I recall feeling moved to do something to help, but what could I do? I was just a kid.

About this same time, there was news about a group of softball players that were attempting to break the state record for the most consecutive innings played in a single softball game. The record was 125 innings. Then I had an idea! If I could inspire my buddies to play in *the most exciting softball game ever* and get them to encourage their parents, relatives and neighborhood adults to pledge money per inning played, then we could not only attempt to break the state record, but also raise money for Nancy!

The idea became reality. In 1971, on the longest Saturday of the year, we played our hearts out from 5:40 a.m. to 9:25 p.m.! Not only did we set the state record with 175 innings in a single softball game, we also raised just over $250 for Nancy. (That was not a bad donation back then.)

Such a book on determination and perseverance could go on by describing how, in the following year, we learned of a fellow high school student who needed a kidney transplant. The medical bills, as a result of her dialysis, were staggering as her parents had no medical insurance. Once again, this same group of awesome guys rallied together to help. We worked harder and smarter than the year before. At the end of the effort, we had raised over $1,200 and smashed our own state record by completing an amazing 205 innings during daylight hours.

I'll never forget, at the age of 16, when I played 37½ hours of continuous ping-pong with my 14-year-old friend Jerry. At the time, we were going for the world record of 42 hours straight. Sorry Jerry, I know how disappointed you were when I nearly collapsed just hours away from entering "the record book." Nevertheless, we raised a bunch of cash for Muscular Dystrophy. Could the details of a story like this inspire others?

If I opted to write such a book on determination and perseverance, I'd certainly include chapters about the Marine Corps; and one of the most significant events in my life—those 81 days called "boot camp!" At the end of all that grueling training, out of 240 men in our four-platoon series, I was selected as the top Marine graduate. This accomplishment paved the way for fast promotions over the remainder of my four years of service, not to mention the confidence instilled deep within me. It was a confidence that I'd carry with me for the rest of my life. Told in a book, just how inspiring might that be to others?

Perhaps the most significant part of any book I'd ever write would deal with the topic of real estate. For over 21 years I have invested myself in this field and have helped families buy and sell homes, lots of homes—over 2500 homes valued in excess of a half a billion dollars and counting. From being the top salesperson in Minnesota (eight times) to Hall of Fame, from Lifetime Achievement to being ranked in the Top 10 in the nation within the RE/MAX organization, my success in real estate has been nothing short of monumental. I have had the privilege and honor of being sought after as a real estate speaker and trainer, inspiring real estate agents and brokers around the world to achieve greater levels of success within their businesses.

I've developed a passion for what I do and for sharing what I have learned. I have truly been blessed.

So back to the initial question: Would events like these be interesting enough to inspire others? Would they be significant enough for me to take the time to put such details on paper and offer them to the world? Possibly, but I have never taken the liberty of doing so. They do however serve a purpose here and now—that is to give you a very brief background of who I am. There is simply no comparison between the events mentioned above and the magnitude of the incredible story that is about to unfold before your eyes.

Foreword

If I were to tell you that it is possible to be healed of a sickness or disease that you or a loved one had been diagnosed with, what would your first reaction be? Better yet, if I told you I was going to share with you the secrets that could produce that much desired healing, would you give me a portion of your time so I could tell you an interesting story?

There is no question; we live in a world of more sickness and disease than ever before, much of which is deemed incurable. I know this first-hand because I was one of those who received such a diagnosis.

In the pages of this book, I will reveal the secrets I have learned that led me to a full and complete recovery from an incurable disease. All of the doctors and specialists that cared for me, both in and out of the hospital, concluded that there was nothing they could do to bring about the healing results I sought. It was medically impossible for me to recover.

What secrets enabled such a healing to occur? What thoughts went through my mind as the doctors described the likely and unfortunate outcome of death? What emotional, physical and spiritual choices were set before me each day? In essence, how did I cope? How did I gain victory over an incurable illness?

Everyone who knows what happened to me has described the account as "unbelievable." For many, my experience is BEYOND BELIEF!

We've all heard the phrase, "Seeing is believing." How then, can one believe without seeing? What does it involve? "Faith" is defined as "the evidence of things not seen." This definition describes a means of "believing *before* seeing" — reverse, if you will, of what most of us use as a means of understanding the world around us.

If faith is the evidence of things not seen and yet we've been conditioned to think in the terms of, "Seeing is believing," then we must change the way we think. We must use unconventional wisdom. We must go BEYOND BELIEF and into the realm of faith in order to experience "the evidence." The evidence I sought was that of a healed and healthy middle-aged man.

The pages of this book will take you on a journey that is truly BEYOND BELIEF. As this captivating story unfolds, you will witness how numerous events wove together in such a way as to bring about a miraculous outcome. Through the very process that I lived through, you will come to learn what I term "the secrets" of healing: the secrets that restored my health 100 percent, without medical explanation. The secrets I will share throughout this book are available to you and to those you care about. In fact, they are life changing to everyone willing to learn and take action.

I share my story with you today as a healed man: one who enjoys life to the fullest with my family, friends and colleagues. Sit back now, brace yourself and get ready for a ride that will take you BEYOND BELIEF—one that will change your life forever.

Jeff Scislow
Apple Valley, MN
www.JourneyToAMiracle.com
Jeff@JourneyToAMiracle.com

The Tsunami of Challenges Begins

"Consider it all joy when you encounter various trials, knowing that the testing of your faith produces endurance."

James 1:2-3

Dot.com Mania

My plane landed safely under the overcast skies of Seattle in March of 2000. I was filled with anticipation at seeing a number of very successful real estate associates from around the country. I knew about a dozen of them and was anxious to meet the others who had also been invited to this special gathering. Equally exciting was the fact that we had been hand-picked to review a new product technology, and to possibly become involved with its anticipated success. My personal invitation to attend this gathering was not only exciting, but an honor. I was part of a tremendous group. There were 20 invitees.

Our first day at the corporate facility was eventful. We met the president and officers of the company and visited with the heads of the technology, accounting and personnel departments. We had the opportunity to tour the entire facility and visit with many of the 50 employees who had developed the new Internet product which would provide online service to real estate agents around the country. This was the ultimate DOT.COM company for the industry which I had come to love. There I was, right in the midst of this incredible opportunity.

Over the next few days, our group of 20 was offered the opportunity to become Advisory Panel members for the company. If we agreed to accept the proposal and responsibilities that came with it, we would receive stock options and other perks such as the opportunity to buy company stock at "pre-offering" prices.

We saw the vision and it was awesome. We understood the need in the real estate industry and recognized how this new product could fill that need. We saw the strategic plan of how the company would grow and how we could empower others to be a part of this growth. We observed how the company and its employees had listened to our ideas and welcomed them. We saw a company that realized they needed our professional input and business acumen. This was a company that was willing to implement our ideas. We began to feel like a family within just a few days.

The company had just signed a major training contract with the National Association of Realtors® which provided instant credibility among the invitees. This contract would provide national exposure to over 700,000 Realtors®, and pave the way for the company to roll out its new products and services; the timing, the people, the product and the need could not have been better. In addition, the Internet product was not limited only to real estate professionals. It was an awesome tool for business in general.

18 invitees out of 20 agreed to serve as Advisory Panel members. This newly appointed group was asked to elect a leader to serve as the primary interface with the company. Due to my background in computers and my good head for business, the group elected me as leader of the newly formed panel. I was honored to be given the responsibility. I intended to put my heart into doing whatever I could to ensure the success of this company and the real estate agents who would utilize its services. Before I left Seattle, I heard the company's Wall Street investment banker tell the president to "give Scislow whatever he needs." He wanted to ensure that the company remained open to my ideas and those of the Advisory Panel. Needless to say, I left Seattle with some pretty high hopes.

Over the next few weeks, many of the attendees made decisions with respect to investing in the company's stock. My personal decision was to invest a sizable amount. I was not alone in this, as other panel members invested handsomely as well. In addition, I spoke with family members and close friends about this opportunity. Several of them wanted in. Having known me and seen numerous successes in my past, they placed their confidence in me and thousands of dollars poured in from family and friends (supplementing my substantial investment) in order to acquire company stock.

Over the next five months, my enthusiasm for the company's product resulted in increased sales both locally and nationally. All subscriber Internet sites were up and running well. Expansion in the technology center was underway. I had booked several speaking and training tours at various locations around the country. I had appointments with several large mortgage companies in town and was preparing an out-of-state presentation for one of the largest banks and mortgage lenders in the nation. The momentum was building and I envisioned potential financial returns in the millions of dollars.

My wife and I both felt good about what I was doing and felt that this new endeavor could draw me in a new direction, away from the day-to-day selling of homes in the Twin Cities area. I recall telling her on several occasions how good it felt to have my business and entrepreneurial skills appreciated.

By mid-August of 2000, my first big out-of-town event had finally arrived—the State Realtor's Convention in Kansas City. For years, I had targeted this part of the country for real estate referrals and relocating transferees. I felt right at home and among friends at the convention and was enthusiastic and fired-up about what I was doing. In the midst of my excitement while working the convention floor, I received a cell phone call from Seattle. The gentleman on the line was professional and direct. He informed me that he was the "acting" CEO of the company. His instructions were simple, "Pack up and go home. Stop selling. The company is unable to support the sale of any of its products and has been taken over by creditors."

I immediately began making phone calls to my contacts in Seattle in an attempt to confirm the shocking news. It was mid-afternoon and all of the company phones were down, voice mail was inoperative and many of the cell phone numbers of key personnel had been disconnected. When I finally reached the Wall Street investment banker on his cell phone, he confirmed the unfortunate news and emphasized that the company had been shut down unexpectedly just hours earlier. It had been taken over by creditors and 90 percent of the employees had been fired and police-escorted out of the building earlier that day. He suggested I get out of Kansas City and take the next plane home. My heart sank.

Over the next few days from my office in Minneapolis, I scrambled to obtain information and provide answers for the many Advisory Panel members who had been calling and emailing, hoping that I might offer a ray of hope in this dire situation. There was nothing good to report.

In addition to fielding these calls, I handled numerous calls from real estate agents and business people who had purchased services as a result of my representation of the company. Providing answers to these folks became a very difficult task; I had nothing to offer them other than my time to listen. It was a very disheartening.

I began to realize that I would never see the thousands of dollars that I had invested in the company. I would never receive the commissions I had earned or be reimbursed for the travel expenses I had incurred. The success I had dreamt about had turned into a nightmare. Worst of all, I was torn up by the fact that others had placed their confidence in me and had bought company stock.

This was not only a financial setback, but an emotional one. Virtually overnight, it took all the wind out of my sails. I felt that I had let others down. I felt I had been taken advantage of and lied to. I was disappointed in myself. I was totally caught by surprise. "I should have seen it coming," I thought. Eventually, I realized that I had neither input, insight, nor clue about the nature of the company's finances. None of the Advisory Panel was privy to that information. To make a long story short, the company simply overspent itself into bankruptcy.

In the midst of this difficult time, I drew strength from a passage of Scripture in the book of James: *"Consider it all joy my brethren, when you encounter various trials, knowing that the testing of your faith produces endurance."* (James 1:2-3)   There was no question that this was a trial. I felt beaten down. Nothing so devastating had happened to me in years. Everything had been going so well!

As a Christian of nearly 20 years, I knew what it meant to stand on God's word. I simply needed to do that now. I knew I'd get through this, but I needed comfort during the process so I chose to put the matter in God's hands. This verse did not simply say to lean on God for His help, but it spoke clearly to me saying, "Consider it JOYFUL during times of trial; rejoice in difficult moments. And as faith is tested by this trial, it will produce endurance."

I did not really know what the "endurance" part of this verse meant, so I simply chose to be "joyful" and trusted God for the rest.

I recall that the fear, frustration and hurt quickly dissipated as a result of the choice to be "joyful" in this time of trial. Although it did not seem to make sense, it worked! It was truly amazing!

As I spoke with the friends, family and business people who had invested in the company, I found them to be more understanding than I had anticipated. At a time when I had been devastated by the sudden turn of events, their understanding was very comforting. Before long, I felt the nightmare was behind me. This one was over, but unfortunately another was on its way.

A Promising Venture

In July of 2000, when everything seemed to be going well with the Seattle Dot.com company and huge financial returns seemed imminent, I stumbled across an opportunity to invest in a start-up company in my own home town of Apple Valley, Minnesota. For the sake of conversation, I will call this start-up company "Venture."

I first became aware of Venture through a close friend who was employed there. There was an awesome new technology that was going to be unveiled—something that had never been offered before.

One day, my friend called and recommended that I speak with the Director of Operations, take a tour of the facility, and review the prospectus and stock offering. Although the private stock offering period had been closed out just days before, the powers-that-be were offering me the ability to purchase stock because of my connection. I agreed to check it out.

First, I reviewed the prospectus and stock offering. Within 24 hours I read approximately 500 pages of plans, objectives, risks, etc. The overall concept and marketing plan for Venture was impressive.

Next, I took a tour of the corporate office with the Director of Operations and deemed the facility and operation equally impressive. Venture's business plan was to provide high-speed downloading of music onto compact discs while the customer watched a small robot complete the task in just a few minutes. The customer would touch-select from a computer screen the type of music—by artist, title, era or style that they wanted to purchase. As each selection was made, an illuminated image would appear on the computer screen showing the amount of disc space remaining on the CD. Once enough selections were made to fill the disc, a single touch by the customer would prompt the music to be burnt onto the CD by the little robot on the other side of the plexiglas window. The result was a custom CD on demand for two-thirds of the cost of a regular stock CD.

Not only did the product seem incredible, the timing for Venture seemed perfect. Throughout much of 2000, Napster and its illegal piracy of music over the Internet was featured in news headlines around the world. Now, with Venture about to be unveiled as a legal alternative to get fast, custom music off the Internet, it was sure to be a hit right off the bat.

Initially, over one million music titles were to be available in Venture's database; a number of record companies had signed on and were ready to participate. Venture's first facility, located in Apple Valley, Minnesota, was scheduled to open in September of 2000. This 50,000 square-foot space would be followed by the opening of four additional facilities within the next 12 months, including locations in Chicago and New York. These large facilities would each include a restaurant, a bar/lounge and a family entertainment center in addition to the multitude of online stations where music could be easily downloaded.

Based on all the information I gathered and reviewed about Venture, I felt comfortable moving ahead with an investment. Although I knew these types of endeavors were always risky, I felt I had been diligent in my research. Simply put, I believed in the product and the people. In addition, I felt a little bolder than I might have otherwise because I anticipated handsome financial returns from the Seattle-based Company.

One of the biggest reasons I moved ahead with the investment in Venture was that the Director of Operations told me a deal had already been "inked" to merge the two companies that would ultimately become Venture. The local, privately-held company that had conceptualized Venture was set to merge with a larger, publicly-traded company and, through the merger, create Venture.

Without this merger, Venture was only a concept. The dollars to successfully birth Venture were coming from the publicly-traded company, not the privately-held one. The news of the merger would be released to Wall Street in just three short days, at which time Venture would become a NASDAQ security and its stock would begin trading soon thereafter.

So, if I made a quick investment in the privately-held company, my shares would revert to Venture shares by the end of that week. Based on projections, it appeared that I would easily double or triple my investment on the first day of trading.

On a summer day in July of 2000, I wrote a check for three times the amount that I had invested in the Seattle-based company. I looked forward to the announcement of the merger with great anticipation. By the end of the week however, the merger had not taken place as scheduled—something had brought about a delay.

The following week I learned that there had been yet another delay, but was assured the merger was still set to take place. One week later I learned that the publicly-traded company had backed out of the deal and there was now no partner for the privately-held company to launch Venture.

By early August, the decision was made by the directors of the privately-held company to move forward with the launch of Venture on a smaller scale, without a partner. Instead, Venture would become a subsidiary and would be funded solely by the privately-held company, its investors and its owners. In my estimation, the concept was still a winner and I remained positive. The grand opening for the first Venture facility was set for Labor Day.

Filled with anticipation, I headed to the 50,000 square-foot facility just a mile and a half from home. I still clearly remember the "Disney-like" description of fascinating lighting, music and mechanical animations that I had read about in the prospectus. This was going to be awesome and I was a big investor in its success!

As I entered the facility, my heart sank into my stomach. I was disappointed in what I saw. The facility looked like a huge warehouse with neon-looking lights above banks of computer terminals scattered around the room. A number of Venture employees wandered around looking clueless, as the Director of Operations ran around trying to determine what went wrong with the robotic CD burners.

Worse yet, I saw the faces of the few customers that had found their way to this "grand" opening. Puzzled looks of confusion abounded. "What's this place all about?" some asked. My mind raced with thoughts of frustration. I wondered who had been in charge of marketing.

The grand opening for Venture took place mere weeks after the demise of the Seattle-based Dot.com company. Thoughts of another financial debacle had unfortunately materialized. It was awful.

In less than two months, the first and only Venture facility closed and the privately-held company which tried launching Venture was buried in over two million dollars of debt. After 20 years of business success, the privately-held company ultimately filed for bankruptcy. All the money employees, their families, their friends and I had invested in the company was gone.

I found myself '0 for 2' in 2000 with respect to companies in which I had believed in. The losses from these two companies, coupled with the overall decline of the stock market in 2000, were enough to make me evaluate how I was living. Was I somehow living in error? I believed I was living right; my faith was strong and intact and I had regularly tithed to the church. I knew that I had been tremendously blessed as a result of tithing and now I seemed to be giving that blessing back for some reason. But, why?

I remember calculating in my head how many years of selling homes it would take to recoup what was lost in those few short months between two unfortunate investments and the stock market. From future commissions, I subtracted the expenses needed to generate the sales and to run the business. After subtracting income taxes and the cost of living expenses for our family of six, I ended up with my answer: *"many, many years."*

Recalling the relief I had felt when I stood on the verse from James chapter 1, I turned to it once again. *"Consider it all JOY my brethren when you encounter various trials, knowing that the testing of your faith produces endurance."*

Just how was my faith being tested, I wondered? I believed that I was being challenged to trust in the Lord and not in money. Not that I had placed all my trust in money before, but now I was challenged to place ALL my trust in the Lord and NONE in the money. I was starting to learn that no matter how much I analyzed the details or terms of an investment, I could not control the outcome. As much as I liked to think I was intelligent enough to make the right choices, I was humbled and reminded that I was not infallible. I was reminded of what the Bible says, *"if I place my trust in Him... and put Him first... then all things will be added to me."* [Compilation of Proverbs 3:5-6 and Matthew 6:33]

In the midst of these major financial setbacks, and in spite of the fact that my wife was not happy with my investment "expertise," I chose to be joyful. I made it a point to do exactly what the verse said I should do, even though it made little sense. I simply said to myself, "On the basis of faith, I will choose not to worry about this at all. I will trust that God is doing something in my life and I choose to trust whatever it is that He is doing—period!"

Once I made that conscious choice in my heart, my spirits once again lifted immediately. I quickly gained emotional momentum and began to move forward again. I knew it would simply take time, and I was okay with that. I would need to sell a lot of homes to recover the dollars that were lost, but I'd do it. I had been selling 100 to 200 homes per year for many years—this was what I was good at! I'd simply focus on selling more homes than ever in order to recover from this setback. Little did I know then, but this was exactly where my next challenge would come from—real estate sales!

It's Time to Sell!

With the disappointing months of August and September of 2000 behind me, as well as a significant setback in our finances, I started the fourth quarter focused on what I did best—selling homes! In the midst of these challenges, I chose to be joyful and faith-filled. I was gaining strength and was ready to get back into the proverbial mode of success. I have never been a quitter and I was not going to become one.

October, however, did not manifest any success. It was not until late in the month, after having no sales at all, that I realized something *very strange* was going on. What was it? I had attended the usual amount of appointments for October but nothing had come together. In an average October, I usually sold 10 to 12 homes, but not this October. It seemed that every buyer or seller selected another agent, decided to take their home off the market or opted to stop looking. It became very evident that business was fleeing from me!

By this time, I had been selling homes for over 14 years, and while I had experienced the occasional dry spell in those years, I had never seen a slow down like this. Typically, the slowest month of the year is December, during which I'd sell three to seven homes. But zero sales in October was unheard of for me! I persisted, while also working on projects that I reserve for slow times, thereby maximizing my time and gaining some self-satisfaction.

One thing I have learned over the years in real estate is that whenever activity slows for a period of time, one day it will suddenly pick up again and things will go right back to normal. This is what I expected for November. Unfortunately, my expectations were a far cry from reality. I sold just two homes that month compared to an average of 12 sales in previous Novembers. Once, in the mid-1990's, I sold 23 homes in a Minnesota November. Now, those were only fond memories.

I knew something inexplicable was happening to me. Just before Thanksgiving, I stopped by the prayer chapel at Hosanna, the church I attended in Lakeville, Minnesota, in order to have someone pray for me. As a frequent visitor to the prayer chapel to get prayer, as well as offer prayer, I wanted to know if God was trying to show me something. Everything seemed to be a challenge, especially from a financial standpoint. Would the Lord reveal something to me that would allow me to escape this onslaught of misfortune?

Upon arriving at the prayer chapel, I met several people I knew and I shared the many bizarre events I had been experiencing with them. I shared the pain of the financial setbacks and the details of how my real estate sales were suffering. I pointed out that while I remained positive and joyful throughout these trials, I desired to know if God was trying to show me something. I told them I was living out the verses from James 1:2-3, *"Consider it all joy when you encounter various trials, knowing that the testing of your faith produces endurance."* I asked them to pray for me so that I might better understand what was happening to me.

Pastor Dave Housholder, one of the pastors of the church, happened to be in the prayer chapel that day. After several members of the prayer team prayed for me, Pastor Dave stated, "I am getting a word from the Lord for Jeff." There was a brief pause, and then he said to me, *"The Lord is preparing you for difficult times that lie ahead."* That was it. I did not know what it meant, but as you will see, those words became a valuable seed that I would draw on for strength and understanding in the weeks ahead.

> ***"The Lord is preparing you***
> ***for difficult times that lie ahead."***

The month of December, statistically the slowest in the year for me, proved to be much like the past two months—I only sold one home. A normal December would produce three to seven sales, so just one sale indicated that nothing had changed; something strange was still present in my life.

When the fourth quarter ended, it went down as the absolute worst in my entire career—just three sales. To make matters worse, one of those sales fell through on the day it was supposed to close, dropping my quarterly number of sales to two. In a quarter when real estate was selling normally for other sales associates, it was not for me—the state's top-selling Realtor over the past decade.

As I sensed the trials of life mounting, I was more determined than ever to stand on the verses in James chapter 1. I made it personal. I quoted it day and night. I shared it with my friends at church and in my men's group. *"I will consider it all JOY when I encounter various trials, for I know that the testing of my faith will produce endurance."*

I still had no idea why I needed to produce endurance, but on the basis of faith, I moved straight ahead. Before the end of December, I would meet my most difficult challenge yet.

We're Out of Here!

While the fourth quarter of 2000 went down as the worst personal performance in my real estate career, I was fortunate to have three sales people on my real estate team who were making sales. I was grateful to receive a portion of the commission from those sales and I felt a small sense of financial security due to having this team in place.

At the beginning of December however, that small "sense of security" evaporated when I was informed that all three were leaving at the end of the month! They made the decision to branch off and start up their *own* sales team. Although this was a bit disheartening, it was not a complete surprise; I had sensed that they might opt to do this someday, but now? The timing could not have been worse. I accepted their decision and planned for their departure by the end of the month.

Unfortunately, the bad news did not end there. Two days later I learned that my former sales team had made a deal with my full-time assistant. For four and a half years she had been my right arm in the running of my successful real estate business. I had employed her to take care of all the office details, including the paperwork for my sales team. The team was now stealing her away. I felt betrayed; by the end of the month I'd have no one left in the office but me!

The timing made this bad news even worse. I learned of my assistant's departure a mere week prior to my family and I flying to Cancun, Mexico for a two-week vacation. "Unbelievable!" I thought, trying to keep my composure in the midst of more bizarre events.

At that point in time, I began reminding myself that if I was going to trust God in *all* things, then this too was one of those "things" in which I needed to trust Him. I recalled that I was supposed to consider this a "joyful" trial! "How can I do that?" I grumbled. I decided to do it anyway, since it had proved beneficial in the past. I certainly could not understand what was happening, nor did I have an inkling of *why* it was happening. I just knew it *was* happening and that I was going to focus and stay the course. Above all, I was going to choose to be joyful.

Over the next few days, I pondered what I should do with my business under these confusing circumstances. In a few short days I would leave for vacation and when I returned, my sales team and assistant would be gone. Clearly I had no time to replace my assistant. Should I stay home and cancel the trip? Should I allow my staff to remain in the office while I was out of town? I ultimately decided that they needed to leave before I left town, since I no longer trusted them to consider my best interests in my absence. I informed them all that they needed to be out before I left for vacation.

On December 14th, the day before flying to Cancun, everyone had left. I forwarded the phones to voice mail and locked the doors to my office, a painful experience. At the last minute, I again considered canceling the trip. "I need to get another assistant hired immediately," I thought to myself. "I need a new sales team and I needed to start selling some homes myself." I had so many immediate "to-do's" on my mind. My mind was racing! Eventually, I realized that canceling our vacation would not be fair to my kids, my wife or me. Staying home was simply not an option; we flew out bright and early on December 15th.

During the flight, I reflected on the past few months and wondered how my vacation might be affected. What were the chances I would have a worry-free vacation? It would be so easy for me to spend my vacation complaining and worrying about all the crazy things that had happened. During my ponderings, it became increasingly clear that *something* was definitely going on. My faith was being tested big-time. I knew this. It had become clearer than ever. But, why?

I consciously decided to meet any challenge head on; no matter what came next, I'd be ready! With faith and trust in God's Word, I would overcome whatever came my way. What other option did I have? I could have spent my time and energy trying to solve these problems in my near state of panic, but I chose instead to lean on the Lord. During my vacation, I praised God, thanking Him for what He was doing, although I did not understand it. I continued to draw strength from Pastor Dave's word of knowledge; I was "being prepared for difficult times that lie ahead." How true those words would prove to be.

Take the Money and Run

For two wonderful weeks, my family and I enjoyed the warmth of the Mexican sunshine and refreshing ocean surf. This was our tenth visit to Cancun and one which I most desperately needed. We had escaped the frigid Minnesota winter briefly and spent time with close friends with whom we vacation each year in Cancun. It was so rewarding not to spend that time worrying about the unfortunate situation waiting for me back home. Once again, I noticed that by turning my problems over to the Lord, and by praising Him in times of difficulty, I made it through the trial just fine. I saw a clear pattern and was amazed by it.

As often happens on vacation, time passed quickly, and once back home, reality began to set in. I needed to re-open the office, hire an administrative assistant and build a sales team. On top of all this, it was really cold!

When my wife and I were married in 1987, she got her real estate license and worked as my office administrator. For nine years we worked together before she chose to stay at home with our children, at which point I hired the assistant who had just left with my sales team. While my wife was not involved with the day-to-day operation of the business for four and a half years, she did, however, maintain an active real estate license. It was a true blessing when she said she'd come back to work in the office until I could find a new licensed assistant.

While January is typically a quiet real estate month in the Twin Cities, this one started out well for me. I put together six sales—three times as many sales as I had the entire fourth quarter of 2000! This was excellent! I felt I was getting back on track. Then another bombshell dropped.

Near the end of January, I realized that I had not received an expected paycheck from my RE/MAX broker—my portion of the sales transacted by a former sales team member while he was on my team. After some inquiries, I learned that the sale had not been reported properly. It had, in fact, been reported as a sale independent of "The Scislow Group". In other words, I would not receive the portion of the commission I was due per the written contract with my former team member.

Believing this was a simple mistake, I asked the broker to speak with the agent in question about this sale and the commission that I failed to receive. Within a couple days, the broker contacted me and informed me that the agent felt the commission belonged solely to him! It was clear to me that this sale was transacted prior to his departure and within the timeframe of our contract.

I became suspicious. I logged onto the Multiple Listing Service and searched each listing the sales team had on the books when they were part of my team. Several of those listings had been reported sold. When I searched the "off-market" date for those sold listings, I discovered they had sold immediately prior to my team's departure. In my opinion, these sales were made while I was their team leader and I deserved a portion of the commission.

Once again, I was dealing with an issue of disappearing money, I could not believe it. I had trusted these people. In fact, I had once even considered making one of the sales team members a partner, or selling the business to the team someday. Now we were arguing over commission splits. I was personally devastated and could not understand why we were having such a dispute.

The broker was unable to mediate a solution, so all commissions from the contested sales that had not yet closed would be held in the broker's escrow account until the matter was settled. I had the option of pursuing this matter in court, so I obtained a legal opinion from an attorney who stated that the contract was clear and well-written. He felt I would prevail and win a judgment in court for the commissions in question.

I needed time to consider what I should do about having thousands of dollars simply disappear. Even with the likelihood of winning in court, was I up for suing my former team for money? Was that the right thing to do? They were waiting for my first move.

"What a thing to be happening," I thought. In the midst of yet another incredible setback I reminded myself, "I need to stay focused, and joyful. These events are beyond my comprehension, but I am up for the challenge. Praise God!"

After much thought and prayer, I opted to write a letter to the sales team giving them the opportunity to search their heart and act upon what they felt was right. I felt the Lord leading me in that direction and in order for this letter to be genuine, I needed to be willing to accept whatever they chose to do. They obviously felt the money belonged to them, so I stated in my letter that I would abide by whatever they felt their hearts were telling them, and that if they felt the money truly belonged to them, they could use the letter as their ticket to have all the money held in escrow released to them. I stated that I would not pursue them in court and that I trusted them to do what was right.

I admit that this was a very difficult letter for me to write. I felt the thousands of commission dollars were unmistakably mine through a clearly spelled out contract and that I simply needed to claim it legally. Since I had lost a small fortune between the business failures, plummeting stock market and the worst quarter in my real estate career, I really needed the money!

The letter was hard to write, but it was even more difficult to send. Once in the mail, there was no turning back. What would the sales team do? Would they do the right thing and pay me what I felt they owed? I sure hoped so. In all this deliberation, I sensed God telling me to send it. I heard Him saying to forgive them and not to worry about money or anything else. He would be taking care of me. I sent the letter to the sales team and sent a copy to my broker.

Nearly a week went by without a reply, at which point I contacted my broker and inquired if he had heard anything from the sales team. He had not, but indicated he would call and solicit their response. Later that day the broker called me back. He stated the sales team's response: "We're all glad that this matter has been resolved." They kept the money! I was shocked!

At this point I became more concerned about the *series* of events that were happening than the events themselves! Why did I keep encountering such completely out of the ordinary events? It was clear to me that I was in the middle of something very, very strange, but what? I was beginning to feel like Job from the Old Testament. Job was a good, righteous man who had been blessed with an abundance of personal belongings and wealth. Then suddenly, disaster struck and one bizarre event after another stole away his family, his possessions and almost his life before the Lord restored Job with double that which he previously had. Then I caught myself and thought, "No, I'm *not* Job."

It was clear however, that I too had been experiencing one peculiar and challenging event after another. In each case, as I searched deep in my heart to find "joy" in the midst of these challenges, the Lord got me through each bump in the road, with an outcome that was better than I expected. "This is no time to change that approach," I thought.

It is difficult to express how strange it seems to praise God in the middle of troubled times. But somehow, according to that verse in the first chapter of James, my faith was being tested in order to produce what would prove to be much-needed endurance.

I searched for more answers in Scripture and found this verse from 1 Peter 4:12-13: *"...do not be surprised at the fiery ordeal among you, which comes upon you for your testing, as though some strange thing were happening to you; but to the degree that you share the sufferings of Christ, keep on rejoicing; so that also at the revelation of His glory, you may rejoice with exultation."* "Some strange thing," seemed like an understatement, but I saw hope in these verses. I envisioned "the revelation of God's glory" as the breakthrough and victory over these trials! It would be a time for me to "rejoice in exultation." I believed that and proceeded on the basis of faith.

A Blow to the Body

I was glad to have January behind me, for it was a period of considerable emotional pain. As I focused more on getting my office up and running again, the personal hurt subsided.

As February arrived, I took a big breath and looked back over the past six months. I saw the avalanche of major setbacks that threatened to overtake me and two things came to mind: First, things had to start improving soon and second, I was determined to get everything back on track. I pressed on.

Before the first week of the month came to a close, I began feeling like I had the stomach flu. The symptoms included slight fever, loss of appetite, nausea and lack of motivation. After about a week and a half of this persistent ill-feeling, I opted to visit the local clinic seeking some antibiotic or other quick fix to help me feel better.

As soon as the doctor saw me, he said I showed signs of having hepatitis. I knew very little about hepatitis, simply that it was not good. I learned that it meant "enlarged liver" and that something may have caused my liver to become inflamed. It was not long before I began to think, "Now even my health is under attack!"

The doctor ordered blood tests to determine if my body had produced any known hepatitis antibodies that would enable the doctors to identify the type of hepatitis that I had apparently contracted. These initial tests were looking for types A, B and C. The results did not confirm hepatitis at all. I was asked to return for additional tests over the next few days.

On February 16th I was tested again for hepatitis A, B and C. By this time the doctor was even more certain that I had hepatitis based on physical observation, but to his amazement, each test came back negative! I was showing all the signs of hepatitis, but it could not be proven. This was puzzling for everyone.

31

Along with the antibody tests, my enzyme counts were tested to determine if I, in fact, had any liver damage. Elevated ALT and AST counts would indicate damage to the liver. These tests revealed that my liver was under attack and had experienced some fairly severe damage. The ALT count was an astronomical 3454 (normal is 0 to 70) and the AST had soared to 1902 (normal is 0 to 55). The doctor at the clinic immediately indicated that I was in need of a specialist.

After a few phone calls, I had the name of the best "hepatitis" doctor in the Twin Cities area. My local doctor made the appropriate referral and I was given a prompt appointment with the specialist. Within a few days I was in the specialist's office where, upon seeing me, he agreed that I had some form of hepatitis. He began ordering a number of tests to determine which type I had contracted. He re-tested for types A, B, and C and proceeded to test for E, G and others. Some tests were sent to local hospitals, others to the University of Minnesota and one was sent to the CDC (Center for Disease Control) in Atlanta, Georgia.

With all these blood tests going on, I was beginning to feel like a pincushion. At one sitting I recall the nurse drawing 11 tubes of blood!

The first test results to return were for types A, B, and C. Just as with the clinic's findings, all results returned negative. At this point the specialist began thinking my liver might be under attack by a parasite. He scheduled me for an abdominal CAT scan the next day. This test also proved to be negative in all respects. Within a few days, all the other hepatitis tests returned negative as well.

Something was definitely wrong, but what? In just three weeks my weight had fallen from 169 to 158. I was not hungry, felt weak and very sick. I had to force myself to eat. My skin was yellow, my urine bright orange. The enzyme counts for my ALT and AST continued to rise to a peak of 3595 and 2174, respectively. My bilirubin count also skyrocketed from a normal range of 0.8—1.2 to 19.8!

Most of those who contract (acute) hepatitis A recover. The other types of hepatitis are oftentimes chronic and result in death over the long term. In my case, they pretty much concluded that I had contracted a new or undetectable form of hepatitis. As a result, they could not provide any sort of prognosis as to what I might expect by way of an outcome.

I felt my faith being tested to a greater degree than ever before, even in light of the past six months. This time it was my health—my very existence! My physical state was terrible, weak and sickly. Emotionally I was wrestling with depression, one of the common symptoms of hepatitis because the patient feels physically incapable of doing anything. An active person often suffers more from this sort of depression due to the inability to keep pace with their normal lifestyle.

Although my physical and emotional states were experiencing quite a battle, my spiritual side was still strong and focused. I had come to recognize that something had been going on in my life beyond my ability to explain or identify. Each time I considered the trial to be "joyful" and praised God in the midst of it, I found myself getting over the hurdle instead of letting it get the best of me. As a result, I was more determined than ever to meet this current challenge head on with joy and faith in my heart.

By the first week of March the specialist confessed, "I am sorry, but we cannot determine what type of hepatitis you have, nor do we really know how you contracted it. We can't say for sure how long it will take to recover, or for that matter, whether you *will* recover. I have a hunch that you will come through this and have a full recovery, but not for at least six months." The specialist scheduled me for weekly blood testing and monitoring.

March 1, 2001 Blood Test Results

⊠ **Fairview** Clinics

Dear ___Jeff Scislow___

DOB __8/1/1956__ Phone No. __952-891-8075__

Date of Test __3-1-01__ Date Sent

Initials

The following tests were checked recently and the results noted below.

*Test explanations are brief and do not reflect all diagnostic uses.

Normal	Abnormal	
☐	☐	Glucose _____ • A screening test for diabetes
☐	☐	Glycosylated hemoglobin _____ % Average blood glucose _____ • Long-term check of average blood sugar 3-6% or less = excellent control or non-diabetic 6-8% = good control 9-14% = poor control
☐	☐	Kidney tests/Electrolytes • Checks how well the kidneys are working and measures body salts which may be affected by medications.
☐	☐	Liver tests • Checks how well the liver is functioning
☐	☐	Thyroid tests • Checks thyroid function and body metabolism
☑	☐	CBC/Hgb _____ • Complete blood cell count (notes presence of infection, anemia, etc.) and checks the number and appearance of blood components and cells.
☑	☐	Hemoglobin 15.4 g/dL [N = 13.7 to 17.5] • Checks the oxygen-carrying capacity of the blood
☐	☐	Urinalysis • Checks for urine abnormalities such as infection, blood or sugar
☐	☐	PSA • Prostate screening test for abnormal antigens
☐	☐	Hemocult • Checks for presence of blood in stool
☐	☐	H. Pylori - Stomach Bacteria
☑	☐	Other Hep A Antibody total ⊖ (sign of older or winfection)
☑	☐	Other Hep A IgM antibody ⊖ (sign of acute infection)
☑	☐	Other Hep B surface antibody ⊖ → sign of food, inf or imm Hep B core antibody ⊖ → no sign of active or prev. infec. Hepatitis C Antibody ⊖

2/22/01

LIPID PROFILE	Desirable	Borderline	Your Result
Cholesterol	Less than 200	200-240	
HDL "Good Chol"	Greater than 35	--	
LDL "Bad Chol"	Less than 130	130-160	
Triglycerides	Below 200	200-400	

Medical Imaging Results / X-Ray

Normal	Abnormal	
☐	☐	X-ray(s) of
☐	☐	Mammogram
☐	☐	Ultrasound
☐	☐	Dexascan
☐	☐	

Comments: 12/6/00 2/16/01 2/19/01 2/23 2/29 3/2

	12/6/00	2/16/01	2/19/01	2/23	2/29	3/2
[N=0-70] ↓ ALT	47	3454	3595	3278	—	2021
[N=0-55] ↓ AST	29	1902	2174	1805	—	1366
[N=0-1.6] ↓ Total Bil	0.8	—	—	11.8	—	12.8
INR [N= 0.8 to 1.2]				2.9	1.5	1.3

☐	No further action is necessary.

☐ Make follow-up appointment with provider.
 ☐ Make follow-up appointment for labs.

☐ Comments and recommended follow up: _____

_____

Please make a follow up appointment if you have additional questions.

Sincerely,

ORIGINAL TO PATIENT - COPY TO FILE

170853 REV. 6/00

TEST RESULTS

By mid-March I began to feel better and acquired a desire for food once again. My lack of appetite had caused my weight to drop all the way to 156 and I was ready to add a few pounds. My weekly visit to the specialist on March 15th revealed that my ALT and AST levels had dropped significantly to 723 and 302, respectively, down from their previously dangerous levels.   I was quite excited about the improvement, especially at how quickly the enzyme levels had fallen. My emotional state quickly improved after hearing this good news.

My spiritual state remained strong as I again considered this challenging trial "joyful," knowing that the testing of my faith was producing endurance. Endurance for what, I still did not know. It would soon be revealed however, as I proceeded down the path of encountering a person's worst nightmare.

Why Me?

The tsunami of bizarre events had taken a financial toll over the past six months: the stock market had been hammered, two back-to-back business failures, the slowest business quarter in my career, learning that I would not be receiving thousands of dollars due to the actions of people that I had previously trusted and missing so much work over the past six weeks. I was taken to the limit of my wits at times, but I continued to trust in the Lord—that He had some "light" at the end of this dark tunnel. I persisted in rejoicing in the face of these trials.

Although weakened by hepatitis, the last half of March found me venturing out, taking listings and selling homes again. I was optimistic that I would be able to recoup all that was lost, no matter how long it took. The financial devastation we had experienced was incredible, but now that my health seemed to be improving, I was motivated to turn things around financially. During the last two weeks of March, business began improving. I listed six homes and sold eight!

During the third week of March, while sitting at my desk, I felt a slight trickle from my nose. Thinking nothing of it, I wiped it with the back of my finger and realized it was blood! "What in the world?" I thought, "I don't get nosebleeds." I worked to get the bleeding under control and concluded it had resulted from an overly dry office environment. I immediately went out and purchased a portable humidifier hoping it would help.

Over the next couple days I noticed my face breaking out. It progressed rapidly over the next week until I had large pimples all over my face. Boils developed, even on my forehead. My face swelled. It was red, puffy and very sore. I had also developed an aggressive cough. I tried lozenges and syrups, but to no avail. I started getting headaches from the progressive coughing. I prayed persistently during this time, asking God to show me what was happening.

At the end of March, I went to the hospital emergency room where the doctor determined that I was battling "tracheitis", a condition in which my trachea was inflamed with a possible infection, the result of a virus going around. He prescribed the antibiotic Doxycycline and sent me home.

At this point in my life, my physical, emotional and spiritual selves were under attack. I said to myself, "I've always been a healthy person. What's happening to me?" Not only was my physical body going through major challenges, but my emotions were torn, as I wondered what was wrong. I simply wanted to be healthy so I could focus on working and replenishing the financial resources that had been stripped away.

My spiritual side was questioning these trying circumstances as well. Not only did I wonder *what* was going on, I wondered *why*. Although I wanted to continue to trust God under all circumstances, I did wonder, "Why me?" from time to time. I made a very conscious effort not to blame God for what was happening. I simply looked to Him as the one who could help me through it and trusted Him to do that. I knew that I might never know exactly why this was happening, but I did have a sense that I would come to an understanding of it at some point.

My world was spinning. Everything was happening all at once. Not only was my nose bleeding off and on during the day and night, but now, as I coughed more, blood began to accompany the coughing as well. In the mornings, I was peeling from my gums what felt like chewing gum, but proved to be dried blood.

I became embarrassed to be seen in public with my face so broken out from the acne and the boils and my eyes so yellow from the effects of the hepatitis. The Doxycycline was not working. I was coughing harder and more frequently. My headaches worsened and my eyes began to ache.

Next I noticed my vision was growing dim. I found it difficult to read and identify road signs as I traveled in the car. I simply concluded that I was just tired, stressed and in need of some catch-up sleep. My main concern was my facial appearance, so I paid much less attention to my dimming vision.

Sunday, April 1st—Before going to bed, I heard the Lord speak to my heart in an ever-so-small-voice telling me to stop taking a particular product that I had begun taking two weeks earlier. He said that it was causing an allergic reaction which was producing the acne and the boils on my face. I stopped using it at once. Amazingly, over the next couple of days, I saw a complete turnaround as my face began to clear up. "Hallelujah!" I cried with much enthusiasm!

Wednesday, April 4th—As I woke that morning, I noticed a lump on my tongue. I quickly went to the mirror and to my horror saw a black-colored, pea-sized lump that resembled a body-pierced black pearl right in the middle of my tongue! Evidently, the lozenge that I had been sucking on for my sore throat and cough had cut my tongue while I was sleeping. This black coloring was the dried blood that had filled up inside my tongue!

I looked at myself in the mirror; then I looked to heaven and shouted, "God! What is going on? I have been faithful! Is there something I need to do that I am not doing? What is going on, Lord?"

It was hard to digest all that was happening in my life. After a few minutes, I regained my composure and once again made the choice to stand on God's Word no matter what. I knew my faith was being tested, and that I was developing endurance, but when would this all conclude? When would I pass the *test*?

I thought about how other people might handle similar situations. What would they do? How would they respond? Could I draw strength from what others had done in the past, or could I draw strength from what I thought others might do?

As my thoughts bounced around on how to respond to these back-to-back challenges, my mind was set at ease as I remembered Psalm 34:19 which says, *"Many are the afflictions of the righteous, but the Lord delivers him out of them all."* "Wow," I thought, "Isn't that the truth!"

I offered up a brief prayer, "Thank you, Lord, for what you are doing. I'm yours and I know that You have a plan. Although I have no idea what it is, I will trust You and give You thanks for being there for me! I trust that, *'all things are going to work together for good,'* according to Romans 8:28—hallelujah!"

The Divine Appointment

Thursday, April 5th—I received a phone call in the morning from a past real estate client. She said, "Jeff, I heard you've been sick. Our pastor is in town today, but is leaving for Arizona tomorrow. He has an incredible gift of healing. I asked him if he would be willing to pray for you and he said he would. How does 7:00 p.m. tonight sound at our church on Lake Street in Minneapolis? I think it is a divine appointment."

At this point I wanted all the prayer I could get and agreed to the meeting. My wife and our neighbor Terri accompanied me to the church that night. Terri wanted to receive prayer as well, since she had been battling pneumonia for weeks.

We met my past client at the entrance to the church. Once inside, we were introduced to Pastor Holmes. We proceeded to his pastoral office. We each took a seat and began sharing our prayer requests.

Pastor Holmes first prayed for Terri and then for me. He asked the Lord to heal us of our respective illnesses—Terri's pneumonia, and my hepatitis, coughing, bleeding, etc.

The prayer for each of us lasted about three to five minutes each. Toward the end of the prayer, I experienced something quite unique—something I can best explain as a vision. During the prayer for a period of approximately 45 seconds, I saw what best resembled a video clip.

This short "movie" was a vivid trip through the inside of a human body, as if it was being viewed with a fiber optic internal camera. After a brief moment, I sensed it was *my* body. I saw five or six white lights that appeared only as dots. They were moving at what I might call the speed of light, and in all directions, leaving comet-like tails behind them!

The clear visual image I was seeing continued through many parts of my body. These little white lights raced all over, down tubes, past my heart and other organs. The pink and red colors of the blood, the tissue and the organs were all so real. The instant the prayer ended, so did the vision.

I shared this with everyone in the room. No one knew what it meant. I only knew that the vision had something to do with the inside of my body. I did not think much more of the vision that night.

As we headed home, Terri indicated she was feeling 100 percent better. The ravaging cough that accompanied her on the way to the church had subsided. It came to pass that she was miraculously healed that night.

I, on the other hand, continued coughing all the way home. I did not feel any different, nor were there any signs of improvement in me. I did not realize at that time, however, that I had just been on a divine appointment—one that would soon manifest into an incredible miracle.

After You Suffer

As we drove home from receiving prayer at the church, I grew very tired. The challenging events that I had been facing were taking their toll on me. I had recently been waking in the middle of the night coughing and had found it difficult to get a good night's rest, reasonably explaining why I had felt so run down and tired during the past couple of weeks.

As soon as we got home, I went straight to bed, hoping for a good night's rest. Once again, however, I was awakened by the cough in the middle of the night. At 4:00 a.m. I went down to the kitchen to grab a banana. That seemed like the best food for my sore throat.

I grabbed the television controller and began flipping through the channels. I landed on a late night channel that had a Bible verse displayed on the screen. It seemed to JUMP OUT at me. As I read it, it came to life! It was my verse! It explained what I had been going through. It was as if I was awakened from my sleep in order to see this verse! *"After you have suffered a little while, the God of all grace, who called you to His eternal glory in Christ, shall Himself, restore, strengthen, perfect, establish and confirm you."* (1 Peter 5:10)

> *"After you have suffered a little while, the God of all grace, who called you to His eternal glory in Christ, shall Himself, restore, strengthen, perfect, establish and confirm you."*

After reading this I responded, "That's me, Lord. I sure have been suffering!" In the midst of excitement over seeing this very specific verse on TV, at this exact point in time in the middle of the night, my thoughts gravitated to the restoration, strengthening and perfecting part of that verse. I sensed that the Lord had heard all my prayers and that He was about to deliver me from all the trials, tribulations and terrible situations I had been going through for many months. Somehow He was going to issue me a "passing grade" on all my tests!

Right smack in the middle of my enthusiasm, in an instant of time, I heard the Lord speak to my heart with these very clear and direct words: *"There is more to come."* "But, Lord...," I immediately thought to myself.

> *"There is more to come."*

I had no idea of what "more" meant, but I knew I was ready for whatever came my way. Sure, I wanted all this to be over, but I knew that the testing of my faith had been producing endurance for something, and I felt strong enough to continue on this most amazing journey. I was determined to get through whatever wilderness or battle I encountered. I knew *"I could do all things through Christ who strengthens me."* (Philippians 4:13)

Some Sweet R & R

Friday, April 6th—I chose to check into a local motel to get some needed rest and relaxation. I knew that two days of no work, no phones, no kids, no pets and an indoor swimming pool, sauna and Jacuzzi would do wonders for me. After getting the okay from my wife, I felt like I was on my way to becoming rejuvenated once again.

That first night was wonderful. The classic, laid back, do-nothing evening included an in-the-room Jacuzzi and movie before retiring early. I scored about nine hours of rest that night, the longest in recent history for me.

Saturday, April 7th—Even with as much rest as I received the night before, I still felt tired and completely worn out once I awoke. I concluded that I had just been through so much that it would take more than one night's rest to get me feeling normal again. I looked forward to my second relaxing day of lounging around the pool, doing nothing and going to bed early.

As I got out of bed and stood up, I felt rather dizzy and lightheaded. "Perhaps I have an ear infection without the pain," I thought, knowing that ear infections could affect one's balance.

In a phone call to my wife, I relayed this sense of dizziness to her. After experiencing so many strange events recently, she was not taking any chances. She offered to pick me up and drive me to the local clinic in Eagan, Minnesota to have me checked out. I agreed.

"You're Really, Really Sick."

Upon seeing the doctor at the clinic, he suggested a blood test based on my appearance and description of symptoms. In a few minutes the results were back. The doctor returned with a concerned look on his face—very concerned. He wanted to bring my wife into the room. I immediately got a sense that more bad news was on the way.

My wife and I sat next to each other, and the doctor sat facing us. He took a deep breath, and with sad, compassion-filled eyes said, "I don't know how to tell you this, but you're really, really sick." He went on to say, "Your blood levels are extremely low and I am going to recommend immediate ambulance transport to the hospital."

When asked which hospital I preferred, I responded, "Burnsville Ridges," since it was the closest facility from my home. He stated, "Burnsville will not have the facilities that you are going to need," and suggested either Fairview Southdale in Edina or United Hospital in St. Paul. His response did not provide any sense of comfort.

We wrestled briefly with the doctor about not wanting to be driven in the ambulance; we preferred to drive ourselves. He cautiously agreed and offered the following words of warning: "Don't trip or fall, drive slowly, and whatever you do, do not get into an accident."

On Saturday, April 7, 2001 at 5:00 p.m. we departed from the clinic in Eagan and headed to United Hospital in St. Paul where the greatest battle of all would begin—the battle for my life! In the days that lay ahead, the limits of my faith would be tested beyond anything I could imagine, and my need for endurance would never be greater.

The Emergency Room

As we drove to the emergency room, both my wife and I were scared. What was wrong with me? What did the blood test reveal that alarmed the doctor so much? What was going to happen? What should I do now?

My wife began to pray. After that we both got on our cell phones and began calling everyone we knew to request prayer. We called family, friends, church members and our pastors. We even called friends as far away as Jamaica and Australia. A number of people who lived in town jumped in their car and headed to the hospital to meet us.

I remember quoting Bible verses out loud—every verse I could think of that provided a promise and a defense. *"Greater is He who is in me, than he who is in the world."* (1 John 4:4) *"No weapon formed against me shall prosper."* (Isaiah 54:17) *"God has not given me a spirit of fear, but of love, power and a sound mind."* (2 Timothy 1:7)

I kept calling on the Lord, through His Word, to direct my thoughts and to help me. I had no idea what was going on. The one thing I knew for sure—it was serious!

Upon arriving at the emergency room, they checked me in and drew more blood. I had become somewhat used to having blood drawn since I had been tested regularly during the bout with hepatitis.

The blood tests came back and the results were shocking. I did not know much about blood at this point, but in the days, weeks and months ahead, I became quite proficient at blood level numbers and what they meant.

All three major components of my blood were at basement levels. My hemoglobin (red) cells, which are responsible for carrying oxygen to the muscles, brain and entire body, were 5.9 (normal is 13.5 to 17.5). When hemoglobin levels fall below 8.0, a person requires a blood transfusion. One was immediately ordered for me.

My blood platelets, which are responsible for blood clotting, were just 2000 (normal is 130,000 to 430,000). My blood was nearly as thin as water with virtually no ability to clot. When levels fall below 25,000, a person requires a platelet transfusion. A platelet transfusion was ordered immediately.

My white cell count, which is indicative of my immune system capability, was 700 (normal is 3,500 to 10,800). Neutrophils are the predominant type of white cell that provide front line defense against infection and germs. A normal neutrophil count ranges from 1.9 to 8.0. My count was 0.0! This meant that I had virtually no immune system and was highly susceptible to any foreign invader such as bacteria, virus or fungus. A common cold could kill me! Worse yet, white cells cannot be transfused since they only have a life span of a few days once they are produced in the body. The ER staff immediately began an intravenous flow of antibiotics to provide protection from potential bacteria that could kill me.

I felt like a human pincushion, having a number of tubes and needles stuck in both my hands and arms. By this time I had stopped wondering what was happening and simply began to realize that something quite serious was taking place. I was reminded of all the bizarre events that I had experienced over the past year and thought to myself, "This is just the next thing in a string of unfortunate mishaps. No matter what I am about to go through, I will conquer it and it shall not conquer me." I knew that the *testing of my faith HAD produced endurance,* and that I was up for any challenge that came my way.

Over the next few hours, a number of concerned family and friends arrived at the hospital to encourage, comfort and pray for me. Even as a tough ex-Marine that was determined to get through this, the emotions of fear and uncertainty continued with their unrelenting assault. These visitors, who dropped what they were doing and came to stand beside me in the emergency room on that Saturday night, played a very significant role in my life. Not only did they supply encouragement and prayerful support, but by being there for me, they established an assurance of their ongoing support, the support I would need for what was just around the corner—the battle of and for my life!

28 Days in the Hospital

"The Lord is my shepherd. I shall not be in want. He makes me lie down in green pastures. He leads me beside quiet waters. He restores my soul. He guides me in paths of righteousness for His name's sake. Even though I walk through the valley of the shadow of death, I will fear no evil, for you are with me; Your rod and Your staff, they comfort me."

Psalms 23: 1-4

Sunday, April 8th

I woke early in my new environment—a hospital bed in the oncology ward at United Hospital in St. Paul. I had lost 14 pounds over the past couple of months and was not looking or feeling my best and now I was in the hospital. The big question remained: "What was going on with me?"

The night before, in the emergency room, the doctors had run a number of tests on me. They followed those tests with several blood transfusions to increase my low blood levels. During the course of this day, I would meet three different doctors to discuss the results further!

Liver Restored!

The first doctor to visit came with results from tests done on my liver. I had told them about my bout with hepatitis the previous month, so they also ran a series of tests to evaluate my liver functions. The hepatitis specialist I had been seeing in February and March had indicated it would be 6 months before my liver function might return to normal. Well, the tests results blew that projection away—they came back completely normal! Wow! Some great news for a change! In just three weeks my sick and ailing liver functions had been restored to completely normal levels! This amazed the doctor, as well as me.

Virus, Leukemia, or Aplastic Anemia

The second doctor to pay a visit was an oncologist, a specialist in the field of diagnosing and treating cancer. He informed me that at that point they did not know for certain with what I had been stricken; but there was no doubt that it was seriously affecting my bone marrow. There was a possibility a virus, such as the one that had most likely attacked my liver, was now suppressing my bone marrow production. On the other hand, it could be something more serious, such as leukemia or aplastic anemia—a disease that attacks the bone marrow and prevents it from producing the blood the body needs to function. A bone marrow biopsy would determine which situation I was facing. One was scheduled for me bright and early the following day.

After hearing the oncologist's comments, my parents began research on the Internet which provided more insight into the two worst case scenarios—leukemia and aplastic anemia. With my ailing vision, I struggled to read what they had found so that I could familiarize myself with what I hoped would NOT be the diagnosis.

Internal Bleeding Stopped

The third doctor to visit me during the day was an internal medicine specialist. His visit was more one of curiosity and amazement. In my conversation with him, he asked me if I had suffered from any recent bleeding. I let him know that about three weeks earlier I had experienced bleeding from my nose, gums and face, as well as coughing it up, but that it had completely stopped just three days ago. That was the part he could not figure out—why the bleeding stopped when in fact, it should have grown worse due to the nose-diving platelet count.

He informed me that the bleeding had probably begun due to my body's platelet count falling so low—the blood no longer had the ability to clot. This caused the blood to begin seeping out from the organs. He simply could not understand why there were no signs of internal bleeding, a symptom on its own that could have caused my death. He concluded that for the bleeding to have started three weeks ago, for the platelet count to have diminished to 2000 during that same time frame, and for the bleeding to have stopped three days ago without any signs of internal bleeding, was a medical impossibility.

After this conversation, it began to dawn on me that something miraculous had occurred after receiving prayer from Pastor Holmes just three days prior. Something took place inside my body when all those little white lights were racing around inside. Although I had the privilege of seeing this vision during the prayer, what really occurred? I did not fully understand the impact of that prayer for another five days.

Monday, April 9th

Bone Marrow Biopsy

The pinnacle of my day was a bone marrow biopsy. I knew it would not be a pleasant experience, but I geared up for it, knowing it would bring me one step closer to a diagnosis and (hopefully) an understanding of what was going on with me.

At 10 a.m., the pathologist and his team arrived and began the procedure with an IV of morphine, followed by an incision on my backside, left of center at the belt line. Next they drilled and removed a 7/8 inch long by 1/8 inch in diameter cylinder of hip bone. They inserted a large needle into the opening and drew out some bone marrow for testing. Needless to say, this was an uncomfortable process.

Gabriel Outside My Door

Later in the afternoon, the morphine had worn off and I was feeling the pain. About that time, I received a phone call from Pat Moe, one of our pastors from church. She had visited me the day before, and spent some time praying with me in my room. She called to convey an absolutely amazing message that was exactly what I needed from the Lord at that specific point in time. God knew what the diagnosis would be before they informed me of it the next day, so He gave me something very special that day—something that would encourage me and strengthen me for what I was about to learn.

Recalling her time in my hospital room, Pastor Moe said, "The glory of the Lord was extremely strong yesterday. I have visited many, many people in hospitals before, but have only experienced the presence and glory of God one other time like I did while in your room. On that other occasion, God miraculously healed that person and I believe He is going to heal you too."

"Awesome! Praise God! I believe that too!" was my response.

She continued, "But that's not all. As I left your room, I saw an eight foot angel standing in the hall next to your door, as if he was guarding it. He appeared to be dressed in some type of battle gear. As I walked toward the elevator, I prayed and asked God what I had just seen. God said, 'That is Gabriel.'"

For a moment I was stunned and shocked. "Gabriel?" Then I replied, "Praise the Lord! Psalms 34:7 says, *'The angel of the Lord encamps around those who fear Him, and rescues them!'* Wow! I am going to be rescued!" I know that *"all things work together for good for those who love God and for those who are called according to His purpose."* (Romans 8:28) This vision and these words from Pastor Moe—which God planned for me to hear at that exact time—were awesome. They gave me the strength I would need after receiving the diagnosis.

Retinal Hemorrhaging

As if I had not had enough excitement for the day already, I was also scheduled to see an ophthalmologist in order to determine why my vision had dimmed so significantly. Upon examination, he discovered that the low blood counts and profuse coughing had caused blood vessels in the back of my retinas to burst. While the bleeding had stopped, scar tissue was preventing light from properly focusing.

As a result, I had an obscured spectrum of sight. I was unable to read a book if I looked straight at it. I could see slightly better if I looked out of the corner of my eyes rather than straight ahead. The ophthalmologist predicted that my vision would clear up in approximately four months as I continued to receive blood transfusions.

Tuesday, April 10th

The "blood cart" rolled in at 6:30 a.m. That's what I called it anyway. Each morning the nurse on duty would roll the blood cart up along my bedside and draw blood for testing. Each morning my veins were met with a sharp needle which would then extract two to five tubes of blood.

Biopsy Results

This day was unforgettable—Tuesday, April 10, 2001. Could you imagine forgetting the day your doctor informed you that you had a disease that would likely take your life?

I remember the moment vividly. It was mid-morning. The lights in the room were dim like the moment I was about to experience. In walked the oncologist with his clipboard and a mundane expression. His initial words were simple and to the point, "Well, you have aplastic anemia."

I knew what this meant! It was awful! I had read the Internet printouts about aplastic anemia the night before. Immediately my heart felt like a molten cup of lead burning deeply as it poured into the depths of my gut. I felt the most unusual and uncomfortable shift in my body's chemistry, like a gripping, dry heat which was engulfing my total existence, sucking the life out of me. I had never felt anything so uncomfortable in my life.

It felt like a bad dream; seconds seemed like an eternity. My thoughts raced in multiple directions, turning from intense fear to thoughts of "control" and calm, to visions of my wife and children without a husband and a dad. I don't think I had ever thought so fast before in my life!

Then, in another instant, I realized I had a choice to make right then and there—in my mind and deep within my very soul. Would I be ruled by fear, or by faith? Would I focus on my circumstances or on God's promises of healing? God had brought me through a year's worth of challenges thus far and I sensed that He had prepared me for this time. My all-knowing God knew that this disease would attack me at this particular time in my life and He had been strengthening me to meet it head on. On top of all this, He had Gabriel standing outside my door! Why should I be fearful?

Within seconds of my mental sabbatical, in a room filled with silence, I propped myself up in my bed, looked the oncologist straight in the eye and with a smile on my face and a heart of determination said, "Wow! Won't this make a great testimony when God heals me!"

The oncologist was shocked at my remark and proceeded to explain the serious nature of the diagnosis. He pointed out that my diagnosis fell into the category of "severe" aplastic anemia, one much worse than most. The severity was due to the fact that my blood numbers were so low when I arrived at the hospital coupled with the fact that no marrow stem cells were found during the biopsy. Both of these factors reduced the chances of successful treatment.

What is Aplastic Anemia?

Aplastic anemia is an autoimmune disease, which means the immune system attacks another part of the body. Specifically, aplastic anemia occurs when the immune system gets confused and begins receiving cell-to-cell communications indicating that the bone marrow is an invader to the human body. The instant the perceived "invader" appears on radar, the immune system attacks it. The bone marrow, however, is the chief manufacturing plant of all blood cells, including the white cells which are the immune system itself. So, in essence, aplastic anemia causes the immune system to commit suicide.

Aplastic anemia can be linked to several factors such as radiation, environmental toxins and hepatitis. Although they could not be certain why I had contracted the disease, they speculated that the bout with hepatitis had set off the aplastic anemia. The likelihood of hepatitis triggering aplastic anemia in a human body is nearly one in three million, and the disease itself is extremely rare, with only 496 reported cases throughout the United States in 2000.

Two Medical Possibilities

I learned from the oncologist that people with aplastic anemia had two possible treatment options. Their outcomes were dependent on age, health and the degree of the disease. With an age of 44, overall good health and physical condition, but a serious diagnosis, the doctor was not optimistic that I would experience any benefits from either treatment option and that I'd likely die.

The first option, which is always preferred, is a treatment called ATG (anti-thymocyte globulin), followed by a drug called Cyclosporine. The second option, and usually the last resort, is a bone marrow transplant. Without success, the patient would eventually be exposed to a germ that would cause complications resulting in death.

My oncologist discussed with me whether or not to even try the ATG option since my bone marrow biopsy had come back showing neither marrow nor stem cells. For the ATG treatment to have a fighting chance of success there needed to be marrow stem cells present. My doctor decided to review the biopsy with a team of specialists at the University of Minnesota Bone Marrow Transplant Center for assistance in making the next move. Upon their review, the doctors concluded there was "nothing to lose, we'll give ATG a shot."

A positive response to the treatment would mean 1) that I had stem cells that were undetected in the biopsy, 2) that the ATG had successfully stopped the aggressive immune cells from attacking the bone marrow, 3) that the few remaining stem cells would begin to produce hemoglobin, platelets and white cells and 4) that my blood count would increase to higher levels.

The doctors made it clear to me, however, that even if my blood levels notched up a bit, they would never return to normal levels due to the degree of damage done. Additionally, if any marrow stem cells did remain, they would be insufficient to produce enough blood cells to return the blood counts to normal levels.

ATG, believe it or not, involves running horse blood through a person's body in a series of eight transfusions, 12 hours apart, with each transfusion taking four hours. The side effects of this treatment include rashes, cold sweats, chills and headaches. The procedure was scheduled to commence on the evening of April 11th and conclude on the morning of April 15th. If successful, signs would appear within two weeks of the completion of the procedure, or by the end of April. Only time would reveal the outcome.

Australian Pastor Doug Stanton

During my stay in the hospital, I had frequent visits from Doug Stanton, a gifted pastor from Australia. He was present when the doctor delivered my diagnosis and prognosis resulting from the biopsy test. After the doctor left, Pastor Doug prayed with me and we talked a bit. What he had to say really touched my heart and I began to cry. The tears later turned to joy as I felt a strong sense that the Lord was going to be using me for big things in the future—of course, after I was miraculously healed!

Wednesday, April 11th

Daily Routine

I started a schedule, a routine, so that I could stay focused on my walk through this "wilderness" on my journey to a miracle. Each day I made of point of doing a number of specific things.

First thing in the morning, of course, was my visit with the nurse and her blood cart. Each day I deposited two or three, sometimes even five, tubes of blood for testing. Each morning the oncologist would pop his head in the door with the results and ask me how I was doing. Before he told me the results, I would say, "Today's the day, my blood numbers are normal!" And he'd say in his low, monotone voice, "Not today." My response was always, "Tomorrow then."

During the day I read the Bible, focusing on verses which promised healing. While it was difficult to see the words clearly, I could still make them out. Each day the Lord impressed on my heart a particular Bible verse and its meaning to me. Each day I wrote the verse (book, chapter and verse) on my ink board on the wall of my hospital room. They accumulated one by one on that ink board for 28 days. I have posted each of these 28 verses, along with the importance that each one had to me, in the appendix.

I also listened to praise and worship music on my CD player each day. I thanked God for all the good things He had done for me and for His promises of healing, as I continued to look for and expect a miracle.

I never even turned on the TV! I had more important things to do. Many of my friends brought me books, and here in the hospital I had time to actually read all of them. Thanks again to all of you who were so thoughtful. The reading was outstanding.

I did my best to move around and stretch at least a couple times per day. It was a bit difficult with an IV in my arm, but I managed.

Taking a shower also had its challenges; I learned to function in the shower with my arm all wrapped up in plastic in order to keep the water out of the IV connectors. I simply rolled the device that held the IV tubes and saline (or whatever medication they had prescribed for that day) into the bathroom and up to the shower entrance.

Once a day my room was dusted and cleaned. I needed to wear a mask while my room was being cleaned and for 30 minutes afterward so the dust would have time to settle. It was essential that the room stayed very clean, because my condition was neutropenic, meaning I had a low neutrophil count and was highly susceptible to germs. Not only was it important to keep my room extremely free from germs, but my food was specially prepared as well. All visitors to my room needed to wash their hands or put on gloves. Everyone was to keep a fair distance from me.

Acts 3:16—It's For Me!

In the middle of the afternoon I was reading my Bible when my eyes crossed over the 16th verse in Acts chapter 3. Those who have seen my Bible can attest to the fact that it looks like a rainbow from all the passages I have highlighted. But Acts 3:16? Not at all; it was simply black on white.

Something amazing happened as I read these words: *"On the basis of faith in His name, it is the name of Jesus which has strengthened this man whom you see and know; and the faith which comes through Him has given him this perfect health in the presence of you all."* (Acts 3:16)

I immediately received this verse in my heart and spoke out in a quiet voice, "That's going to be me. That's talking about me!" Instantly, I heard that still, small voice of the Lord say these incredible words to me: *"That's the verse you're going to share with everyone on the day you're made whole."* Wow! It was so real. My eyes teared up with joy! Our God is an awesome God!

> *"That's the verse you're going to share*
> *with everyone on the day you're made whole."*

ATG Treatment Begins

My first horse blood (ATG) transfusion began at 4:00 p.m. and lasted four hours. The battery of eight transfusions would be administered every 12 hours over the next four days, which meant I would be awakened at 4 a.m. for the next four days as well. That seemed to me an odd schedule, but what could I say? I was just the patient.

I fell asleep early that evening, but woke shortly after midnight with a nasty bout of hives. I was experiencing a fairly bad reaction to the ATG. They immediately administered an IV bag of Benadryl. Slowly the itching and swelling subsided and I fell back to sleep for a few hours, before the next round of ATG.

I geared myself up to remain faith-filled and positive over those next four days. I expected the ATG treatments to bring about the much desired increase in my blood levels, thereby reducing my need to receive blood transfusions so frequently. There are risks to receiving any blood transfusion, but the risk increases with time and frequency.

Transfusions

Without functioning blood cells, one dies. Since I lacked marrow, and therefore the ability to produce blood cells on my own, I required regular blood transfusions. Ultimately, I required a blood transfusion every three to four days on average. I needed platelet transfusions more frequently than hemoglobin (red cell) transfusions, as platelets have a much shorter lifespan.

After each transfusion, my hemoglobin and/or platelet levels rose, but then slowly declined over a period of days, before I needed another transfusion. The doctors pointed out that the human body often begins to reject transfused blood. After two to three months of transfusions, my body could fail to respond to the new blood or it could reject it all together, bringing on a new set of completely different life-threatening complications.

I also learned that blood levels attained after a successful transfusion may be less in the future. For example, if my platelet count reached 50,000 after any given transfusion, it may only rise to 40,000 after a future transfusion. If this began to occur, I would need more frequent transfusions to keep the levels safe. Fewer transfusions are always best, but if I needed the blood, they had to transfuse if it is still safe to do so.

After having a red blood transfusion, my hemoglobin level typically rose to a range of 9.5 to 11.5, before falling again. Normal levels in men are 13.5 to 17.5. Once my level fell back below 8.0, it was time for another blood transfusion. The standard two-bag, red cell transfusion takes roughly eight hours to complete.

After having a platelet transfusion, my levels on average only rose to 24,000. This was disheartening for two reasons: (1) my level was so far from the normal range of 130,000 to 430,000, and (2) this low count required me to receive more frequent platelet transfusions. A platelet transfusion is required when levels fall under 25,000 (10,000 while in a controlled hospital environment). A typical one-bag platelet transfusion only takes 30 to 40 minutes to complete.

Blood testing is a big part of evaluating and monitoring "progress." Astoundingly, since early March I'd had 58 tubes of blood drawn from my arms, wrists and hands. I had three blood transfusions in less than five days, not counting my four-day ATG treatment which had just begun.

Beyond Belief

The doctors were very careful not to give me more transfusions than I really needed, working to keep a balance between proper life support, and over-transfusing in an effort to prevent my body from rejecting the donated blood.

I am so grateful to everyone who donates blood. Whoever you are, wherever you are, thank you! If it weren't for you, many would not be alive today, including me.

Thursday, April 12th

A Letter to the Hospital Staff

After the Lord spoke to me about Acts 3:16, and how I would share with everyone on the day I was made whole, I was unable to stop thinking about its significance.

I got a sense from the Lord that I would be writing a letter of some kind to the hospital staff and that the Bible verses I added to the ink board in my room each day would be a part of the letter. It was impressed upon my heart that the letter would need to explain how I was miraculously healed, since the medical world would not be able to explain why or what happened once my tests were normal again. I sensed that I was supposed to prepare this letter immediately, and that when I was healed completely, I would deliver the letter which I had already prepared during the time I was sick and still in the hospital.

Initially this seemed a bit far out, but yet it wasn't. It was exactly in line with what I believed, so I acted on my belief and asked my wife to bring my laptop to the hospital. I told her that God was going to help me write a letter to the doctors and nurses who worked there and were caring for me.

Do the Deeds You Did at First

Later in the evening as I was jumping about in the Scriptures, I came across Revelation 2. These passages *were* all highlighted in my Bible and I was very familiar with them. This time as I read them, I felt as if *my name* was being inserted into the verses. It became very personal. In Revelation chapters 2 and 3 Jesus spoke to the seven churches; He delivered seven messages (called "Letters"), one to each church. At the end of each letter, He said, *"He who has an ear, let him hear what the Spirit says to the churches."* The churches in this sense are Christians— believers.

The first letter, written to the church at Ephesus, begins in Revelation chapter 2. As I read it, it was personalized this way: *"The One (Jesus) who holds the seven stars in His right hand, the One (Jesus) who walks among the seven golden lampstands, says this: 'Jeff, I know your deeds and your toil and perseverance, and that you cannot tolerate evil men, and you put to the test those who call themselves apostles, and they are not, and you found them to be false; and Jeff you have perseverance and have endured for My name's sake, and have not grown weary. But I have this against you Jeff, that you have left your first love. Therefore remember from where you have fallen, and repent and do the deeds you did at first; or else I am coming to you and will remove your lampstand out of its place—unless you repent. He who has an ear, let him hear what the Spirit says to the churches. To him who overcomes Jeff, I will grant to eat of the Tree of Life which is in the Paradise of God.'"* [Emphasis added]

As I read this passage it re-affirmed what I had felt two days earlier when Doug Stanton prayed with me after receiving the diagnosis. God spoke to my heart and told me to do more for Him by way of ministry—the kind of ministry I had done when I first became a believer in 1981. At that time, my heart was truly on fire for God. Jesus was the love of my life. It was a time when I continually shared my faith with others and told them of the goodness and love of God; God had used me on a regular basis to lead people into a personal relationship with their Creator. I was now reminded that I had "left my first love" and that Jesus wanted to be first in my life again, just like He was when I first accepted Him into my life. He reminded me to "do the deeds I did at first".

This was a special, personal moment with God; it was emotional, spiritual and powerful all at the same time. I repented and asked forgiveness for my self-serving ways. I asked God to help me make the necessary changes in my life. He heard me and He comforted me as I prayed. I drew strength from His Spirit and from His love.

The Lord's Imminent Return

I sensed that the Lord's return was near—nearer than I and many Christians might think. I had written a book about prophecy in 1982 and I was aware that the signs were all around us, but I had become a bit sidetracked and had lost focus on the importance of always being ready. Throughout the Bible it says that Jesus will return at an hour no one will expect, like a thief in the night, and we are to make sure we are ready at all times for His unannounced return.

In the book of Daniel, when describing the last days, it is written, *"Those who have insight will shine brightly like the brightness of the expanse of heaven, and those who lead the many to righteousness, like the stars forever and ever."* (Daniel 12:3) The question I pondered was, "Do I have insight?"

As I sat in my hospital bed thinking about all this, I recalled 2 Peter 3:9 which states, *"The Lord is not slow about His promise, as some count slowness, but is patient toward you, not wishing for any to perish, but for all to come to repentance."* I felt God teaching me and warning me at the same time. Another verse (Luke 12:39-40) followed, *"But be sure of this, that if the head of the house had known at what hour the thief was coming, he would not have allowed his house to be broken into. You too, be ready; for the Son of Man is coming at an hour that you do not expect."* And then a final verse came to me, *"...The harvest is plentiful, but the laborers are few."* (Matthew 9:37)

I then understood. The Lord showed me these verses in rapid succession because He was calling me to share the wonderful message of His love with those I knew, those I would meet, and even those I didn't yet know. Not just now and then, or here and there, but in a more fervent and committed way. I still had time and work to do. Not only did I understand my responsibility, but I was even more certain now that God's hand was upon me and that I would be miraculously healed.

With this revelation, I prayed and told the Lord that as He opened doors for me, I would share His unconditional love with those who did not have a personal relationship with Him, as well as with those believers who might have lost their focus and closeness in their relationship with Him.

Friday, April 13th

Surprise Call from Pastor Holmes

I am not superstitious, so I treated Friday the 13th as just another day. However, that day would prove to be a far cry from "just another day."

About midday I received a phone call from Pastor Holmes, the pastor who prayed for me two days prior to my being admitted to the hospital. From his car in Scottsdale, Arizona, he called my office and was transferred to my hospital room phone. We had not spoken since he had prayed for me, at the meeting at his church on Lake Street in Minneapolis. His message for me was profound.

He told me the Lord had spoken to him and told him, *"Jeff received a partial healing, and the rest of his healing will come if he is obedient to what you are to tell him."* I instantly realized that the partial healing was the stoppage of the internal bleeding that the doctors could not explain. It all began to make sense now; it was during Pastor Holmes' prayer—when I envisioned all those little white lights—that the "partial healing" had taken place! Right after that event my nose, face and mouth had stopped bleeding.

Pastor Holmes had no idea I was in the hospital before making the call to me that day; he had no knowledge of my blood, marrow, nothing! He only knew what the Lord had told him: that I had received a partial healing and that the remaining healing would happen if I was obedient to what the Lord asked me to do.

Nearly in shock I responded, "I'm all ears. What am I supposed to do?"

He humbly replied, "The Lord is asking you to sow into our new ministry here in Arizona—a ministry designed to get kids off the

71

streets." He pointed out that he, himself, was not requesting the money, but that the Lord was. He said I could send $5, $10, $1 or whatever. "Whether you wish to sow is your choice, as is the amount." When I initially heard this, I mentally backed off a bit, but continued to listen.

He briefly explained the relationship between Abraham and Melchizedek as written about in Genesis 14 and Hebrews 7. He said the Lord had used this Biblical illustration as the basis for the request He was making of me. Although I did not completely understand this, I wanted to learn. I knew for a fact that a miracle had already occurred, that my internal bleeding had stopped. This provided instant credibility to what Pastor Holmes told me. I told him that I would read these passages, pray about it and let him know tomorrow. He said, "Fine, no problem."

I read the chapters right away. The Bible says (Genesis 15:6; Romans 4:3; Galatians 3:6) *"Abraham believed God, and it was reckoned* [credited] *to him as righteousness,"* [Explanation added] and as a result, he received the "promise" of being the father of many nations. This relationship goes on to show that Abraham, the patriarch, tithed 1/10 of his wealth to Melchizedek, and in return, Melchizedek "blessed" the promise which Abraham had received from God. (Hebrews 7:3) Melchizedek, the king of peace and righteousness, was, *"without father, without mother, without genealogy, having neither beginning of days nor end of life, but made like the Son of God, he remains a priest perpetually."* This was extremely interesting.

Being Obedient & Releasing the Money

When my wife arrived at the hospital later that evening, I shared with her what Pastor Holmes had told me. After discussing the specifics of all the interesting circumstances over the past eight days, we concluded that God was asking for our obedience with respect to helping this ministry in Arizona. Since we've always been givers, we looked forward to helping in this way. After agreeing on a dollar amount, my wife planned to call Pastor Holmes first thing in the morning with the news. Her phone call set a series of events in motion—events that are quite simply, "Beyond Belief."

Saturday, April 14ᵗʰ

The Rest of the Healing

Once each month, on a Saturday morning, I attended the 8 a.m. men's prayer breakfast held at Hosanna, my church in Lakeville, Minnesota. Obviously I was not in attendance that day. I later learned that around 9 a.m., the guys at this breakfast held a special prayer for me, knowing that I was recently admitted to the hospital and diagnosed with a serious disease.

During their prayer for me, the Holy Spirit fell upon one of the attendees—Paul. The Lord spoke clearly and powerfully to Paul saying, *"Paul, I want you to go to the hospital where Jeff Scislow is, pray for him, lay your left hand on his head and tell him that he has been healed!"* Immediately Paul's left arm heated up with fire and a tingle, as if electricity were filling his arm! This incredible sensation was present from the tip of his fingers right up through his shoulder.

Now, Paul did not know me. He knew *of* me as a well-known Realtor, but did not know me personally. He had no idea what hospital I was in or how to find me. He was a bit frightened, but wanted to obey this direct command from the Lord.

At the end of the men's breakfast, with his left arm still hot and electrified, an alarmed Paul walked around the church seeking a pastor with whom he could speak. With no success, he returned home to tell his wife what had happened. Still not knowing what to do, he decided to wash his car in the warmth of the springtime day that had finally arrived in the Twin Cities. Even after washing his car, the powerful tingle that had engulfed his left arm did not subside. He decided to eat lunch while considering what he should do.

After lunch the condition of his arm had not changed. At 1:30 p.m., Paul decided to go back to church and look again for a pastor. After combing the halls and offices, something prompted Paul to stick his head into the prayer chapel. He saw a familiar face and approached Greg, a man who had recently led a Bible study that Paul had attended. Feeling a sense of relief, Paul shared what had happened with Greg.

As Paul was sharing this story with Greg, a smile appeared on Greg's face. When Paul finished speaking, Greg informed Paul that, "Jeff Scislow is in room 4526 at United Hospital." Paul nearly fell over in astonishment! "What?" Paul responded. Greg repeated himself, "Jeff Scislow is in room 4526 at United Hospital. I know that because I work there." Paul had an assignment and God was going to ensure it was completed.

At 7:30 p.m., Paul knocked on the door of room 4526. "Come in," I said. Paul slowly entered the room, humble and nervous, and told me his incredible story. He told me that his left arm was still hot and electrified. Tears of excitement and anticipation filled my eyes as I praised God for what was about to happen. Paul prayed and when he placed his left hand on my head, the Holy Spirit—with fire and electricity—flowed out of Paul's hand and into my body. I cried tears of joy that soon turned to uncontrolled laughter. It was truly incredible!

It dawned on me that "the rest of my healing" had just occurred. God had moved powerfully in response to my obedience to His request that had come from Pastor Holmes' phone call. "It's happening just as God said it would," I expressed to Paul. "I've just been healed! Praise God! Hallelujah! This is so awesome!"

Write the Letter!

Later that evening, after Paul departed and just before I planned to sleep, the Lord said to me, *"Write the letter!"* Filled with excitement over all that had happened, I quickly grabbed my laptop computer (which my wife had brought to me) and began to write a letter. This letter would not be given to the doctors and nurses until my bone marrow was restored and my blood levels were back to normal and no medical explanation.

I titled the letter, "I've Been Miraculously Healed" and dated it that day, April 14, 2001. As I composed the letter, I eagerly anticipated how exciting it would be both for me to deliver the letter, and for the doctors and nurses to read it!

I worked on it for a couple of hours before I felt it was just right, then saved it on my computer for that special day—the one I was greatly anticipating. Here is the letter and that special verse (Acts 3:16) that I would "share with everyone on the day I'm made whole!"

I've Been Miraculously Healed!

"On the basis of faith in His name, it is the name of Jesus which has strengthened this man whom you see and know; and the faith which comes through Him has given him (me) this perfect health in the presence of you all." (Acts 3:16)

I am writing this on Saturday April 14, 2001. As you know, I was admitted to my room 4526, United Hospital just one week ago today. I have been diagnosed as having no bone marrow (aplastic anemia), an extremely rare and deadly disease. I could not imagine how difficult this diagnosis would be for a patient that did not have a personal relationship & faith in Jesus Christ. My faith is enabling me to stand on God's promises as I believe for a full and complete healing, all in God's perfect timing. As each of you know, there is no fear residing in me.

The moment I arrived in my room I began adding Bible verses to the white ink board on the wall in my room for two reasons; one for my strength to endure this testing period and two, so that I could share them with you. Now that I have been in this room for one week, the Lord is telling me to write this very letter to you now, but not share it with you until my bone marrow and blood counts are once again normal. Due to the fact that you're now reading this, I have been undoubtedly and miraculously healed! Praise God!

I was blessed by each of you. Each doctor and each nurse who took care of me and tended to me shall not lose their reward for their kindness. God is faithful. Below are some of those verses that I have written on my wall, along with a few others. My prayer for each of you is that you come to know the Lord Jesus in an even more personal way. He loves you and He does perform on all His promises if we trust Him wholeheartedly! His Word is powerful & alive!

My Miracle Verses

"Consider it all joy, my brethren when you encounter various trials, knowing that the testing of your faith produces endurance, and let endurance have its perfect result, that you may be perfect and complete, lacking in nothing." (James 1:2-4)

"Therefore humble yourselves under the mighty hand of God, that He may exalt you at the proper time, casting all your anxiety upon Him, because He cares for you... After you have suffered a little while, the God of all grace, who called you to His eternal glory in Christ, will Himself perfect, confirm, strengthen and establish you." (1 Peter 5:6-7, 10)

"For the Word of God is living and active and sharper than any two-edged sword, and piercing as far as the division ofsoul and spirit, of both joints and <u>marrow,</u> and able to judge the thoughts and intentions of the heart." (Hebrews 4:12) [Emphasis added]

"No weapon formed against you [me] *shall prosper."* (Isaiah 54:17) [Emphasis added]

"The angel of the Lord encamps around those who fear Him, and rescues them." (Psalms 34:7)

"The righteous cry, and the Lord hears and delivers them out of all their troubles." (Psalms 34:17)

"Many are the afflictions of the righteous; but the Lord delivers him out of them all." (Psalms 34:19)

"For I know the plans that I have for you," declares the Lord, *"plans for welfare and not for calamity, to give you a future and a hope."* (Jeremiah 29:11)

"My son, give attention to My words; incline your ear to My sayings; do not let them depart from your sight; keep them in the midst of your heart. For they are life to those who find them and health to all their whole body." (Proverbs 4:20-22)

"Beloved, do not be surprised at the fiery ordeal among you, which comes upon you for your testing, as though some strange thing were happening to you; but to the degree you share in the sufferings of Christ, keep on rejoicing, so that also at the revelation of His glory, you may rejoice with exultation." (1 Peter 4:12-13)

"Therefore I say to you, all things for which you pray and ask, believe that you have received them, and they will be granted you." (Mark 11:24)

"Whatever you ask in My name, that will I do, so that the Father may be glorified in the Son. If you ask Me anything in My name, I will do it." (John 14:13-14)

"If you abide in Me, and My words abide in you, ask whatever you wish, and it will be done for you." (John 15:7)

"For we walk by faith, not by sight." (2 Corinthians 5:7)

"For God has not given us the spirit of fear; but of power, and of love, and of a sound mind." (2 Timothy 1:7)

"Therefore, do not throw away your confidence, which has great reward. For you have need of endurance, so that when you have done the will of God, you may receive what was promised." (Hebrews 10:35-36)

— **Former Patient, Jeff Scislow**

Sunday, April 15th

Easter Sunday

After the amazing day I just had, I could not wait for the doctor to roll in mid-morning and deliver me the miraculous results of my 6:30 a.m. blood draw. I felt especially "honored" to be able to experience my miracle on "Easter Sunday". I was so filled with anticipation I began buzzing the nurse on the call button and asking when the doctor would arrive.

The doctor arrived, but no miracle. In fact, my blood levels had dropped considerably from the day before. Multiple transfusions were ordered, both platelets and hemoglobin. These transfusions were in addition to the final ATG transfusion that was scheduled for 4 p.m.

For most of the day, as I received bag after bag of blood, I thought to myself, "What happened?" I played the events of the last few days over and over in my mind. They were so closely tied to one another yet they were miraculous in themselves. Paul was given a clear message for me, "Jeff, you are healed!" I could not figure that part out. I had expected to be healed, but I was still very sick, lying there in bed with all kinds of needles in me receiving multiple blood transfusions. It was Easter Sunday and I was expecting it to be *the* day. "What happened?"

During the course of this long day, I was reminded of what 1 Peter 5:6 says: *"Therefore, humble yourselves under the mighty hand of God, that He may exalt you at the proper time."* I realized that I needed to be patient and continue trusting God, especially for His timing on the healing I was expecting. The Word clearly says, *"… at the proper time"*. Even though God knows exactly when that time is, I optimistically believed that my miracle—being that it did not arrive that day—would arrive the following day!

Monday, April 16th

Filled once again with the anticipation of receiving my miraculous healing, I looked forward to the doctor's visit and reporting of the day's blood draw. To my disappointment, there was no indication of a "healing." The blood numbers were only slightly higher, even after receiving all the blood transfusions the day before.

Take Your Thoughts Captive

My emotions began to slip. I started to feel like I was fighting a losing battle. Maybe the doctors were right. Fear was knocking on my door; I was slipping into what I call, "no man's land." It is not the place anyone wants to be. After experiencing these thoughts for a few minutes, I caught myself from falling deeper into the trap of negativity. I needed to stay positive and take those thoughts *"captive to the obedience of Christ"* as it says in 2 Corinthians 10:5.

Taking "thoughts captive" simply means that *any* thoughts inconsistent with God's promises need to be "captured" and aligned with what God says. Negative thoughts would wage war against my faith, as they would be in direct opposition to what God had promised to do. They would bring on feelings of fear, doubt and worry. When I chose to stand on God's promises instead, the negative thoughts and emotions would be replaced with those of peace, joy and confidence!

Each time I had a fearful, anxious or doubting thought, I made a conscious effort to "capture" and resist it. I would counter-punch such thoughts with Bible verses that promised something positive, often speaking the verses out loud. I needed to make a regular, determined effort to do this—to capture any negative thinking and to do it each and every day, for as many days as it took, until the victory was mine.

Taking thoughts "captive" is a learned behavior. As I continued to practice this, I gained strength each and every time. As I resisted the devil (his lies and the negative thoughts he initiated), he fled from me, just like it promises in James 4:7. In the midst of these emotional and spiritual battles, I regularly spoke these words out loud: *"The Lord has not given me a spirit of fear, but of love, power and a sound mind."* (2 Timothy 1:7)

Taking my thoughts captive to the obedience of Christ did not ensure that I would not be attacked by my emotions again at some future date. I have come to learn that it is an ongoing battle, but one I am promised to win in the end if I do not give up.

A Messenger in the Night

It was well past visiting hours when a friend unexpectedly showed up in my room. He explained to me how he had to negotiate with the security guard in order to pass and how he could only stay a few minutes. He went on to tell me that the Lord had prompted him to bring me a particular cassette tape that he had sitting around his house—one that had a sermon by Chip Brim on it. I thanked him and told him I'd listen to it. Little did I know, at that time, the revelation I'd receive from hearing the message.

Tuesday, April 17th

Daniel Waits 21 Days for Answer to Prayer

After providing my 75th tube of blood since March, I popped in the cassette my friend had delivered to me the night before. In his message, Chip Brim spoke about the significance of the 10th chapter of the book of Daniel and how it relates to prayer being answered.

I carefully read Daniel 10 over and over again. From this chapter, I learned that Daniel prayed to God for a revelation, but did not get an answer to his prayer for 21 days. Daniel's prayer was "heard on the 1st day," but Daniel did not receive the response until the 21st day. What happened? Why the delay? This is where it gets interesting.

Immediately after Daniel began to pray, the answer to his prayer was sent from heaven with "the angel of the Lord" (presumed to be Gabriel). However, before Gabriel was able to deliver the revelation (answer to his prayer) to Daniel, he encountered the Prince of Persia, a demonic force in the heavenly realm who opposed the delivery of the answered prayer. During these 21 days, another demonic force—the King of Persia—entered the battle.

As the battle between angelic and demonic forces waged on, Daniel persisted in prayer, fasting while he prayed, choosing not to give up, and continuing to expect an answer to his prayer—an answer he desperately needed.

On the 21st day of Daniel's persistent prayer, Michael the archangel, was dispatched from heaven to fight alongside Gabriel. These two powerful angels overpowered the demonic forces, allowing Daniel to receive the answer to his prayer! This is a wonderful image of spiritual warfare and the subsequent spiritual breakthrough that resulted.

The Goal Line Defense

In his sermon, Brim, a former football coach, described a vision that the Lord had given him years before. In the vision, the Lord took Brim to a very interesting football game during which he was neither on the field, nor in the bleachers, but rather hovering above the field with a clear view of everything. From this perspective in the vision, the Lord illustrated to Brim what he already knew from his own experience: It is much easier to move the football from your own end of the field or even from mid-field, but as you enter your opponent's end of the field, it becomes more difficult to move the ball. In fact, when you get down to the one yard line, the defense puts in its biggest and toughest players to prevent you from scoring a touchdown.

"The same is true in the spiritual world," the Lord told Brim. When people in need are on the cusp of receiving their miracle, their healing, their answered prayer, the enemy (Satan) will put in his best defensive players to prevent a touchdown. He will dispatch his evil, demonic warriors to instill doubt, fear, uncertainty and chaos to get them to give up, cave in, quit, and throw in the towel. But if they do, they lose and the enemy wins. However, if one perseveres like Daniel, the touchdown will be scored, the miracle will arrive and the faithful recipient will tell the world what Jesus had done! That is the last thing Satan wants, so he will put up a fight.

In Brim's vision, the Lord then revealed millions and millions of people, young and old, who had died on the one-yard line. They never made it. They got close, but never got over the goal line. They never scored their touchdown, never received their healing and never got their miracle. When the enemy challenged their emotions and faith with all his weapons, he overcame them.

"Wow," I thought, "This is really heavy." I gained strength both from Brim's message and the 10th chapter of Daniel. I would not be a casualty on the one-yard line; my faith would not fail! I would trust

God completely, unwaveringly, expecting a miracle no matter how long it took! I was drawn to the verse that says, *"My righteous one shall live by faith; and if he shrinks back, My soul has no pleasure in him. But we are not of those who shrink back to destruction, but of those who have faith to the preserving of the soul."* (Hebrews 10:38-39)

Our Battles are Spiritual in Nature

Ephesians 6:12 reads, *"For our struggle is not against flesh and blood, but against the rulers, against the powers, against the world forces of this darkness, against the spiritual forces of wickedness in the heavenly places."* This is exactly what Daniel experienced in his 21 days of spiritual battle. Daniel did not give up and neither would I!

Brim's message encouraged me to stand fast, stand firm and trust the Lord. I needed to be patient and believe God in His perfect timing. I needed to firmly adopt this mindset so that I would be less prone to being overcome by circumstances. I truly needed to *"walk by faith, not by sight."* (2 Corinthians 5:7)

Hebrews 6:11-12 says to *"...show the same diligence so as to realize the full assurance of hope until the end, so that you may not be sluggish, but imitators of those who through faith and patience inherit the promises."* Hebrews 10:35-36 reads, *"Therefore, do not throw away your confidence, which has great reward. For you have need for endurance, so that when you have done the will of God, you may receive what was promised."*

Wednesday, April 18th

I Am Healed!

My mind continually replayed the events that had occurred since I had arrived at the hospital. I repeatedly went over the details in an attempt to gain a better understanding of what was happening to me and what I needed to do next.

I was particularly intrigued and perplexed by what Paul had told me the prior Saturday night. The Lord told Paul, "Pray for Jeff. Lay your left hand on his head and tell him he is healed."

"Maybe Paul got it wrong," I thought. "Did he say it correctly? Maybe he was supposed to say, 'Jeff, you *will* be healed.'"

"Tell Jeff he *is* healed." If this was what Paul was supposed to say— and say it, he did—then why was I still without bone marrow five days later? Paul must have gotten something wrong. It did not make sense. My thoughts on this matter would not rest.

Abruptly, I took my wandering, circular thoughts captive and said to myself, "Stop!" Paul was miraculously directed to deliver a message from the Lord to me—"Tell Jeff he is healed." I had to believe that what Paul said was exactly what he was supposed to say. The Lord did not orchestrate all those intricate, interwoven details simply to screw up the punch line. No way! Paul got it right, because the Lord would have ensured he got it right; it was the Lord's message, not Paul's! So then, what was the significance of telling me I was healed when in fact I was not yet healed? I was still without bone marrow, without an immune system, and susceptible to dying at any time!

Then, finally, it dawned on me! It was as if the Lord downloaded a profound answer to the perplexing question I had been trying to solve. The Lord's message to me was very simple: *"Jeff, you are healed."* Paul was instructed to "tell Jeff he is healed." The past tense of this message was powerful! I was *already* healed! "Jeff IS healed." Not "will be healed," but IS ALREADY HEALED!

Immediately I thought of a familiar verse in 1 Peter 2:24 which states, *"...by His wounds you were healed."* By Jesus' wounds or stripes (from flogging, beating and crucifixion), we are healed. His sacrifice on the cross paid the price for my healing! Jesus did not *just* die for my sins, but also for my sicknesses! I turned to Isaiah 53:5 and learned from this verse that Jesus died on the cross for three things: my sins, my sicknesses, and my well-being!

The price for the sickness that's trying to kill me had already been paid for on the cross by Jesus Christ! Jesus' death paid the price for my being healed of aplastic anemia! By His wounds (stripes), I am healed! Then the revelation I was receiving ratcheted up another notch.

After I failed to initially understand the significance of Paul's words from the Lord, "Jeff, you are healed," God sent my friend to me with another clue—the cassette-recorded message from Chip Brim. Brim's message conveyed that on the first day that Daniel prayed in faith, believing God would answer him, his answer was granted and immediately sent. However, it was met with great opposition in the heavenly realm by demonic forces in an attempt to keep Daniel from receiving his answer. A battle raged on for 21 days. The forces of evil were simply hoping Daniel would grow weary, lose heart, give up and become one of the millions (from Brim's vision) who ended up on the one-yard line, never to receive the answer to his prayer.

The Apostle Paul emphasizes in Ephesians 6:12 that our battle is not against flesh and blood, but against powers, principalities and evil forces in the heavenly realm—the very thing we see taking place in Daniel chapter 10.

I had a greater sense of God's goodness. He had sent other obedient believers to deliver several messages to me in order to facilitate my understanding of something incredibly powerful. The faith and complete belief that I had up to this point—that God would heal me of this killer disease—rose to new heights. I knew now that I had *already* been healed in the *spiritual* sense. Due to God's Word, the sacrifice Jesus made when He died on the cross, and my own solid faith, I had already been healed!

I realized I was in a spiritual battle, positioned on the one-yard line, attempting to score a touchdown. Through faith and persistence I knew I would cross the goal line, score the touchdown and receive *physical* healing! If I maintained this belief and did not give up, I knew I would win the battle.

I intensely and diligently sought an answer of the meaning "Tell Jeff he is healed," and was rewarded with a revelation of great intensity! When I realized this, I cried with joy and thanksgiving at the goodness and awesome nature of God.

Saturday, April 21ˢᵗ

Nothing of significance occurred for a few days. I followed my personal routine religiously. Each day I had blood drawn, listened to praise music, read the Bible, posted one verse on my ink board, read from a book or two, and worked on my thoughts. Yes, I worked on my *thoughts*. I wanted to ensure each and every thought was aligned with the expectation of what I was telling everyone I believed! I found this to be extremely important for my own well-being. Whatever promise I found in the Bible, which applied to my situation or my need, I stood on without wavering.

The Prayer of Jabez

I began sensing that the Lord wanted to work on my heart. He was about to reveal things to me that would help me endure and understand my current journey.

A few days before, one of my visitors had brought me the popular little book, *The Prayer of Jabez*. I had initially placed it on the ledge along the wall in my room, but tonight I decided to pick it up and read it. Although my vision was still challenged when it came to reading, I was able to finish the book before going to bed that night.

In the entire Bible, Jabez is only mentioned in one verse— 1 Chronicles 4:10. In this passage, Jabez boldly petitions the Lord; his petition, or prayer, has been termed "The Prayer of Jabez." This single Bible verse inspired the book entitled *The Prayer of Jabez* which had already sold over eight million copies!

That night I prayed the Prayer of Jabez, this one simple little Bible verse. I prayed it out loud. I prayed it intensely just as I imagined Jabez himself must have prayed it, expecting to receive the very things for which I petitioned in this prayer: *"Oh that You would bless me indeed and enlarge my border, and that Your hand might be with me, that You would keep me from harm that it may not pain me! And God granted him what he requested!"* 1 Chronicles 4:10

My interpretation is: "LORD, BLESS ME INDEED (give me what You know I need, and give it to me now), ENLARGE MY BORDER (give me more opportunities to expand my outreach for You—open doors for me to share Your love with others), THAT YOUR HAND MIGHT BE WITH ME (that You would bless all that I do and guide and direct my paths for You), THAT YOU WOULD KEEP ME FROM HARM (that You would keep me out of the arena of the evil one and protect me), THAT IT MIGHT NOT PAIN ME (that I cause no disappointment or pain to You, to me or to others). AND GOD GRANTED JABEZ HIS REQUEST!

That's it! Short, simple and direct. This is a powerful prayer!

Sunday, April 22nd

Hindered Prayer?

The day after diligently praying the Jabez prayer, I experienced some interesting things that kept me focused on my anticipated miracle of healing. I remember feeling drawn to read 1 Corinthians chapter 11:30-31 where the Apostle Paul writes, *"For this reason many among you are weak and sick, and a number sleep* [have died]. *But if we judged ourselves rightly, we would not be judged."* [Explanation added]

This passage showed me the importance of evaluating and examining myself! I was already familiar with Bible passages such as, *"He who turns away his ear from listening to the law, even his prayer is an abomination"* (Proverbs 28:9) and, *"There is a way which seems right to a man, but its end is the way of death."* (Proverbs 14:12) *"My people are destroyed for lack of knowledge...."* (Hosea 4:6) and, *"...show her* [your wife] *honor... so that your prayers will not be hindered."* (1 Peter 3:7) [Explanation added]

From these verses and from Paul's message to the Corinthians, I saw that prayer could be hindered. Since I obviously did not want mine to be hindered, I set out to examine myself, asking God to reveal anything He wanted me to work on. He showed me several important things about myself.

Honor Your Wife

The first area toward which the Lord directed my attention was the relationship between my wife and my parents, and how I had been dealing with the challenges presented. For over 14 years I tried to bridge the gap between them during times of disagreement and misunderstanding. In each instance I played the peacemaker, trying to mediate or negotiate. I always asked that they forgive each other, forget the matter and move on. This peacemaker role had been causing friction between my wife and me for years.

That afternoon, during a phone call with my wife, the topic strayed to disharmonious family matters once again. Instead of automatically shifting into peacemaker mode, I felt compelled to just listen. After listening at length to my wife, the familiar stories which I had heard many times before took on a new and different meaning. The way I processed the same information was different—so different that it brought tears to my eyes. Unlike before, I was unable to say, "We've discussed this enough, haven't we?" or "Do we have to go through this now?"

As she went on, I realized that my mediation tactics were actually contributing to her frustration and causing even more challenges between us. I realized that day, by divine revelation, that my wife simply wanted me to defend her position—to take her side. Although my intentions were good, it was not the best approach for me and my family. As the phone conversation continued, my tears turned to laughter and the joy of the Lord was upon me. A fresh internal healing occurred both in me and my wife.

What I had learned that day clarified a verse from Ephesians 5:31 that says, *"For this reason a man shall leave his father and mother and shall be joined to his wife, and the two shall become one flesh."*

Later I spoke with my parents about what had transpired. I expressed to my parents that I loved them very much and respected their position as well, but that my true role was that of my wife's defender. Although it must have been surprising after so many years, they handled it very well. They understood and respected what I had to say.

Late that evening before going to bed I recalled my prayer the night before: "Lord, bless me INDEED!" And indeed, that is what He did. In the course of a few hours, I experienced a breakthrough for a problem that had gone on for 14 years. I had never thought to pray about my peacemaking role, believing I was 100% correct. I had never recognized, in all those years that I was the one who needed to change. After simply asking the Lord to bless me indeed, He gave me a desire to examine myself, and as a result I had a wonderful breakthrough. Is God good or what?

Tuesday, April 24th

The 95th tube of blood taken from my body during this journey showed that my blood counts were still at dangerously low levels with no sign that the ATG treatment was having any success. A platelet transfusion was ordered for me later that morning.

That day marked my 17th day at United Hospital. Although I was supposed to be "really, really sick," I felt stronger all the time—not necessarily in a physical sense, but mentally, emotionally and spiritually. My inner experiences were more like those of someone at Bible camp or ministry training school than in a hospital waiting to die. I had more time to read the Word, to hear God's voice and to pray than when I was actively at home in good health.

How's Business?

Since my arrival at the hospital, the springtime real estate market in the Twin Cities had been quite robust. I was mindful that I had a commissioned position and needed to do whatever I could to continue receiving an income, as my insurance did not cover loss of commissions.

While in the confines of my hospital room, I took calls from existing clients who had questions regarding the marketing of their home. When prospects or clients called in and asked, "Where is Jeff?" my office staff would reply, "Actually, he is in the hospital for a few days for observation. His white counts are a bit low, but he is fine. Would you like to speak with him?" We had a game plan and it worked.

When an offer came in on one of my listings, my staff faxed it to me in the hospital. I presented it over the phone to my client and my staff obtained signatures back at the office upon agreement of all the terms. When a seller wanted to list their home, my staff filled out our standard Listing Worksheet, pulled their tax record and faxed the forms to the hospital. With that information in hand I simply completed the Market Analysis on my laptop computer and forwarded my conclusions via email to my wife. She in turn met with the seller, showed them my evaluation and indicated my suggested list price for their home. We continued to get listings this way!

The business was blessed—certainly more than the previous fall! We continued to tell our clients and prospects that I was simply being held for observation for a few more days. From a disadvantaged position, our new "system" had produced four listings and four sales in April! God is good!

Thursday, April 26th

My platelet count continued to diminish rapidly after each transfusion. The count after the morning blood draw was just 7000. I saw that the transfused platelets were not going as high as they once had nor did they last as long. This was clearly not a good sign, but I refused to worry. I kept thanking the Lord for all the good things that were happening. I stood on His Word and stayed the course of expecting a miracle!

Mid-morning I was informed that I would be moved to a new room. I did not want to move! I had become accustomed to this room, number 4526. I had not left the room a single time in the 19 days I was there and simply felt comfortable in it. When all my resistant efforts failed, I was moved across the hall to room 4536.

To my delight, the new room had a real sense of life and energy in it; something rare for a room in the oncology ward. A much better space than the one I had been in; it was larger and even had a better view! I realized that something as simple as a little hospital room can mean so much when your whole world is shifting. I was happy about the move and thanked the nurses for their persistence.

Friday, April 27th

For days I continually sought guidance from the Lord to help me see anything else that could be standing in the way of my prayer for healing to be answered. I wanted any hindrance to be identified so that I could do what I needed to do to remove it.

Humble Yourself

Just after 11:00 p.m. I finished listening to a wonderful tape series by my friend, Pastor Joe Braucht. The tapes, entitled "Renewing a Right Heart," discussed the importance of "being right" with God and the steps we can take to get into that right relationship with Him. This is exactly what I sought—a deeper walk with Him in all areas of my life.

Then the Lord revealed something about which He was concerned. I heard that still, small voice say, *"Why do you think of yourself as more important than others?"*

I was puzzled at first, but then experienced many insightful thoughts and emotions about how I truly viewed myself. For years I had been praised by others for my successes. I had grown proud of my accomplishments. I compared myself with others—consciously as well as unconsciously. Even though I aimed for humility, pride had a way of sneaking up on me.

The Lord was very kind and gentle as He asked me again, *"Why do you think of yourself as more important than others?"* I had no answer other than, "I am sorry." Feeling badly, I was overcome with emotion and cried, feeling saddened by my past actions. I buried my head in my pillow, trying to keep quiet so the nurses would not hear me crying. I did not want them to think I was afraid of dying, especially since they all knew that I believed God would provide a miraculous healing. My crying had nothing to do with dying. It had everything to do with what God was doing with that pride buried deep within my heart.

For 30 minutes I cried. Then a sense of relief and joy fell over me and I began laughing out loud. Once again the joy of the Lord came as a confirmation of a good work completed within me.

The Scripture teaches that *"...God is opposed to the proud, but gives grace to the humble."* (James 4:6) I needed God's grace, and knew the last thing I should do was run around with pride inside. In Philippians 2:3-4 it says, *"Do nothing from selfishness or empty conceit, but with humility of mind regard one another as more important than yourselves; do not merely look out for your own personal interests, but also for the interests of others."*

As I examined myself and my heart, the Lord revealed pieces of my life that He wanted to see me improve. I did not want to end up like the Corinthians to whom Paul spoke—the weak, sick or those that had died. I wanted healing to manifest in my life and I was willing to do whatever I needed to do.

Love

More verses from God's Word came to me to strengthen me as I examined myself. In Luke 10:27-28 Jesus says, *"You shall love the Lord your God with all your heart, and with all your soul, and with all your strength, and with all your mind; and love your neighbor as yourself... Do this and you will live."*

In 1 Corinthians 13:1-3 Paul writes, *"If I speak with the tongues of men and of angels, but do not have LOVE, I have become a noisy gong or a clanging cymbal. If I have the gift of prophecy, and know all mysteries and all knowledge; and if I have all faith, so as to remove mountains, but do not have LOVE, I am nothing. And if I give all my possessions to feed the poor, and if I surrender my body to be burned, but do not have LOVE, it profits me NOTHING!"* [Emphasis added]

After reading these verses I thought about how busy society had become, how the "love" of so many has grown cold and how everyone seemed to be self-absorbed.

Note this Biblical description of society in the days preceding the return of Jesus Christ: *"But realize this, that in the last days difficult times will come. For men will be lovers of self, lovers of money, boastful, arrogant, revilers, disobedient to parents, ungrateful, unholy, unloving, irreconcilable, malicious gossips, without self-control, brutal, haters of good, treacherous, reckless, conceited, lovers of pleasure rather than lovers of God; holding to a form of godliness, although they have denied its power; avoid such men as these... always learning and never able to come to the knowledge of the truth."* (2 Timothy 3:1-7) How does this description match up with your observation of the society we live in today?

Tuesday, May 1st

Platelets Nosedive

My morning blood draw revealed the lowest platelet count since arriving at the hospital. It was a mere 5000. I fought discouragement. I realized that the ATG had failed. The specialists at the University of Minnesota, along with the oncologists at United, all concluded that if the ATG worked, we would know within two weeks. Two weeks were now over and there had been no change.

A White Halo of Light

Later in the morning, Erin, the young woman who regularly cleaned my room, was going about her cleaning responsibilities as she and I talked. I shared with her a number of things I had experienced while staying in the hospital, along with my full expectation of a complete healing.

While we were talking she suddenly stopped and stared for a moment, as if she was assessing something. I asked her, "What's up?" She began to describe a vision of what she was seeing in the room.

"I see a circular aura, like a halo over your head and a white beam of light ascending up into the sky," she said. She was surprised by this and indicated that she had never seen anything like it. I asked her where the beam of light went and she replied, "I think it goes right to the throne of God."

Upon hearing this, all discouragement from my low platelet count disappeared. I was amazed at how I continued to receive messages, visitors, tapes, visions and revelations from God just when I needed them most! This day was no exception!

The Search for Marrow Donor

When it became apparent that the ATG treatment had failed to produce results, the doctors conducted a search on the worldwide database to locate a matching marrow donor for me. No match was found. They then requested that my three siblings, Jyl, Jim and Ed, be tested as a hopeful match. The tests had been performed and the results were due to arrive in two days.

Even with a perfect "six-point" marrow match, based upon my age, there was only a slight chance of successfully surviving the procedure. If I survived the procedure and the marrow was not rejected immediately, I was told I might have two years before I would become susceptible to bone marrow rejection or relapse.

By the time one ran all the mathematical probabilities, the odds were slim to none that I would live very long, if at all. What is worse is that these "odds" were based on obtaining a perfect marrow match, something that had not yet been located.

But I chose to believe in God's Word—His promises for all my needs! God *"is able to do far more abundantly beyond all we ask or think..."* (Ephesians 3:20); and *"I can do all things through Christ who strengthens me,"* (Philippians 4:13); and *"He sent His Word and healed them* [me] *and delivered them* [me] *from their* [my] *destructions."* (Psalms 107:20) [Emphasis added]

As strange as it may sound, I had been so blessed during the proceeding few weeks. I felt like the luckiest person on earth. I had seen the Lord there for me every time I was in need—whether it was a physical, emotional or spiritual need. God had been there right on schedule. It was truly amazing!

I continued to wait on the Lord. I read from Isaiah 40:31, *"Yet those who wait on the Lord will gain new strength; they will mount up with wings like eagles, they will run and not get tired, they will walk and not become weary."* What a promise! That would be me!

Blood Test Results While in the Hospital

UNITED HOSPITAL
St. Paul, Minnesota

PROTOCOL NUMBER: _____
DIAGNOSIS: _____

DATE:	4-8	4-8	4-9	4-10	4-11	4-12	4-13	4-14	4/15	4/17	4/8	4/19	4/20	4/21	4/22
HEMATOLOGY															
HGB (F:12-16, M:14-18)	5.9	8.5	8.0		9.5	9.6	8.7	8.4	8.0	11.1	11.2	9.9	11.1	10.7	10.2
WBC (4.8-10.8)	700	400	400		500	500	200	300	300	400	500	500	700	900	600
Polys															
Bands															
Lymphs															
Monos															
Periph Blasts															
Platelets (150,000 — / 300,000)	2,000	26,000	22,000		3,000	7,000	23,000	16,000	7,000	40,000		19,000	14,000	900	23,000
Protime (11-13)															
PTT (24-36)															
Thrombin Time (8-14)															
FSP (< 10)															
Fibrinogen (200-600)															
BLOOD PRODUCTS REQUIRED	15D plt	3 units prbc													

DATE:	4/23	4/24	4/25	4/26	4/27	4-28	4-29	4-30	5/1	5/2	5/3	5/4			
HEMATOLOGY															
HGB (F:12-16, M:14-18)	9.9	9.3	9.2	8.7	7.6	9.5	9.5	9.1	9.0	8.9	8.5	10.6			
WBC (4.8-10.8)	900	900	900	1100	800	1.1	1.5	1.3	1.3	1.1	1.0	1.3			
Polys															
Bands															
Lymphs															
Monos															
Periph Blasts															
Platelets (150,000 — / 300,000)	10K	26K	14K	7K	26K	200	14K	12K	5,000	43K	32K	24K			
Protime (11-13)															
PTT (24-36)															
Thrombin Time (8-14)															
FSP (< 10)															
Fibrinogen (200-600)															
BLOOD PRODUCTS REQUIRED															
BONE MARROW BIOPSY Blasts															
Specify Protocol and agents.															

102

Wednesday, May 3rd

They drew my 115th tube of blood as they continued to monitor the ravaging effects of the aplastic anemia. The test results revealed a continued drop in my hemoglobin level and a double-bag transfusion of red cells was ordered.

God Considers Me Unique

The doctor stopped by my room later than normal that day with the results of my brothers' and sister's bone marrow tests. My siblings' tests were the last option available to the doctors that could provide me with any type of "odds" of survival. The ATG had failed. No possible marrow donor existed in any of the worldwide databases. So lastly, it came down to my siblings.

The doctor said, in his same monotone voice, "I'm sorry, there is no match." Somehow expecting this, I quickly responded by saying, "Amen! God considers me unique! He is just making it clear to everyone that it will be Him and Him alone that will heal me." The doctor just stared at me in silence for a moment before informing me that I was going home the next day.

"Going home, why?" I asked. Since there is nothing else they could do for me, the doctor simply said, "We cannot just keep you here; besides, we've tried everything." He told me to prepare to go home the next morning.

I had become so comfortable. I did not want to leave. "There are germs outside! In this room, on this floor, there are controls that keep people without immune systems safe... they're just throwing me out to the wolves," I thought. I began to believe I would be healed miraculously by morning. This was God's perfect timing! Tomorrow would be the day!

Thursday, May 4th

They loaded up on six tubes of blood for some reason, a total of 121 since this excitement began. I guess they wanted some extra for good measure. It did not matter how many tubes they drew, because I believed that this was the day I would see the miraculous healing manifested.

The doctor arrived with the test results. There was no change in my condition; I was still without bone marrow and my blood numbers had declined again. The platelets had fallen to the point where I required another transfusion. The doctor planned to meet with me after the transfusion in order to give me crucial instructions for my survival.

A Mini Prognosis

Afternoon had arrived, the platelets had been transfused and I was about to be discharged from the security of the oncology ward at United Hospital.

First I met with the nurse. She gave me three informational, *pre-printed* pages on "How to Deal with Low RED Blood Cells," "How to Deal with Low WHITE Blood Cells" and "How to Deal with Low PLATELETS." It is interesting to note that my sheets had been edited.

On the RED cell sheet, the following words were crossed out in red ink, "Your red blood cell count will get better." On the WHITE cell sheet, "Your white blood cell count will get better," was crossed out. And on the PLATELET sheet, "Your platelet count will get better," was crossed out. Although they never spoke to me about this, they were sending me a clear message that I was not going to get better!

Can you imagine that? At first I just blew it off, but in time it began to make some sense... they really did not believe I was going to get better. I did not let this bother me in the least. God had a plan and a promise for me—a plan for me to be healed 100% from this affliction!

The Doctor's Departing Words

"Keep an eye on your temperature. Should you develop a fever of 101 degrees, get back in here right away. If you experience any pain, rashes or uncontrolled bleeding, get back here as quickly as possible."

"We will continue to look for a marrow match for you and will let you know if we locate a donor."

"But for now, stay away from your kids, don't kiss your wife, get rid of your pets and don't go out in public unless you absolutely have to; and if you do, wear a mask."

So with these parting words, I walked out of the fortress I had called home for the proceeding 28 days and set my sights on what I would need to do to bring about the manifestation of the promised miracle. I needed to remember that "I *am* healed!" No matter what I encountered, no matter what others said, I was going to stand on God's promises and would never give up!

"Stay away from your kids, don't kiss your wife, get rid of your pets and don't go out in public unless you absolutely have to; and if you do, wear a mask."

Sent Home Without Hope

"... do not throw away your confidence, which has a great reward. For you have need of endurance, so that when you have done the will of God, you may receive what was promised."

Hebrews 10:35-36

22,000 Emails!

My "Journey to a Miracle" continued after the doctors sent me home from the hospital without any hope of survival. I was told to, "Stay away from your kids, don't kiss your wife, get rid of your pets and don't go out in public unless you absolutely have to; and if you do, wear a mask." I was basically told to live inside a bubble. As a result, this next part of my journey began in the basement of my home.

After a few days at home, I decided to send a brief email to a select handful of friends. I provided a few paragraphs of recap of what I was dealing with. I went into very little detail. I did not share the diagnosis or prognosis of the aplastic anemia. I simply asked for their prayers. I did not want to reveal much information about my personal battle with this disease, as I wanted this part of my life to remain private.

It was at this point, after having sent the first brief email that the Lord told me to open up, be transparent and share with *everyone* what was happening in my life. I wrestled with this. I simply wanted to keep my condition and situation private. I felt that I had already shared enough, but the Lord kept prompting me to tell everyone everything.

I then petitioned the Lord, *"I know You are going to heal me; I absolutely believe it. But just in case You choose not to, for whatever reason, I do not want You to look bad in the eyes of all those who You want me to tell; I would not want to create a stumbling block for them or cause their faith to falter. Are You sure You want me to tell everyone about this?"*

I did not hear anything from the Lord. I waited, but continued to hear nothing. A few days passed and still nothing. I thought deeply about what I was asking God. Then, it dawned on me: "Where is your faith, man!" I exclaimed to myself. Why would I even question whether or not God would heal me when I had been saying all along, "He *will* heal me?"

I asked God to forgive me for such a foolish thought on my part. "God is able to take care of Himself," I chuckled to myself. He does not need me to watch His back! I only needed to do my part—believe. IF I did my part, THEN God would do His part!

I also asked the Lord to forgive me for questioning His request to "tell everyone everything," and I agreed to do it. It was then that God spoke to my heart saying, *"I am going to show Myself strong through you, before the eyes of many people."* With this, I cried in joy and humility as I began to prepare the pages of this book from the basement of my home the first week of May 2001.

> ***"I am going to show Myself strong through you, before the eyes of many people."***

In response to the Lord's request, I composed a second email. This multi-page email went into much more detail than the first in respect to what had transpired over the past year, including my 28-day stay in the hospital. It was sent to 22,000 recipients! I had a large database of friends and real estate agents from around the country and I made sure they each heard from me. I needed to bring *everyone* up to speed on what had occurred in my life in order to set the stage for what was about to happen.

Anyone reading the second email would conclude that, according to the medical world, I was destined to die, but that according to what I believed, I was going to live! Basically, that second email was a mini-version of what you have read so far in this book.

What you are now about to read are the *actual* emails I sent from the basement of my home. These emails not only describe the amazing events that took place after being discharged from the hospital, but they capture the thoughts and actions that took place while on my "Journey to a Miracle."

May 19, 2001

To All My Family and Friends,

I want to thank you as a group, but also individually, for your continued prayers of support for the miracle I am expecting! Give thanks and praise.... *"Now FAITH is the assurance of things hoped for, the conviction of things not seen."* (Hebrews 11:1) [Emphasis added]

Allow this to serve as my pledge to you—I will keep you updated through email and tell you everything that transpires. A miracle is forthcoming and we will experience it together!

In this email I will recap various events that have taken place since being discharged from the hospital on May 4th. Needless to say, I need to be very careful. The doctors certainly gave me a fair amount of unpleasant advice. I am not to go out in crowds without wearing a mask. I'm supposed to stay away from people, including my children. It's been strongly suggested that I get rid of our two dogs, something I am not going to do. I'm not to go near anyone with a cold or the flu. I'm to wash my hands frequently and brush my teeth with a "feather-like" toothbrush so my gums don't bleed. I'm to be very careful not to "push" when having a bowel movement and when using toilet tissue, as there is a high risk of bleeding. I'm to monitor my temperature regularly. If it hits 101 degrees, I'm to go directly to the emergency room. If that is not enough—no kissing or sexual intercourse!

I've made a plan to sleep at our second home, which I use as my real estate office, should a family member get sick.

Walking by Faith, not by Sight

As I listen to all the reports, opinions and advice "from the medical world," it is quite clear that the odds are greatly against surviving this strange and rare disease. The doctors would need to locate a perfect match marrow donor and perform a successful transplant. If the marrow is not rejected, perhaps I would live for two more years.

I know that all the details provided to me thus far by the doctors are sound. They have provided me with an accurate medical analysis. Is it good news? No way. It really stinks. The diagnosis and prognosis are reality and I cannot go into denial; I must deal with the circumstances at hand. All the findings and analysis come from the world we know and understand as the "sight" realm, but there is another realm out there, it's called the "faith" realm.

According to 2 Corinthians 5:7, Christians are to "...*walk by faith, and NOT by sight.*" [Emphasis added] We are to trust in what God says in His Word, even if it seems to go against what we believe to be reality. I am choosing to believe God, especially when His Word says, "*...without faith it is impossible to please Him, for he who comes to God must believe that He is, and that He is a rewarder of those who DILIGENTLY seek Him.*" (Hebrews 11:6) [Emphasis added] I will continue to believe God as I diligently seek Him for my miracle!

At this point in time, I really don't need to remind you of the other miracles that have been happening as a result of walking in the "faith" realm. Nothing is impossible with God, and I trust that what His Word says will occur in the days or weeks ahead. I trust you will see the love, power and purpose of God in this matter as my journey plays out. I could not be a more blessed person as a result of the awesome experiences I have been through so far. In fact, I am the most fortunate person in the world, amidst all the trouble that surrounds my failing health.

If my perspective seems a bit strange, I invite you to read on and stick with me. I'd like you to experience along with me what the Lord will do right before your eyes! He said He was going to show Himself strong through me before the eyes of many people; and I believe Him!

Just How Many People Did Jesus Heal?

Time and time again Scripture tells us that Jesus healed ALL of them. *ALL* their sicknesses were healed. John 1:1, 14 says, *"In the beginning was the Word, and the Word was with God, and the Word was God. And the Word became flesh, and dwelt among us...."*

Jesus is the living Word of God. He *IS* the Word. Jesus healed them with *"His Word."* (Matthew 8:16) *"He [God] sent His Word and healed them, and delivered them from their destructions."* (Psalm 107:20) [Explanation added]

Now if it were known that Jesus was going to show up personally at your church this Sunday for a healing service, how many people do you think would go there "expecting" to be healed? I gather most people would.

Jesus is the *"same yesterday and today and forever."* (Hebrews 13:8) God says in Malachi 3:6, *"I change not."* So you can see, Jesus is the Word, and He healed ALL who were afflicted with sickness. He does not need to be physically present to heal me or anyone else. *"With His Word He healed them."* Physical healing is as available today as it was 2000 years ago!

There are SO MANY verses in the Bible that promise healing and provide answers to our ever-increasing number of requests, hurts and needs. Yet how many "really" believe in these promises? How many take them to heart? Do we even know they exist? Please understand, for *"...unless you are converted and become like a child* [quit trying to figure it all out in our heads], *you will not enter the kingdom of heaven."* (Matthew 18:3) [Comment added] Child-like faith enables one to humbly come before God for salvation, but for all prayer requests as well. We must do it in faith, believing.

Verses with Big Promises

One of the simplest verses that I clung to while in the hospital (and still do today, not just for the healing, but for anything), is John 15:7, which says, *"If you abide in Me, and My words abide in you, ask whatever you wish, AND IT WILL BE DONE FOR YOU."* [Emphasis added] This is pretty direct; no gray area. "Abide" means to trust, to follow, to lean on, to latch onto and to obey. IF I do this, THEN God says He will grant any request I bring before Him. Likewise, from 1 John 3:22, we see that IF we do our part, THEN God will do His part: *" and whatever we ask we receive from Him, because we keep His commandments and do the things that are pleasing in His sight."*

Another terrific passage that ends in a promise, providing you do your part, is: *"Ask, and it will be given to you; seek, and you will find; knock, and it will be opened to you. For everyone who asks receives, and he who seeks finds, and to him who knocks it will be opened. Or what man is there among you who, when his son asks for a loaf, will give him a stone? Or if he asks for a fish, he will not give him a snake, will he? If you then, being evil, know how to give good gifts to your children, how much more will your Father who is in heaven give WHAT IS GOOD to those who ask Him!"* (Matthew 7:7-11) [Emphasis added]

Faith Check

I felt it important to share some of these verses with you. God does hear us when we ask. He wants a relationship with us through His Son.

I have been receiving many emails and communications from you— and I thank you dearly from the bottom of my heart—but I really sense a need for me to do what I can to boost *your* faith! Don't worry about me! God is faithful to His Word. You WILL see it manifested in my healing; so there is no need for concern on my behalf.

The miracle will arrive not because of *me*, nor because I am a special favorite of God, but because God is able and willing to do it FOR HIS GLORY, because He loves me and because He has already promised to do so in His Word! I'm simply standing firm on His promise! I know, He *"... is able to do far more abundantly BEYOND all we ask or think...."* (Ephesians 3:20) [Emphasis added] So I must ask, how many of us really trust Him? With everything? With anything? He wants to do WONDERS in our lives!

Stay Away from Crowds

When I left the hospital with a dangerously low white blood cell count, I was told to stay away from crowds because of all the germs, etc. I could very easily pick up an unwanted cold or flu virus which, of course, would result in my returning to the hospital emergency room and possibly dying. My plan was to spend most of my time in my basement.

The third day out of the hospital, however, was different. I felt compelled to go to a local Sunday evening church service to hear a minister from Indiana by the name of Steve Munsey. I did not know who he was. I had never heard him speak. I just felt I needed to go.

This was the first time I ventured out of my house and was around a crowd, so it was necessary for me to wear my surgical mask to fend off airborne germs. I must admit this was a humbling experience. Soon after the service began however, I stopped thinking about the awful "mask" I was wearing. With over 200 people in one place for such a long time, I am glad to inform you that I was completely protected from any cold or flu bugs, as my body temperature has remained steady at 98.6. Amen!

Not only did Pastor Munsey deliver an incredible message that night, he said something profound; something that appeared to come out of nowhere. In the middle of his powerful and animated delivery—and believe me he was on a roll—he suddenly froze in his tracks for a few seconds as if he was listening to something. The room was dead silent. He then said this. *The Lord is telling me that there is someone here tonight who the doctors have told does not have long to live. But God is going to remove that sickness that has come against you and add 15 years to your life.* Then he continued preaching right where he had left off. This was not a healing service!

> *"The Lord is telling me that there is someone here tonight who the doctors have told does not have long to live. But God is going to remove that sickness that has come against you and add 15 years to your life."*

All along, God has provided little signs, words or messages to help me, to keep me strong, to perfect my faith. Was this Word spoken by Pastor Munsey for me? Absolutely! By faith I chose to take ownership of that prophetic Word—it was meant for me—Amen!

I find it most interesting, that up until that night, I had no desire to leave the confines of my home. For some reason, I was drawn to attend. I now believe that the Lord not only wanted me to hear the general message, but He wanted to deliver me a personal one through Pastor Munsey!

Your Kids Could Send You Back to the Hospital

The warning to stay away from my children was a tough one to deal with. I have four terrific kids! The three boys are 8, 6 and 4 years old; and our little princess is just 10 months old. Any coughing or sneezing by them could land me back in the hospital due to my compromised immune system. In addition to the four children, we had two dogs and two additional adults (a sister and a niece) living under one roof! Germ possibilities? You bet!

My family and many others continue to pray for my protection from viruses, bacteria and any other thing that might want to attack and send me back to the hospital, or worse. I want to thank you for those prayers! The kids have been coughing and sneezing from time to time, especially the past couple days and I am not isolated from them. Today, two of the boys got sick and threw up. The flu bug is in our house! I did not leave, but stayed and kept trusting the Lord for protection. As I write this now I can gladly say, I feel wonderful!

Getting an Uneasy Feeling

After a couple days of being out of the hospital and living (basically) out of my basement, I began getting an uneasy feeling about a powerful drug the doctors had recently prescribed for me. The drug, called Cyclosporine, is a preparatory drug used on patients who may undergo a bone marrow transplant, as it further suppresses any immune activity. Since I had virtually no immune system, I was not really sure why I was on this drug in the first place. I simply went along with the doctor's recommendation.

This uneasy feeling was not a physical one, but spiritual. I simply sensed that this was the wrong thing to be doing. Up until now, I had always taken every pill or medication the doctors prescribed; but this time something was different.

One of My Tenants Stops By

On Saturday May 5th I had a brief business conversation on the phone with Monique, a tenant of one of my rental properties. During our talk, I mentioned the diagnosis I had received from the doctors. Two days later, Monique showed up at my home. She told me that for the past two days she had been praying about whether or not to bring some "interesting material" over to me. She went on to tell me she had not been getting an answer to her prayer. So tonight, while driving in her car, she began praying again, saying, "God, just tell me YES or NO. Should I bring this material to Jeff?" As she pulled up to the next intersection, the car immediately in front of her had a bumper sticker with one word on it: YES! That was the answer to her prayer!

The "interesting material" that Monique shared was a book and VHS tape on herbs and natural healing. She and her husband Tom had been given this information by someone at their church. As a result, they have been using a variety of herbal products ever since and felt wonderful.

I had personally used herbs in the past and was open to the video and reading the material. Over the next few days, as I reviewed the material, I prayed about the direction I ought to be taking.

The Fork in the Road

By the middle of the next day, Wednesday, May 9th, I had started contemplating what I should do next. I recognized a proverbial fork in the road. I had been feeling uneasy about taking the Cyclosporine, and now I was being presented with material on how natural herbs had healed over 10,000 of this particular "herbal" doctor's patients! These patients had cancer, AIDS, heart conditions, tumors, Alzheimer's, blood disorders and numerous other diseases. It was quite intriguing to read through the medical information that was presented along with the numerous testimonials.

Some of the points this herbal doctor made were well taken. For example, he emphatically pointed out that the medical industry does not have any idea of how to heal anyone from a disease, they only treat the symptoms. They use drugs (most with side effects) and oftentimes revert to cutting, radiating or poisoning parts of a person's body to achieve an oftentimes temporary result.

He also pointed out that God put natural plants, roots, etc. on the earth for a reason: to heal people when they get sick. The doctor's extensive background in herbal medicine was making me rather comfortable with this approach. I continued to study "herbs" on the Internet and reviewed this herbal doctor's material again. As I did, I received quite an education on nutrition as well. I realized how poor my diet was and how I most likely had a lot of accumulated "junk" and build-up inside my body.

His preference for natural healing over medical treatment was clearly radical. He was not at all fond of the medical profession; one he had been part of for years. Medical professionals on the other hand had an equally strong position of support for their industry. I believe that both natural healing and medical science have their place and am not advocating one over the other.

As I continued to comb through the information on natural healing, I kept in mind the circumstances under which I had received it— through yet another believer who prayed for direction and was led to deliver this information into my hands. This, in itself, was consistent with how the Lord had been using other believers during my most interesting journey. So I continued reading and praying about this "natural approach."

Later in the day my wife and I began talking about the Cyclosporine. She too had developed an uneasy feeling about my taking it. We could not quite pin it down, however. Nevertheless, I made the decision to cut my daily dosage from 800 mg to 600 mg without discussing it with my oncologist.

Off the Meds

On the morning of May 10th I began doing additional research on the Internet; particularly research on the use of Cyclosporine. Then something prompted me to pick up the Cyclosporine box, remove the packaging material and read the printed warnings about this drug (I needed a magnifying glass to read the 5 or 6 point type which was printed in faint blue ink). What I read was shocking!

Numerous warnings and side effects from Cyclosporine were listed which included renal dysfunction, structural kidney damage, nephrotoxicity, hepatotoxicity, high blood pressure, neoplasms such as lymphoma and carcinomas of the skin and several others. I know that many drugs have varying degrees of side effects, but to me, these were very severe. The only side effect of Cyclosporine that was discussed with me at the time it was prescribed was possible high blood pressure. This, too, concerned me quite a bit.

Midday, I realized that I had not taken my morning dosage of this drug (the 300 mg I had planned to take). Strangely enough, I completely forgot! I had never forgotten to take a medicine when I was supposed to, yet I just did. At this point, I thought I would just take the 300 mg evening dosage and forget about the morning dosage since I had already missed it. Right then, that uncomfortable feeling began stirring again, telling me that something was wrong. I made the choice right then to stop taking Cyclosporine altogether. In addition, I opted to quit taking Prilosec, another drug I had been prescribed. It was something for indigestion, yet I never had a bout of indigestion in or out of the hospital.

Emotionally, stopping the medication caused me to feel as though I had lost a life line. While taking the meds, I was able to maintain hope that something positive would result, like a return to the healthy condition I so desperately desired. But now that I had chosen to stop taking them the wishful, hopeful life line had been cut. It's just one of those little emotions that I needed to work through.

There were four reasons I chose to stop taking the Cyclosporine:

1. There had been no results to date, something the doctors had somewhat expected from the beginning.

2. There were potential side effects.
3. I was planning to visit a couple more doctors and get their opinions over the next two weeks and could always go back on the drug if needed.
4. Something continued to tell me that something was wrong with my taking this drug. I followed my gut instinct.

Side Effects Soar

During this time I had been feeling quite tense and on edge. Later in the day on Thursday, May 10th, while at the doctor's office to receive a platelet transfusion, I had my blood pressure tested. To my amazement it was 170/108! The next day on Friday morning I began noticing an intense dull pain in my kidneys. No position (sitting or standing) could rid me of the pain. I felt extremely tense. I tested my blood pressure at home and found that it had jumped to 183/123! No wonder I was tense! I realized I was experiencing the side effects of Cyclosporine and began to understand why I had been getting that funny feeling about the drug. I thanked the Lord for prompting me with that little feeling. For if I had not stopped taking the drug when I did, who knows how high my BP would have gone or how painful my kidneys would have become.

I was told while at the doctor's office on Thursday that they would be calling me with a prescription to lower my blood pressure. They never called.

In the week since I stopped taking Cyclosporine, my kidney pain went away, a rash that had begun developing almost dried up and my blood pressure dropped steadily to where it belongs at 120/78!

Herbal Order Placed

By Friday afternoon on May 11th, I finally came to the decision to order the herbal program which would cleanse my body and build it up with natural herbs. This is what my heart was telling me to do. I wanted to provide you with the web sites of two different herbal doctors. Both are nationally known. You will get an idea of what I have been reading, studying and evaluating before deciding whether to make the choice I did. One is www.drday.com and the other is www.HerbDoc.com.

By the way, I am not suggesting that anyone stop taking prescribed medication as a result of what I have shared in this email! I am only sharing the choice I personally made and why I made it.

Required Herbal Warnings

In determining whether I should use herbs, it was necessary for me to hurdle past (in faith) the "warnings" that the FDA require those who practice natural healing to display in their printed material and on their web site(s). The following is one such warning I read.

A WARNING from our Lawyers:

This book is published under the First Amendment of the United States Constitution, which grants the rights to discuss openly and freely all matters of public concern and to express viewpoints no matter how controversial or unaccepted they may be. However, medical groups and pharmaceutical companies have finally infiltrated and violated our sacred Constitution. Therefore, we are forced to give you the following WARNINGS:

"If you are ill or have been diagnosed with any disease, please consult a medical doctor before attempting any natural healing program."

"Many foods, herbs or other natural substances can occasionally cause dangerous allergic reactions or side effects in some people. People have even died from allergic reactions to peanuts and strawberries."

"Any one of the programs in this book could be potentially dangerous, even lethal, especially if you are seriously ill."

"Therefore, any natural method you learn about in this book may cause harm, instead of the benefit you seek. ASK YOUR DOCTOR FIRST, but remember that the vast majority of doctors have no education in natural healing methods and herbal medicine. They will probably discourage you from trying any of the programs."

My oncologist highly discouraged my using natural herbal remedies and pointed out that, "When you have aplastic anemia, you never want to take herbs; there could be serious side effects."

Till the Soil

Even though I felt that the Lord had paved the way for me to get off medication and begin an herbal program, I was still praying for a confirmation that I was making the right choice. The warnings and risks of taking herbs seemed very real and I did not feel I was in a position to make any mistakes. Yet the herbal catalog and supportive material made reference to *numerous accounts where people were healed miraculously by using these herbs.*

As a result of reading this, I needed to know what to tell others once the healing was manifested in my body. I could not have a mixed or convoluted message in the future. Since I firmly believe I will be miraculously healed by the Lord, I don't want any doubt later on that the healing came as a result of the herbs. I needed to know this NOW, in advance of my being healed. I did not want to second guess it later. So I persisted in praying, both for a confirmation that I was doing the right thing by taking the herbs, and also for the Lord to tell me it was Him, not the herbs that would perform the miracle in me.

While praying before bed on Sunday, May 13th the Lord responded to my prayers with an incredible answer. In fact, I wrote it down immediately. This is what He said, *"The herbal program will not heal you, but it will prepare your body to function properly—in a healthy mode. A farmer does not plant a seed in the field until he tills it, readies it and then takes care of the field. You do likewise with your body and I will plant the seed of marrow and it will grow 100-fold!"* Oh my gosh!! I can't explain the feeling of excitement I got after getting this Word from God. It confirmed what I was doing by taking the herbs, as well as a miraculous outcome! IF I do my part, THEN God will do His part! If I do all I can do, God will do that which only He can do! After I wrote this down, I sprang from my knees and shared this amazing news with my wife. What a profound moment!

> *"A farmer does not plant a seed in the field until he tills it, readies it and then takes care of the field. You do likewise with your body, and I will plant the seed of marrow and it will grow 100-fold!"*

Doctor Notified I Stopped Taking Meds

On Monday, May 14th, while in for my scheduled platelet transfusion and meeting with one of the doctors, I mentioned that I had stopped taking the Cyclosporine. He was a bit surprised, but since he was a fill-in for my primary doctor, he was not too upset by my decision. He suggested I get back on the medication right away. I told him I was planning to get some additional opinions from other doctors over the next two weeks, as I did not think Cyclosporine was right for me.

Herbal Detox Program Begins

On Tuesday, May 15th, I began a five-day detoxification program designed to cleanse the colon, liver, gallbladder, blood and a few other parts of the body. It is a comprehensive flush designed to remove wastes, toxins, parasites, etc. from the body. On day one I ate only fruits and vegetables. On days two through four I fasted, consuming liquids and juices only. On day five, I was able to eat fruits and vegetables again. I am in the middle of this detox program and it seems to be going well. Even though I am in the fast period, I am not hungry. I drink roughly 1.25 gallons of liquids per day mixed with a variety of herbs. I am very optimistic and feel good about what I am doing.

My "Second" Opinion

On Wednesday, May 16th, I made my way to the University of Minnesota Bone Marrow Transplant Center to obtain my *first* "second opinion" and to discuss the nature and stipulations of a bone marrow transplant. In addition, I was considering changing oncologists from the one I had been seeing at United Hospital. Today, I had the good fortune of meeting with an internationally renowned transplant surgeon at the University of Minnesota and felt comfortable with him. After briefly examining me and reviewing my records, he agreed with the aplastic anemia diagnosis.

We then spent time talking about the marrow transplant donor program (locating a non-relative match on one of the world's databases) and a bit about the transplant procedure itself. My wife and I informed the doctor that we do not believe a transplant will be necessary and that we expect God to heal me miraculously without a transplant. He showed some signs of amazement, but continued on with his overview of medical procedures, likely outcomes, etc.

The transplant surgeon indicated that he would not have prescribed anything different than what I had been prescribed. He indicated that it was good that I got off the Cyclosporine for the time being since I was experiencing side effects, but that I ought to get back on the drug relatively soon. He added that I should consider undergoing another ATG treatment and follow that with Cyclosporine once again since I had very few options available. He pointed out that if I did opt for another attempt at the ATG treatment, there would be a lesser chance of success than the first round, and that the side effects may be worse. He also suggested I have another bone marrow biopsy done and offered to perform one right then and there.

I was not up for another bone marrow biopsy. I failed to see the benefit. I felt it would only reveal the absence of bone marrow and stem cells, something everyone already knew. Additionally, I refused another ATG treatment and was not up for taking more Cyclosporine. I kindly let him know that as well.

The surgeon was hoping I'd consider using his services and the University of Minnesota Transplant Center to have the bone marrow transplant performed. There were many considerations that would ultimately lead to my making a decision.

Since I was susceptible to germs and dying at any time, they knew how important it was to find a marrow match as soon as possible. But how selective should they be with respect to the donor's marrow? This was the big question. Even with a perfect match, the odds of a successful transplant were quite low due to numerous factors. If a "perfect match" could not be located, finding a "close match" might be the best option. If the donor's marrow was only a close match there would be a greater likelihood of my body rejecting the transplanted marrow, which could also result in death. Any way you look at it, there is risk involved.

The surgeon queried me as to what I would like him to do. Should he keep looking for a perfect match, hoping I did not get sick before one was located, or try finding a donor whose marrow is reasonably close to mine and proceed with the transplant with greater risk of marrow rejection? It was a lot to think about.

I simply asked the surgeon to inform me once they located a match, or a possible match, and I would make my decision based upon the available facts at that time. In my heart I did not believe they would find a match, or even a close match, because I believed that God planned to perform a miraculous healing in me against all odds.

The surgeon then asked me to make my decision by June 1st as to which surgeon and facility I wished to utilize for the transplant procedure. This way, they'd have me registered and ready to move forward quickly once the matching marrow was located.

My "Third" Opinion

On Thursday, May 17th, my wife and I met with another very warm and capable surgeon. He did not have anything new to say. He agreed with the diagnosis and prognosis that I had received. He also suggested I repeat the ATG/Cyclosporine treatment. He referred to the internationally renowned surgeon that I had seen the day before at the University of Minnesota as "the best." He said that if he had aplastic anemia, that is who he'd go with to have a marrow transplant. At the conclusion of our discussion that day and in a nice way, this surgeon termed my rare condition as *"an unfortunate case of bad luck."*

I made a plan to visit one more blood specialist (hematologist) at the end of May. At that point I will decide whether to stay with my current oncologist or make a switch. In the meanwhile, I am standing FIRMLY on the Word of God with His abundance of loving, caring and healing promises—that He will move in my physical body and manifest that which is promised! Hallelujah!

Our Regional RE/MAX Director, David Linger, put it so well when he was visiting me in the hospital. He said, "God is rarely early (in His perfect timing), but He is never late." That is a profound truth that I hang on to. The Bible tells us to *"wait on the Lord," "be patient," "trust," "lean on,"* and that *"He will exalt you in due season," "He is faithful and true,"* and that *"He will not allow the righteous to be shaken."*

I still stand firm on the verse the Lord gave me at 4:00 a.m. (on the TV), two days prior to my entering the hospital: *"After you have suffered a little while, the God of all grace, who has called you to His eternal glory in Christ Jesus, shall HIMSELF restore, strengthen, perfect, establish and confirm you."*

Blood Numbers

May 17th	My Blood Counts	Notes	Normal Range
Red	10.4	Last Transfusion: 14 Days	13.5 – 17.5
White	1,000	Cannot Transfuse	3,500 – 10,800
Platelets	23,000	2 Transfusions per week	130,000 – 430,000
Neutrophils	0.1	Most abundant white cell	1.9 – 8.0

Weight Numbers

For someone whose weight never changed much for years, it is interesting to see all of the ups and downs of my weight in 2001! After returning from Cancun around the 1st of the year I weighed 174 pounds. During my bout with hepatitis in March, my weight fell to 157 pounds. By April 7th, the day I was admitted to the hospital, it had increased to 161 pounds. While in the hospital it increased to 169 pounds due to Prednisone, Cyclosporine and lack of exercise. In the two weeks since leaving the hospital, my weight has plummeted to 153 pounds! Don't be alarmed! Much of the excess weight was from water weight and effects of the steroids. I am eating very healthy and continue to take the herbs. Overall I feel terrific!

Summary

All of us are standing firmly on God's Word for my complete 100% healing—without a bone marrow transplant! Please keep me in your prayers. Pray specifically for:

1. Protection for my family and me from the enemy, as he continues to try to sow seeds of doubt at every juncture *"for we are not ignorant of his schemes."* (2 Corinthians 2:11)
2. Me to cross over the goal line to score the touchdown of healing which the Lord shall perform for His Glory and in His perfect timing!
3. The Lord to help me in writing these email updates so they touch the hearts of many! *"The Spirit and bride say, 'Come'; And let the one who hears say, 'Come'; And let the one who is thirsty come; let the one who wishes take the water of life without cost."* (Revelation 22:17)

As I write these last few words of this email, I would like to say I am feeling extremely well. I still try to protect my health by not going out too much and staying away from large crowds. I try not to shake people's hands, but if I do I wash them right away.

Our real estate business is going very well! God has His hand on all of our affairs. He has blessed us with a lot of business during my physical absence. My wife is going on the listing appointments and showing a few homes! She meets with our clients to get all of the papers signed. I do the market evaluations and speak with the clients on the phone, oftentimes in negotiations. Our teamwork is awesome. Praise God!

As I have said before, "I am one blessed individual." I am so happy to be hearing from so many of you after you learned of my health challenge. More importantly, I am blessed to hear how the Lord has touched many of you as a result of my faith walk. Remember, I am just a person who is choosing to trust God at His Word—and to do that each hour of each day. I won't give up! You have my word on that. I will continue to rejoice in the midst of this trial. Victory is at hand. We will see it together!

Closing Verses

"... Humble yourselves under the mighty hand of God, that He may exalt you at the proper time." (1 Peter 5:6)

"...Today if you hear His voice, do not harden your hearts." (Hebrews 4:7)

"But as many as received Him, to them He gave the right to become children of God." (John 1:12)

"How will we escape if we neglect so great a salvation?" (Hebrews 2:3)

===

Your Friend,

Jeff Scislow

P.S. Feel free to forward this email to whomever you wish. Blessings!

May 28, 2001

Greetings & Happy Memorial Day!

How about that weather! We finally broke out of a week's worth of clouds and rain here in the Twin Cities... and today looks like a "10"!!!

Over the past week and a half I have been feeling great (this is nothing new) as I await a miraculous turnaround in the midst of a dire situation. At the end of this email update I will be sharing some exciting news, so please read on. And of course, I hope this finds you and your family doing fantastic! You are all winners!

Detox Complete!

The five-day (herbal) detoxification program went well. I began the program on May 15th and finished on May 19th. It involved drinking a lot of water, juiced vegetables and fruits, taking a variety of herbs and garlic, drinking herbal detox tea, eating no meat, drinking a "SuperFood" drink of herbs, vitamins and minerals and fasting the middle three days of the five-day detox period.

The only complication I encountered during detox was that I burned the inside of my mouth as the doses of garlic increased. I did not realize the potency of garlic, especially after juicing it in a blender. I did not rinse my mouth after drinking it and my lips, tongue and mouth were burned as a result, making it very painful for several days after the program ended. Any cut or burn to the skin is reason for alarm, as infection can easily set in, something I must avoid at all cost. Additionally, the time it takes to heal from a cut or burn is much longer when a person has a low or lacking immune system. But praise God, I am better now and did not experience any infection!

There are a number of detox programs. This particular one was focused on cleansing the liver and gall bladder, and removing any potential parasites. My weight fell as low as 153 during the program, but I did not feel weak. I trust I am "good and clean" now as those herbs had a way of "cleaning" me out... if you know what I mean.

I am continuing each day with one to two SuperFood drink mixes, lots of water and of course plenty of juiced fruits and vegetables. I also eat bananas, asparagus, broccoli, carrots, etc. No junk food (what a change). My weight is maintaining itself between 154-156 (the lightest in many years).

What Really Needs to be Done to be Healed?

This is the million dollar question—one that seems to be in the minds of many of my friends. In fact, numerous friends and folks I don't really know have provided advice on what I ought to be doing in order to be healed. The advice has basically been supportive and helpful, yet once in a while I receive what I will simply term, "strange" input. I have received medical advice, spiritual advice and "words from the Lord." Over time, the accumulation of all the advice was becoming confusing.

I know that "... *God is not a God of confusion*," (1 Corinthians 14:33) so I am simply praying for clarity, trusting my gut and following my heart with respect to whether or not I should follow any particular advice. I primarily listen to my wife and a few trusted friends whose advice I greatly respect.

What did become clear in this process of receiving "advice" was this: I do not need to "do" anything else to "earn" my healing. It is a done deal. In fact, it was done on Calvary about 2000 years ago. "...*by His wounds you were* [I AM] *healed.*" (1 Peter 2:24) [Emphasis added] In the same way that I cannot "earn" my salvation by being "good," neither can I earn my healing by doing anything for it. I must receive it by faith!

What has begun to crystallize in my mind is that I need to "thank the Lord" for what He HAS DONE in me. *"Rejoice in the Lord always; again I will say, rejoice!"* (Philippians 4:4) In James 1:9 it says, *"But the brother of humble circumstances is to glory in his high position."* Well then, I should be singing praises and rejoicing, correct? Exactly! And that is just what I AM DOING!

Remember Paul and Silas—they had been beaten with rods, thrown into prison, bound in chains and stocks, in the darkness of night, most likely with rats and snakes about them. What did they do in their darkest hour? Did they whine? Did they complain about their lashings and the pain? Did they fear their circumstances? No, no and no!

Listen to what happened: *"But about midnight Paul and Silas were praying and singing hymns of praise to God, and the prisoners were listening to them; and suddenly there came a great earthquake, so that the foundations of the prison house were shaken; and immediately all the doors were opened and everyone's chains were unfastened! When the jailer awoke and saw the prison doors opened, he drew his sword and was about to kill himself, supposing that the prisoners had escaped. But Paul cried out with a loud voice, saying, 'Do not harm yourself, for we are all here!' And he called for lights and rushed in, and trembling with fear he fell down before Paul and Silas, and after he brought them out, he said, 'Sirs, what must I do to be saved?' And they said, 'Believe in the Lord Jesus, and you will be saved, you and your household.'"* (Acts 16:25-31) In the midst of terrible circumstances, their joy and faith brought about a miraculous outcome—one which I, too, am expecting in the midst of my circumstances!

The Latest on My Eyes

As you recall, I was also diagnosed with retinal hemorrhaging on April 9th. As a result, it has been difficult to focus properly—both up close as well as at distances. Even more bizarre than the obscured vision with my eyes open is what I see with my eyes closed! With my eyes closed, I see a constant image of a roaring lion! I really cannot explain this. It appears to be in the form or substance of scar tissue.

Did the scar tissue form in such a way as to create the image of a roaring lion? I doubt that. Or am I seeing a type of spiritual reflection of a Bible verse that says, *"Be of sober spirit, be on the alert. Your adversary, the devil prowls around like a roaring lion, seeking someone to devour."* (1 Peter 5:8) I am more inclined to believe this. My sense is I am simply being reminded that I am under spiritual attack and that I am to *"...resist him, firm in faith..."* (1 Peter 5:9) As a result, I speak against the devil with authority and rebuke him so that I will not fear this "image" when I close my eyes. It works!

On May 25th I made my way back to the ophthalmologist for a scheduled follow-up eye exam. I did not say anything about the image of a roaring lion, as I could have ended up in another ward (ha ha). The test results showed no new damage or retinal bleeding and very slow signs that the scar tissue is dissolving. There is still a good chance that my vision could return to normal, but the doctor now feels it will take longer than the initial four month projection. Much of the outcome in my vision depends on the success of the ongoing blood transfusions. Normal blood levels do quite a bit for the human body, including the promotion of healing to a variety of body tissues. Low blood levels prolong or even inhibit the healing of body tissues.

I can read reasonably well with my head turned slightly to one side, but I am extra cautious when driving as I truly have a few "blind spots" with which to deal.

Enemy Attacks

Satan does make his attempts to beat me up and wear me down. I have found that the more time I spend studying my medical diagnosis and prognosis, the more pessimistic and worrisome I have a tendency to become. While at the U of M Transplant Center a couple weeks ago, I was given reading material and a VHS tape which were designed to mentally prepare me for a transplant. The tape would cover the chemotherapy phase, the radiation phase, the transplant phase, the odds of surviving and the support groups for patients and surviving families.

Did I delve into this material wanting to learn what the medical profession said my life was "going to be like" before, during and after a bone marrow transplant? No, I did not. I did not care, nor did I want to mentally go there; as I was NOT there— physically, emotionally nor spiritually. I am here in my home, outside of the hospital, feeling incredibly well and extremely optimistic that God's timing will be perfect and that I will be healed! His Word says, *"So do not worry about tomorrow; for tomorrow will care for itself. Each day has enough trouble of its own."* (Matthew 6:34) I agree; so that settles that!

It is imperative that I keep standing on God's Word during these times. Remember when Jesus was in the wilderness and Satan attacked him with tests and temptations, Jesus was victorious by quoting Scripture! *"...And the Sword of the Spirit, which is the Word of God"* (Ephesians 6:17), is a weapon of warfare—the weapon I fully intend to use!

I can't emphasize this enough: If we focus on our problems in life instead of on God's promises for victory OVER our problems, we not only invite the enemy in to remind us of our failures, our inadequacies, our inability to have God help us, but we might as well concede right then and there. There is NO WAY we will be victorious over any sickness, financial situation, relationship or issue if we are focusing on the problem, feeling overwhelmed and beat up. This is exactly where Satan wants us: depressed, filled with anxiety, full of doubt, with no sense of hope. He is a LIAR!!! Don't listen to him! He has lied from the beginning! Every word he speaks is a LIE!! He is speaking from his nature! (John 8:44)

If you *want* to be set FREE, *allow* the Son to set you FREE! Abide in His Word and you SHALL KNOW THE TRUTH and the truth SHALL SET YOU FREE! (John 8:31-36) God loves us so much and wants to give us the desires of our heart. (Psalm 37:4) He tells us that when we are TIRED and HEAVY LADEN, when we are WEARY, to come to Him. He offers us REST for our tired souls. He offers His gentleness and His humility from His heart. He will not burden us with a heavy load, but will relieve us from one. (Matthew 11:28-30)

Return to the Hospital?

The oncologists and surgeons at the University of Minnesota, along with my current doctor, have recommended that I undergo another ATG treatment and resume taking Cyclosporine to try to suppress the immune system once again to see if there is any chance of reviving any (potential) marrow stem cells. This would mean a trip back to the hospital for a minimum of five days. The chance of success from a second treatment of ATG and Cyclosporine is reduced by half over the first treatment. Since the first treatment produced no results, what are the odds of a second treatment producing results? Go figure. Not only does a second attempt have less chance of success, but it poses a higher risk of side effects. I had a few side effects from the ATG treatment I received while in the hospital, including night-sweats, hives, heartburn and some minor rashes.

As it stands right now, I do not feel inclined to check back into the hospital. By not doing the ATG/Cyclosporine again, the doctors admit there is nothing else that can be done. There is no marrow donor to be found. The only thing available is continued blood transfusions twice per week. This is a limited therapy. Each doctor has said that in time my body will begin to fight against the transfused platelets and red cells. When this rejection occurs, life cannot be sustained. There is no way of telling "when" this will occur; it simply begins to occur in time. Additionally, they've all reminded me that I will continue to be susceptible to infections and germs due to my very low white cell count. To date, I have received 24 blood transfusions and have had 146 tubes of blood drawn for test purposes.

The search continues for a matching bone marrow donor. The doctors wonder whether I will return to the hospital for another round of treatment, have future transfused blood rejected or succumb to a germ I encounter in the process. I stay faithfully at home, trusting God, on no medication. I am eating well, feeling good, continuing the herbal program, seeking alternative opinions and expecting a miracle!

Jesus asked, "Why Do You Call Me Good?"

"And someone came to Him and said, 'Teacher, what good thing shall I do that I may obtain eternal life?' And He said to him, 'Why are you asking Me about what is good? There is only One who is good; but if you wish to enter into life, keep the commandments.'" (Matthew 19:16-17)

I began to think of this passage as a result of my receiving so much supportive email. What does this passage have to do with the email, letters and cards I have received? Through my ordeal, some have looked up to me as someone special as a result of my faith, attitude and will to fight this disease. I can take no credit for this fight, or for my attitude towards it. I am simply standing on God's promises. It is a choice I make. He is the One who is "good," not me. And remember, I am not fighting this battle alone, the Lord is beside me in this fight! *"I can do all things through Him who strengthens me"* (Philippians 4:13), and when I have faith and trust in Him, the victory is handed over to me! When? At the proper time! *"...and this is the victory that has overcome the world—our faith."* (1 John 5:4) This battle has already been won, as long as I don't lose heart and give up!

Like a Bad Dream

In many ways my life could be thought of as a "bad dream." Some mornings when I wake up, especially while I was in the hospital, my mind races through all the things the doctors have told me and the unfortunate outcome I will likely experience. If I elect to spend time "dwelling" on those spoken words or the unpleasant prognosis reports found on the Internet, I will most certainly be feeding my mind with fear, doubt and anxiety. In essence, I'd be setting myself up for defeat.

Each day when negative or fearful thoughts arise, I have a choice to make. First, I choose to apply a verse from Philippians 3:13 into my life: "...forgetting what lies behind and reaching forward to what lies ahead." In addition, I choose to take "every thought captive to the obedience of Christ" (2 Corinthians 10:5); and to "...walk by faith, not by sight." (2 Corinthians 5:7) You too can make choices such as these to combat the fears and negative thoughts you may be experiencing. So if you're going through some tough times right now, stand on God's Word. Never back down, no matter what the circumstances! Get right with God and trust Him.

The Bible says that, "For those who are according to the flesh set their minds on the things of the flesh, but those who are according to the Spirit, the things of the Spirit. For the mind set on the flesh is death, but the mind set on the Spirit is life and peace." (Romans 8:5-6) I simply choose, by faith, to set my mind on the things of the Spirit in order that I have life and peace, and you can too!

A New Doctor?

On Tuesday, May 29th, I will be meeting with yet another doctor to see what he has to say about my situation. He has quite an interesting background. Although he is a chiropractor, he is also certified in herbal and homeopathic medicines, acupuncture, immune disorders, blood disorders and several other specialties. If I understand correctly, he is only one of two such doctors in the Twin Cities with his type of training.

He intends to "dig in" to my personal background (mostly from a health perspective) to determine what may have caused my marrow and blood levels to be affected. In advance of my appointment I have to complete a 45—page questionnaire! What a contrast from a typical new patient information form used by most medical doctors.

I'll keep you posted on this upcoming appointment!

A New Record on "Reds"

On May 24th they needed to fill me up again with red cells. Where's the good news in getting a blood transfusion? The good news is the length of time since having the last red cell transfusion. The longer I can go between transfusions the better. My first three red cell transfusions lasted 8, 12 and 6 days, respectively. My last one lasted 21 days! Hoorah! Although the doctors said nothing about this, I am keeping very close tabs on any sign of progress. To me, this is good news.

I'm Not Going to Be Sick!

In March of 1976, when I was 19 years old and stationed in Kansas City, Missouri in the U.S. Marine Corps, I contracted a sickness that really wore me down. My throat was incredibly sore and became infected. My tonsils, which had turned milky white in color, had swollen to the point of nearly closing off the back of my throat.

I drove to the local (military) medical clinic at Richards-Gebaur Air Force Base to have it checked out. The doctor ran a few tests including a blood test. He came back and told me my white count was sky high because I had infectious mononucleosis (mono for short). I asked him what we needed to do to get rid of it because tennis season was starting and I intended to play on the Marine Corps team!

His first words were, "You won't be playing tennis this year." I promptly responded, "Oh yes I will." He retorted back, "You don't seem to understand, you have mono. You won't be playing any tennis for quite some time." I quickly responded stating, "You don't understand, tennis starts next month and I'm not going to be sick!" "Hey kid, you can die from this if you don't take care of yourself and get some rest!" he firmly stated. "I'll see you in two weeks," he added. As I walked out the door, I looked back at him and pointedly said, "I'm not going to be sick."

My first stop after leaving the Air Base was the public library. I remember my attitude of determination. I did not want to be sick but I did want to play tennis. Nothing else mattered; my focus was quite intense!

I read about mono in the library. I wanted to learn whatever I could to fight it. I saw microscopic images of the mono cells in the encyclopedia. From the library I went directly to the supermarket and loaded up on protein foods (steaks, meats, etc). When I got home I began eating foods rich in protein. I called my chiropractor (yes, I had one back then) to set up an appointment for me to get an "adjustment". I wanted my spine and the spinal fluid to flow perfectly because "I was not going to be sick." I wanted to do everything I possibly could to enhance my chances of beating this thing.

On two separate occasions, while sitting up in my bed, I engaged in a mental battle to attack and kill the mono cells. First I pictured in my mind what those mono cells looked like (from the encyclopedia at the library). Then I pictured what my antibodies looked like. Then I visualized my *strong* antibodies attacking the mono cells that had invaded my body. I visually saw a battle within my bloodstream with the antibodies winning. I visualized this on two occasions until the antibodies had killed all the mono cells. Each of these occasions lasted about 20 minutes, depleted a great deal of my energy and caused me to sweat considerably.

I returned to the Air Force base thirteen days after my "mono diagnosis" and saw the same doctor. After a blood test was taken, the doctor entered the room where I was waiting and said, "I don't understand it, your blood levels are normal?????" I promptly responded, "I told you I was not going to be sick!" In a loud and disappointed voice he said, "Get out of here!"

Tennis started two weeks later. For what it is worth, and if you don't mind me saying, I went on to win the Marine Corps tournament that year for the Mid-States Region and was flown to California for a wonderful week to play tennis with the top USMC players from around the country. My competition whipped me good on the courts, but I sure had fun and I certainly was not sick!

I wanted to share this story simply because I feel the same way today. I'm not going to be sick! Since I do not specifically know what my "foe" is this time around—the doctors tell me that the "foe" is my own immune system—it makes it a bit difficult to "attack" it. The big advantage I have, however, is that the Lord does know the specifics of my "foe" and He is the One who will fight this battle along with me! I only need to trust Him to do so!

More Sickness on the Home Front

As you recall from my previous email, some of my children have been sick. Two of them threw up. Last week my other son threw up as well. I'm happy to say that they are ALL better now—thank you, Jesus! None of the cold or flu germs got to me. I was protected again. I have maintained a perfectly healthy body temperature of 98.6 degrees! Praise God!

It is interesting to note, that when I was in the hospital, two different individuals that prayed for me at different times envisioned some very interesting things. I did not share them with you before because

I saw no place to do so, but I do now. One person saw a bubble around me—a clear, transparent bubble of "protection." The other person saw me inside of a cocoon, protected and awaiting to emerge.

Now I cannot really tell you what these images mean, but I am getting a sense that it is just another wonderful and awesome act of God Almighty. I love Him and praise His name!

The last time I met with the doctor I told him that I had several sick children at home and that I felt fine. He admitted, "Well, you do look good." This was one of the few positive comments I have ever heard from him. Praise God; wait until he sees the miracle!

Blood Numbers

May 24th	My Blood Counts	Notes	Normal Range
Red	7.5*	Last Transfusion: 21 Days	13.5 – 17.5
White	800	Cannot Transfuse	3,500 – 10,800
Platelets	28,000*	2 Transfusions per week	130,000 – 430,000
Neutrophils	0.2	Most abundant white cell	1.9 – 8.0

* 2 bags of Red Cells and 1 bag of Platelets transfused on May 24th
* Tubes of Blood Drawn since Illness: 146

Weight Numbers

Daily range 154-156 lbs. Feeling very well.

Closing Verses

"For all have sinned and fall short of the glory of God." (Romans 3:23)

"For the wages of sin is death, but the free gift of God is eternal life in Christ Jesus our Lord." (Romans 6:23)

"For God so loved the world, that He gave His only begotten Son, that whoever believes in Him shall not perish, but have eternal life." (John 3:16)

"How will we escape if we neglect so great a salvation?" (Hebrews 2:3)

===

Blessings,

Jeff Scislow

June 3, 2001

What an awesome morning of sunshine here in the Twin Cities, Minnesota! Where has the past week gone? Time sure has been flying by! Later in this email I will share something incredible that I discovered since I last updated you. Before I do, allow me to bring you up to speed on some other things that have been going on.

Lymph Node Swollen

About a week ago the lymph node near my left tonsil began to swell. To my knowledge, a lymph node typically swells as a result of it producing infection-fighting lymphocytes in an attempt to fight off an infection or other germs. Being that I had neither been feeling sick, nor did I have any type of fever, I had no idea what was causing the swelling. Nevertheless, a swollen lymph node brought about some concern as to what was happening.

A few days after the node began to swell I developed a nasty toothache on the same left side. Perhaps this was the reason the lymph node was working hard to produce lymphocytes, to fight against a tooth infection. It was my best guess.

After a couple days of persistent tooth pain and no change in the size of the lymph node, I decided to visit my dentist the following day. That night however, I prayed for the toothache to go away, and the next morning it was gone! I have had no pain since! Praise God!

While at the doctor's office last week for blood testing and a platelet transfusion, not only had the swollen lymph node produced an increase in the lymphocyte count, but the neutrophil count as well. Although the doctor was unavailable for comment, I consider this a good sign.

My white count moved to 1300 from 800 just five days earlier. The white count, which is still very low, has hovered around 800 for the

145

past two to three weeks. Over the past two months, my highest count was 1500, my lowest 200. Normal is 3500—10,800. The most interesting part of this last blood test however, was the jump in neutrophils.

The biopsy done on April 9th showed no bone marrow, no stem cells, a near absence of white cells and a neutrophil count of 0.0. For the next six weeks, the neutrophil count remained at 0.0. Then it inched up to 0.1 and was there for about two weeks. Then it moved ever so slightly to 0.2 and remained there for just over a week. On the 29th of May it had increased to 0.4! I know that this is a long way from normal (1.9 to 8.0), but it is a move in the right direction!

As the neutrophil counts have inched upward, I asked the doctor if this was good news. He said, "It does not mean anything since it is so insignificant." I asked if there was any way a neutrophil count could appear (or increase) outside of bone marrow producing it. He answered NO. To me this was not a mystery; the ONLY way that neutrophils can appear is if there is MARROW present!

This is awesome! I know it is very premature because the levels are still very low, but there must be marrow! How else would neutrophils be showing up? While the doctors continue to declare "you have no bone marrow," they have yet to render an opinion as to why the neutrophil count is inching upward.

God told me that if I till the soil of my body He would plant the seed of marrow and it would grow 100-fold! Is this what's happening? God only knows, but I absolutely know that His hand is on this entire matter and I trust Him for a complete 100% recovery! We will be watching these blood levels with great anticipation!

Natural Homeopathic Doctor Passed Up

As I mentioned in my last email, I had planned to visit with a natural health Chiropractor (the one with the 45-page questionnaire). We did in fact meet and had a lengthy discussion, but I opted not to utilize his services. I felt like I was going to become an experiment. I know that testing is part of the fact-finding process, but after praying for discernment I sensed his experience level was not what I was looking for.

I am scheduled to meet with another natural health professional on June 5th. A fellow RE/MAX agent, as well as a past client, strongly recommended him. The RE/MAX agent had a serious condition a few years back and was healed of a challenging disease after getting advice from this doctor. My past client had been suffering from ill symptoms for some time and was helped by this doctor and is well today. Unfortunately, she met this *natural* doctor after medical practitioners had removed her tonsils in an attempt to make her well!

At this point, I am absolutely convinced that the "natural way" is the correct way for me. I have seen and heard enough now to understand that God was directing me this way initially, when our tenant brought the herbal book to our home a few weeks ago. At first it was scary making the decision to go this route and stop taking the medical doctor's prescriptions, but it has been confirmed over and over again! Praise God! He is leading the charge!

I promise to keep you posted on all my doctor visits. I am looking forward to finding the right person to help me and I believe God will direct me to him or her.

Another Biopsy?

The medical doctors have just requested another bone marrow biopsy from me in order to determine why the neutrophil count has been rising. It is nice to know that they are acknowledging that something positive might be occurring inside my bones. The likelihood is good that I will comply with their request and have this procedure done within the next week or so.

The biopsy is an outpatient procedure performed at the hospital. It should answer some questions that the doctors now have and will help them to determine what to suggest to me next.

A Discerning Process

This has been an interesting process of evaluation and discernment for me. There have been many professional opinions offered to me. Most seem sound, but not all can be correct. Which, if any, will be the one(s) that work?

On the one hand (from a medical profession standpoint), I am not taking the prescribed medication, nor am I agreeing to another ATG treatment as recommended. On the other hand, I am gaining confidence in the area of natural healing. These two professional fields are quite opposed to one another. With an open mind, I am trying to locate the right professional(s) in each field, so their individual recommendations will compliment one another and work positively in my behalf. So far this has been quite challenging. I will keep you posted.

What's the Body to Do?

What I am about to share with you came as an incredible revelation. If you, or anyone you know, are suffering from an autoimmune disease, these words will have very special meaning and purpose.

Let's begin with a look at how the *Body of Christ* is called to be "fitted together" as one. We as Christians are called to work together in unity and to build up one another in love. From Ephesians 4:11-16 we read, *"And He gave some as apostles, and some as prophets, and some as evangelists, and some as pastors and teachers, for the equipping of the saints for the work of service, to the building up of the body of Christ; until we all attain to the unity of the faith, and of the knowledge of the Son of God, to a mature man, to the measure of the stature which belongs to the fullness of Christ."*

"As a result, we are no longer to be children, tossed here and there by waves and carried about by every wind of doctrine, by the trickery of men, by craftiness in deceitful scheming; but speaking the truth in love, we are to grow up in all aspects into Him, who is the Head, even Christ, from whom the whole body, being fitted and held together by what every joint supplies, according to the proper working of each individual part, causes the growth of the body for the building up of itself in love."

Next, let's look at another depiction of how the *Body of Christ* is to function in harmony. Note how the analogy of the human body is used once again as a guide for Christians to live and work together. Then, focus closely on the analogy itself. The analogy of the function of the human body is foundational according to the following passage. God's Word clearly states that the human body was designed to function in harmony with other parts of the body. If the body fails to function properly and attacks another part of the body, it is operating inconsistently with God's design. We as believers, in faith, have the authority over the malfunctioning part of the body to command it to line up in accordance with the way God created it. Why? Because it is written in the following verses:

"For even as the body is one and yet has many members, and all the members of the body, though they are many, are one body, so also is Christ... for the body is not one member, but many. If the foot should say, 'Because I am not a hand, I am not a part of the body,' it is not for this reason any the less a part of the body. And if the ear should say, 'Because I am not an eye, I am not a part of the body,' it is not for this reason any the less a part of the body."

"If the whole body were an eye, where would the hearing be? If the whole body were hearing, where would the sense of smell be? But now God has placed members, each one of them, in the body, just as He desired... and now there are many members, but one body. AND THE EYE CANNOT SAY TO THE HAND, 'I HAVE NO NEED OF YOU,' or again, THE HEAD

TO THE FEET, 'I HAVE NO NEED OF YOU,' (OR THE IMMUNE SYSTEM TO THE BONE MARROW 'I HAVE NO NEED OF YOU!')" (These are my words.) [Emphasis added]

> ## *"THE IMMUNE SYSTEM CANNOT SAY TO THE BONE MARROW 'I HAVE NO NEED OF YOU"'*
> *- Jeff Scislow*

"On the contrary, it is much truer that the members of the body which seem to be weaker are necessary; and those members of the body, which we deem less honorable, on these we bestow more abundant honor, and our less presentable members become much more presentable whereas our more presentable members have no need of it. But God has so composed the body, giving more abundant honor to that member which lacked, so that there may be no division in the body, but that the members should have the same care for one another."

"And if one member suffers, all the members suffer with it; if one member is honored, all the members rejoice with it. Now you are Christ's body, and individually members of it." (1 Corinthians 12:12-27)

This is SO POWERFUL! God is SO GOOD! This passage, although it addresses how Christians should be "getting along with one another," derives its analogy from the HUMAN BODY and the way God foundationally created it.

So with these passages and the authority that I have over my body, by the Word of God and its ultimate authority, I am able to address the parts of my body in prayer and command them to act in accordance with this passage in God's Word!

I have already done this! In prayer, I have commanded my immune system to "no longer attack the bone marrow, for he is your brother; but rather, build up and support your brother as we are commanded to do in Scripture!"

More specifically, in my prayer I have spoken to my immune system telling it that "I am sorry for putting bad things into my body over the years which have caused you to work overtime: my poor diet, my lack of diet, even the prescription drugs that I have recently taken which were designed to suppress and kill you!" I then commanded my immune system to "work in accordance with the way God created it and to HELP THE BONE MARROW to gain strength, as it is fitting with the Word of God, and to build up and edify all parts of the body!"

In the same prayer, I spoke to the bone marrow as one of the weaker parts of the body at this time. I informed it that "the immune system is now under the authority of the Word of God and that it will not attack you anymore!" And that according to 1 Corinthians 12:24-25, *"God has so composed the body, giving more abundant honor to that member which lacked (that is you bone marrow!), that there should be NO DIVISION IN THE BODY, BUT THAT THE MEMBERS SHOULD HAVE THE SAME CARE FOR ONE ANOTHER!"*[Emphasis added]

These passages from 1 Corinthians 12 are promises that can be received by any person who is battling with an autoimmune disease (one whereby the immune system or some part of the body is attacking another part of the body). If you are experiencing something in your body that is clearly inconsistent with the way God created it; with the way your body was meant to function, then you can take authority over that condition and speak God's Word over it. Remember, *"He [God] sent His Word and healed them [us] and delivered them [us] from their [our] destructions"* (Psalm 107:20) [Emphasis added], and *"...calls into being that which does not exist."* (Romans 4:17)

In other words, God can call things that are not "healthy," as though they were "healthy." He is able to speak them into "healthy" existence! Do you believe this?

You and I have this same power and authority! We have the power and authority to do exactly the same; and even greater! How? Because Jesus said we could! It is promised to us in John 14:12!

When referencing the incredible miracles He had been doing, Jesus said something extremely profound, *"...he who believes in Me, the works that I do, he will do also; and greater works than these he will do; because I go to the Father."* Jesus told us that we will do greater works than He did, because He will bring our requests before the Father. As a result, you not only have the power and authority to speak life and healing to your body, but to do many miraculous works as well!

Therefore, if you are fighting MS, rheumatoid arthritis, fibromyalgia, lupus, aplastic anemia or any number of autoimmune diseases—take authority over the attacking immune system, reminding it that it is operating against God's design and that it "can no longer say to another part of your body, 'I have no need of you!'" Exercise your rightful authority in Christ!

Wow! What a revelation God has shown me! This is God's Word in action and power! These passages in 1 Corinthians 12 speak so clearly to my situation!

I must quote the following Scripture again right now, with tears of joy in my eyes...

"For the Word of God is LIVING and ACTIVE and sharper than any two-edged sword, and piercing as far as the division of soul and spirit, of joints and MARROW, and able to judge the thoughts and intentions of the heart!" (Hebrews 4:12) [Emphasis added].

REALTORS® Respond!

I have sent my emails to over 20,000 RE/MAX friends around the nation asking for their prayerful support during this most challenging episode of my life. I have received a huge outpouring of love and support not only from RE/MAX, but from my friends in Star Power, Keller Williams, Coldwell Banker and many other superb real estate organizations. Thank you so much for personally responding.

In addition to the individual prayers of many, some have added my name to their church prayer lists and others have committed to praying in their small groups. I have even learned I was placed on several large prayer chains of over 1,000 individuals each! That's simply awesome! As the word gets out that one is in need, I cannot express how amazing the support has been. I extend a great big thank you to each of you and a joyous praise to God! I love you guys! You are all winners! We will see a miracle together! It's coming!

Blood Numbers

May 29th	My Blood Counts	Notes	Normal Range
Red	9.7	Last Transfusion: 5 Days	13.5 – 17.5
White	1,300	Count 5 Days Ago: 800	3,500 – 10,800
Platelets	25,000*	Last Transfusion: 5 Days	130,000 – 430,000
Neutrophils	0.4	Highest in 2 Months!	1.9 – 8.0

* 1 bag of Platelets was transfused May 29th

Weight Numbers

Daily range 154-156 lbs. Feeling very well.

Eyes

It is difficult to determine if there has been any improvement. Retinal hemorrhaging is still evident in the form of scar tissue causing "floaters" and blind spots. The image of a "roaring lion" is slowly dissipating!

Closing Verses

"Therefore if you have been raised up with Christ, keep seeking the things above where Christ is... set your mind on the things above, not on the things that are on earth... therefore consider the members of your earthly body as dead to immorality, impurity, passion, evil desire and greed... for it is on account of these things that the wrath of God will come... put them all aside: anger, wrath, malice, slander and abusive speech from your mouth. Do not lie to one another, since you have laid aside the old self with its evil practices, and put on the new self... put on a heart of compassion, kindness, humility, gentleness and patience; bearing with one another, and forgiving each other... just as the Lord forgave you... And beyond all these things, put on love, which is the perfect bond of unity." (Colossians 3:1-14)

"Behold, I stand at the door and knock; if anyone hears My voice and opens the door, I will come in to him, and will dine with him, and he with Me." (Revelation 3:20)

"How will we escape if we neglect so great a salvation?" (Hebrews 2:3)

===

Blessings,

Jeff Scislow

June 10, 2001

Greetings!

As I enter my third month in the battle against aplastic anemia, I am in great spirits and feeling quite well overall. I am taking the necessary precautions not to become "infected" with any virus or bacteria, as it could cause serious complications, even death. I thank the Lord for His sustained protection; as a result, I'm doing great!

I have yet to experience the physical manifestation of my healing, but as I have said before—I believe it is at hand. So what delays this manifestation? This is a very interesting and challenging question; one that I aim to explore with you in detail with this, my fourth email update.

Principles of Healing

Needless to say, the extraordinary topic of healing has been front and center in my life over the past couple months. My main objective has been to search the Scriptures and uncover a key principle, or principles, that will pave the way for me to realize the complete healing in my body. To date, I have explored and applied several principles of healing. I will continue to search for answers and revelations, as I press on toward the physical manifestation of perfect health.

I am sure you will agree, from the material that you will read below, obtaining the "physical" manifestation is challenging. I am not sure if the "goal line stand" imposed by the enemy is simply so strong and that I need to continue pressing on before I score the proverbial touchdown or if God is possibly waiting for me to come to some "understanding" of what He wishes to show me in order to receive a breakthrough resulting in my miracle? Some believe it's one way, others believe it's another; still others believe it is a combination of healing *principles* that will bring about the miracle I so desperately need.

This I believe for sure; God is able to bring about a miracle any way He wishes, and it will be in accordance with His Word. As a result, my effort and strength must remain focused on His Word and on the *variety* of Biblical principles found there. Below, I will share with you Biblical principles that pertain to miraculous healing. Keep in mind, these are all Christian principles. I have not and will not seek any "other principles," although "the world" is filled with so many "healing principles" that it can make one's head spin.

Principle 1: Faith Alone

The Bible says in Hebrews 11:6, *"And without faith it is impossible to please Him, for he that comes to God must believe that He is and that He is a rewarder of those who seek Him."* God promises to reward those who diligently seek Him in faith; something I am doing. As a result, I believe that the promise in this verse alone is enough for me to be healed.

"Now faith is the assurance of things hoped for, the conviction of things not seen," as stated in Hebrews 11:1. This means simply believing, without wavering, in things we expect to happen, although they have not yet happened or physically materialized (unseen).

We see example after example of miracles and healings in Matthew chapters 8 and 9. Both Jesus and the disciples were performing all kinds of signs and wonders and healings! Jesus healed ALL that were sick!

Now listen closely to this story from Mark chapter 9, starting at verse 17: *"Teacher, I brought You my son, possessed with a spirit which makes him mute; and whenever it seizes him, it dashes him to the ground and he foams at the mouth, and grinds his teeth, and stiffens out. And I told Your* disciples to cast it out, and they could not do it. And Jesus answered them and said, 'O unbelieving generation, how long shall I be with you? How long shall I put up with you? Bring him to Me!'"

"And they brought the boy to Him. And when he saw Him, immediately the spirit threw the boy into a convulsion, and falling to the ground, he began rolling about and foaming at the mouth. And He asked his father, 'How long has this been happening to him?' And he said, 'From childhood. And it has often thrown him both into the fire and into the water to destroy him. But if You can do anything, take pity on us and help us!'"

"And Jesus said to him, 'If You can? All things are possible to him who believes.' Immediately the boy's father cried out and began saying, 'I do believe; HELP MY UNBELIEF!'"

"And Jesus rebuked the unclean spirit, saying to it, 'You deaf and dumb spirit, I command you, come out of him and do not enter him again.' And after crying out and throwing him into terrible convulsions, it came out; and the boy became so much like a corpse that most of them said, 'He is dead'. But Jesus took him by the hand and raised him; and he got up." [Emphasis added].

We see from this example two important things. First, we see that the man said, *"I believe, help my UNBELIEF,"* and that Jesus said, *"All things are possible for him who believes."* The boy's father asked Jesus to help his UNBELIEF. I see this as an illustration of God being able to work miracles and heal even if our faith is not perfect, for *"...Jesus is the author and perfecter of our faith...."* (Hebrews 12:2) He perfects our faith before the Father for us! This man's heart was pure and he spoke truth from his heart, seeking Jesus' help! Jesus honored his request!

Secondly, we see from Jesus' words, *"All things are possible..."* This means that God is not limited as to *how* He will perform that which He will perform, nor is He limited to *what* He can do.

Believing is nonetheless crucial, but even in our weakness (as it relates to faith) God is able and willing to move miraculously! This boy was healed because His father acted on faith alone, and even though the father admitted his faith might be short of what God might have expected, God honored the sincerity of his heart and had compassion on him and his son!

Principle 2: Conditional Upon an Action

While I was in the hospital I made a point of diligently praying the same prayer that Jabez prayed to the Lord. (1 Chronicles 4:10) Within days, I began experiencing some interesting things taking place; things that caused me to evaluate myself and re-align areas of my life that needed correction. The issue of self-examination is not necessarily a topic we look forward to, but one I believe is very important to receiving breakthroughs in our lives.

The Apostle Paul spoke to the Corinthians about this; how failure to examine themselves was resulting in many of them being sick and even dying: *"...many among you are weak and sick, and a number sleep* [have died]. *But if we judged ourselves rightly, we would not be judged."* (1 Corinthians 11:28-31) [Emphasis added]

The topic of self-examination, and subsequent repentance of any sin as a condition to receive healing, is explored in detail in a book I began reading this past week. This excellent book, written by Pastor Henry Wright, was recommended to me by two separate individuals a couple weeks ago.

Below are excerpts of Pastor Wright's introduction to his book, *"A More Excellent Way—A Teaching on the Spiritual Roots of Disease."* It is clear to see from this segment that conditions may exist in our lives that can prevent healing and miracles from manifesting; and once certain conditions are met, (spiritual) doors are opened to receive the miraculous.

"When I began in ministry in the early 1980's, I was part of a church that believed that God did get involved in people's lives, and that there was something happening between conversion and heaven. But even in that church of over 1500 people, coming week after week, the elders anointing them with oil, praying the prayer of faith, fasting and prayer, and standing on the Word, people WERE NOT GETTING WELL from incurable diseases."

"I observed that as I crossed America, regardless of denomination, regardless of the Church, less than 5% of all of God's people (forget about the world, the unbelievers) were getting healed of their diseases. It is even worse than that today! I don't know if you have ever been prayed for because of a disease and did not get well. If you went before God and believed Him, believed that He loved you and He would heal you and it did not happen, that was a staggering attack on your faith and your trust in the living God."

"Scripture tells us that God loves us, that He came and died for us in the person of the Lord Jesus Christ. He healed the people of their diseases and cast out their evil spirits. The disciples did it, the 70 did it, and the early church did it. Then we entered into a Dark Age of time from which I don't think we have ever recovered."

"When I began in ministry, I wanted to know why God said in Psalm 103:3 that He not only forgives us of all our iniquities, but He heals us of all our diseases."

"In 1 Thessalonians 5:23, we're told — 'may the God of Peace sanctify you wholly in spirit, in soul, and in body.' Well, I did not see much sanctification of the body, I did not see much sanctification of the soul and I found a need for sanctification in God's people in holiness. You know, I am sure everyone in here is holy by faith, but I have found that God's people struggle with the things of life, (as Paul noted in Romans chapter 7)."

"When I began to become involved with people, getting involved in their lives, I prayed for people, and I believed God would heal them. Less than 5% of anyone I prayed for got well. I preached the Gospel that got people saved

and got them to heaven, but left them stranded between conversion and heaven. Would that be the Gospel I would preach? Would I come up with a doctrine that would establish it? It would be easy to say, 'Sorry, no help for you, no hope for you.' But in my heart, the Scriptures I read seemed to indicate differently."

"I went to God one day and said, 'You'd better talk to me, Boss, because if you have called me to represent You to Your people, and to those yet unsaved, you would better show me a little more fruit. If it's not happening, you would better tell me why or else I'm going to go back into sales and marketing. I will go to church, I will love You, I will be a good Christian, I might even be a deacon, but You can forget about me speaking. I'm not speaking for You if my words are not being honored, because that is fraud.'"

"I went to God in the early 1980's and God began to show me His truth about disease from the Scriptures. It was not that He could not heal. It was that we had to become sanctified in certain areas of our lives before He would heal. DISEASES IN OUR LIVES CAN BE THE RESULT OF A SEPARATION FROM HIM AND HIS WORD IN SPECIFIC AREAS OF OUR LIVES. God would have to become double-minded, would have to become evil in condoning evil, in order to bless us in our sins. Except for those times when He would—have mercy on whom He would have mercy—disease was an issue to do with circumcision of the heart."

"One day my eyes were opened and I saw something and I have never looked back from the ministry God set before me."

"The Lord came and He demonstrated the love of God and power over the devil and disease in spite of sin. He demonstrated in Matthew, Mark, Luke and John; His disciples and the early church also demonstrated it in Acts. Then, from Romans all the way through Jude, you will find the Scriptures teaching us about sanctification. You can't have Matthew, Mark, Luke, John and Acts until you have dealt with Romans to Jude. You cannot expect God to bless us if we are separated from Him in an area that needs to be dealt with. I like to say it this way, 'We have been taught so much about God's promises and not much about His Spirit of discernment and the consequences of sin.'"

160

"As a pastor, if somebody came to me with simple arthritis, and asked me to pray for them, I would say, 'No, I'm not going to do it.' If they said, 'But the Word says to come before the elders and be anointed with oil and be prayed for.' I would respond, 'No, I have been there, done that.' Do you know how many times I have prayed for people with arthritis in the past? None of them were healed. I quit praying for them; it was a waste of my time."

"But one day God opened my heart. I was ministering in 1985, when five ladies came up to me. Each of them had arthritis. Two of the ladies had gnarly disfiguration. I said to them, 'You know there is sometimes a responsibility before God for healing.'"

"I want to tell you, healing and things you get from God, to a degree, are CONDITIONAL TO YOUR OBEDIENCE. I am not into legalism. I'm into grace and mercy. But I want to tell you that with freedom comes a degree of responsibility."

"I told the five ladies with arthritis 'that there would be a condition to their healing.' I asked them to think about the people who had injured each of them in their lifetime, either through word or deed—someone who did not treat them right, victimized them, lied about them, abused them, either emotionally, physically, verbally, or maybe even sexually."

"I asked them, 'When you think of their name, or their face, whether they're living or dead, what do you feel? Do any of you have that high-octane ping going off inside?' They all said, 'Yes, there is somebody I have not had resolution with.' There was bitterness and unforgiveness. I told them in exchange for their healing, they would have to get that right with God, right then, or else we were wasting our time. They were going to have to forgive that person."

"The Scriptures say: 'But if you forgive not men their trespasses, neither will your Father forgive your trespasses.' (Matthew 6:15) Have you ever read that Scripture? Do you think it is there just for the fun of it? Do you think it is a situational Scripture that only applies to some and not to all?"

"When you take a look at these Scriptures you will find that consequences of unforgiveness may bind you to a disease that is a result of this sin of bitterness and unforgiveness."

"Christians, for the most part, believe we are saved by grace and by faith. Just because you are born again and your spirit has become alive in God, it does not mean you have resolved the consequences of the sin issue in your life. Otherwise, we would not need sanctification, would we? (Hebrews 12:14)"

"I told the 5 ladies that an exchange would happen for their obedience. I said, 'If you, from the heart, will forgive that person of their trespasses, sincerely, whether you feel like it or not, I'm going to ask God to heal you. But, if you just do it because you want the healing for selfish reasons and you are using this kind of like a mechanism, or a system, or a mantra, we're still wasting our time.' The Bible says, 'If you, from the heart'—from your spirit forgive."

"Your head might still be pitching a fit about what they did to you because that's in your memory. The Bible says—as many who are led by the Spirit of God, they are the sons of God. Are you being led by your psychology (soul) or is the Spirit of God leading you? Who lives within your human spirit and makes you sons and daughters of God? Are you being led by the Spirit of God or by the intellect and other thoughts? I ask the question because it's an important question."

"I led the five ladies into a prayer of repentance and forgiveness. I am here to tell you that when I finished the prayer, I looked up to them and said, 'How's your arthritis doing?' All of a sudden it dawned on them that they had no more pain. Fingers had straightened, the pain was gone, and all five ladies stood there totally freed from crippling arthritis and its pain. I NEVER MINISTERED HEALING TO THEM ONCE!"

"When they met the conditions of His nature, He was there to heal! That's the reason why I'm not too impressed by (and I say this carefully) healing crusades that don't take into account that disease may be a result of sin that has not been dealt with."

162

As I read through this portion of the introduction, I was challenged again, just like I was while in the hospital, to search my heart and to ask God if there was anything in my life that I needed to repent; anything that might have possibly brought this affliction upon me or was now standing in the way of my being healed. I was again reminded of what the Apostle Paul had said to the Corinthians; *"...many among you are weak and sick, and a number sleep [have died]. But if we judged ourselves rightly, we would not be judged."* [Explanation added] I was determined to examine and judge myself rightly!

Principle 3: Calling it Into Existence

This past week I read a wonderful book by Charles Capps, called *"God's Creative Power for Healing."* Here are a few points from this book:

"God's Word will heal your body. Healing can be received into the human spirit through the Word. Once it is conceived there, it permeates the physical body; it must be applied on a regular basis; and spoken to your individual circumstance—someone else cannot do it for you."

"When God's Word concerning healing takes root in your flesh, it becomes greater than disease and healing is the result. When you speak God's Word from your heart, then faith gives substance to the promises of God; your words create images and eventually you will live out the reality of that image."

"An example of this is found in Mark 5:25-28, where the woman with an issue of blood said, 'If I may touch but His clothes, I shall be whole.' She continued to speak until she saw herself well. The Amplified Bible says, 'For she kept saying, 'If I only touch His garments, I shall be restored to health.''"

"That hope was her goal, but she did not feel healed, she did not look healed, but she began filling hope with faith filled words, 'I shall be restored to health; I shall be restored to health; I shall be; I shall be.''"

"I am sure her head said, 'When? You don't look any better, you are NOT any better!' Then she began to answer human reasoning by being more specific—"When I touch His garment I shall be restored to health.'"

"She was filling her hope with a faith image. She set her own point of contact to receive her healing. Her words penetrated her spirit and she began to see herself well. That 'grow worse' image of despair and defeat had to give way to the faith filled words that came from her mouth. When she touched His clothes, her touch of faith made a demand on the covenant of God and the anointing that was upon Jesus."

"What she was saying was her faith talking. When she acted out what she said, and touched His garment, that faith that was in her BECAME THE SUBSTANCE of her hope and her words became a living reality. Notice it was her faith that made a demand on the healing anointing that was upon Jesus. Faith gave substance to her hope and healing was manifested in her body."

"Her hope was to be healed, but hope DID NOT HEAL HER! Faith gave substance to her hope. Her faith gave substance to and brought about the manifestation of healing that was already hers because of the covenant. But she had to call for it (all things are possible to them that believe—Mark 9:23). And Jesus said to her (after she had touched His garment), 'Daughter, your faith has made you whole.'"

Later in his book, Charles Capps goes on to say, *"There is probably no other subject more important to your healing and health than the principle of CALLING THINGS THAT ARE NOT. Abraham became fully persuaded that God would do what He had promised. The way he became fully persuaded was by calling those things, which were not manifest, as though they were."*

"Giving voice to God's Word is a method of calling for things that God has given by promise and is not yet manifest. When you do this, some may say that you are denying what exists (the illness), but that is not true at all. You are establishing what God has said to be true concerning healing even though

it is not yet a reality in your body. You don't deny that sickness exists, but you deny its right to exist in your body, because you have been redeemed from the curse of the law and delivered from the authority of darkness." (Galatians 3:13; Colossians 1:13)

"When you are sick and confess that you are healed by the stripes of Jesus, you are calling for what God has already given you, even though it is not yet manifest. This is God's method of calling things that are not as though they were until they are."

"There are some who have misunderstood this principle, and they call things that are, as though they are not. In other words, they deny what exists. But there is NO POWER in denying that sickness exists. The power is in calling for healing and health by mixing faith with God's Word."

"Denying sickness won't make you well. But by mixing faith with God's Word, you are calling for the promise of God to be manifest in your body. This will cause you to be fully persuaded, and healing is the result."

"There are some who would say you are lying if you confess you are healed when you are sick. No, you are simply calling for healing that God has already provided, even though it is not manifest in your body. What you are doing is practicing God's medicine. You are calling your body well according to Luke 17:5-6 and Mark 11:23. Your body is listening to you and it will obey you if you believe and doubt not in your heart. Your words have more effect on your body than anyone else's words."

"But God's method is to call for positive things, even though they are not yet a reality in your body. You call them until they are manifest. You have a God-given right to exercise authority over your body. If you feed the spirit man God's Word, it will make demands on the flesh to line up with the Word of God. But you must make demand on it before it will respond."

"No, it won't happen just because you say it, but saying it is involved in causing it to happen. Saying it is the way you plant the seed for what you

need. The spoken Word of God imparts spirit life into your physical body (John 6:33), for His Word is incorruptible seed, and it produces after its kind."

After reading Capp's book I made the decision to write out a number of affirmations and demands according to the Word of God and His covenant/promise for healing. I have used large post-it notes and put them around the house so that I can see them often during the day. I *speak them out loud* and with authority! Below are a few of these affirmations:

1. My Word shall not come back void—but shall accomplish that which I have intended!
2. And this is the VICTORY that overcomes the world—my faith!
3. I thank you, Lord, for full and complete healing! According to Thy Word—I'm healed!
4. I rejoice with gladness, I sing with praise, for the great and mighty things My God has done for me!
5. I feel strong! Well! Blessed! Whole! Healed! Hallelujah!
6. Jesus came to give LIFE and give it abundantly! Thank you, Lord!
7. It's a DONE DEAL! Born in Heaven! Thank you, Jesus!
8. Glory! Glory! Glory! To the Lamb that set me free!
9. By body and flesh and bones operate in strength, in harmony and in unity as ordained from the foundation of the world!
10. With my lips I shall sing praises unto the Lord all the days of my life; for He hath set me free and hath restored my health!
11. *"After you have suffered a little while, the God of all grace, who called you according to His glory in Christ, shall Himself, restore, strengthen, perfect, establish and confirm you."*
12. My body is the temple of the Holy Spirit, where NO darkness or disease can dwell!
13. I know the plans I have for you saith the Lord, plans for hope and a future!
14. Hallelujah! Praise God! I'm healed in Jesus' name! Oh my God—I praise Your name!

15. The hand cannot say to the foot "I don't need you;" the eye cannot say to the ear "I don't need you;" nor can the Immune System say to the Bone Marrow "I don't need you!"
16. Blood numbers: White=8000, Red=15.5, Platelets=250,000!!!!
17. By Jesus' stripes I'm healed!!!
18. Jesus has set me free from the law of sin and death!
19. No weapon formed against me shall prosper!
20. Thank you, Father, for giving me this wonderful body of strength and health, and for protecting me from all sorts of sickness!
21. I bind all sickness and disease that shall come against me in the name of Jesus, and cast them into the pit!
22. Thank you, Father, for planting fresh, clean, strong bone marrow in my bones!
23. My immune system shall support all other organs, cells and fibers in my body according to 1 Corinthians chapter 12!
24. My immune system is working perfectly! Thank you, Jesus!
25. Greater is He that is in me, than he who is in the world!
26. Fear the Lord and depart from evil, for it shall be health to the navel and marrow to the bones! (Proverbs 3:7-8)
27. *"Pleasant words are a honeycomb, sweet to the soul and healing to the bones."* (Proverbs 16:24)
28. I shall not be sick because God hath spoken life and healing into my body!
29. I have never felt better, stronger or more blessed in my life! Thank you, Father, for your miraculous healing!
30. And the man said, "Lord, if thou will, you can make me whole." And Jesus said, "I WILL!"

Post It Affirmations

Jesus came to give LIFE and give it Abundantly! Thank-you Lord!!

I thank you Lord for full & complete Healing! According to Thy Word... I'm healed!

And this is the VICTORY that overcomes the world — My Faith!

Thank you Father for the Fresh, Powerful & healthy Bone Marrow!

I know the
plans I have
for you saith
the Lord —
Plans for Hope
and for a
Future!

"Let there be
Marrow!"
And it was
granted unto him
according to his
Faith!

Jesus
has set
me Free
from the
Law of Sin
and Death!

My body
is the
temple of
the Holy Spirit,
where NO
darkness or
disease can
dwell!

My
Immune System
shall support
all other
organs, cells
and every fiber
in my body
(I Corin 12)

NO
Weapon
formed against
Me
shall prosper!

(Isa 54:17)

The Lord
has delivered
me from every
Kind of
Sickness & disease!

I'm healed!

The hand cannot
say to the foot
"I don't need you"

The eye cannot
say to the ear
"I don't need you"

nor can...

The immune system
say to the bone marrow
"I don't need you"

(I Corin 12)

And the man
said, "Lord,
if thou will,
Ye can make me
whole."
And Jesus said,
"I WILL"

Greater
is He
who is in
Me
than he who
is in the world
(I John 4:4)

By Jesus'
STRIPES
I'm Healed

(I Peter 2:24)

I Bind
All Sickness
and Disease
that shall come
Against me in
the Name of Jesus,
and cast it into
the Pit!

Nutrition & Natural Substances

Shortly after my release in May, I began using herbs to detoxify my body from the various toxins that can build up over time. Between this, juicing fruits and vegetables and eating well, I actually feel very good most of the time.

I still experience symptoms of aplastic anemia, which include light-headedness, an impaired memory with forgetfulness (due to low oxygen levels to the brain), impaired vision and becoming tired easily. I know these symptoms will pass as I return to normal!

I have read a lot about how the body can heal itself. God created our bodies to function victoriously when under attack from a variety of viruses, bacteria, environmental toxins, etc. I believe this even more so since becoming sick and have modified my daily diet and supplemented it with herbs to enhance my overall health and nutrition.

I am reading *Live Right 4 Your Type* by Dr. Peter D'Adamo, a book that teaches that our bodies chemically react to what we eat and drink based upon our individual blood type. Why is it that you feel sleepy after one meal, energized after a different meal or bloated after yet another? I'm amazed at D'Adamo's accuracy in the personality characteristics for O blood types. I now realize how many of the wrong kinds of foods I have been eating for my O blood type. This book has sold over two million copies and is the sequel to *Eat Right 4 Your Type*.

I recalled that if I tilled the soil of my body by eating right and taking care of it that He will plant the seed of marrow and that it will grow 100-fold! According to D'Adamo's book, I was off base on what foods are best suited for my blood type, so I have made yet another adjustment.

Clearly, I am very teachable at this stage. From food to herbs, lifestyle to spiritual matters, I am open. I am seeking the Lord for His provision. He will reward me as I diligently seek Him through faith (Hebrews 11:6). I believe in the end He will clearly reveal to me what His plan was all along. Even if I prove to be a slow learner, I know He is patient with me and will instruct me properly unto a full recovery!

Generational Curses & Deliverance

The Bible says God will visit the iniquities of the fathers on the children and on the grandchildren to the third and fourth generations (Exodus 20:5; 34:7; Numbers 14:18; Deuteronomy 5:9). This past week, my wife and I met with Marjorie Cole, lecturer, counseling minister and author of *Taking the Devil to Court* (and winning) to discuss generational curses.

Marjorie has exceptional insight into this often overlooked area of Scripture. We learned a lot in the two hours we spent together, even though we only touched on the surface of this deep subject. As an example of her knowledge and insight, she ascertained with certainty that I had "royalty" in my blood, simply due to the doctor's diagnosis. I had actually forgotten that I was related to Queen Elizabeth! She pointed out that many blood disorders have been passed down through the generations within royal families. I found this most interesting, as I was familiar with Bible passages that indicate that certain diseases are the results of generational curses.

This week I learned that my grandmother on my dad's side died of a blood disorder. I never met her; she died the year I was born at the same age I am now! I am gathering our family tree records and will allow Marjorie to guide us through this process and pray with us. I will keep you posted on this very interesting aspect of the healing process!

Getting Out and About

I made the choice to start getting out of the house and I trust God to protect me from germs. I watched my boys' soccer games this past week, and went shopping at the store for the first time since I was admitted to the hospital. I even went on listing appointments in other people's homes! In the natural mind it is scary, but I have concluded that I must live as though I will live, not as though I will die. I have prayed for protection and have asked God to keep me at home if I am acting irresponsibly. Since I have had peace, I have ventured out—without a mask of course!

> **I even went on listing appointments in other people's homes... I do not want to be foolish; dying as a result of stupidity would be a terrible way to go!**

When I venture out of the house, it is like walking out on a branch of a tree—going a little further, a little further, while trusting God to keep the branch from breaking. I do not want to be foolish; dying as a result of stupidity would be a terrible way to go. I keep my hands clean with bottled liquid disinfectant and always pray that God will keep me from accidentally rubbing my eyes or putting my hands near my nose or mouth.

Blood Numbers Not Holding

In my last email I indicated that my white count had jumped to 1300 on May 29th from a previous level of 800 and that the neutrophils had risen to 0.4 from 0.2. Unfortunately, on my next visit on June 4th these levels had dropped to 1000 and 0.3 respectively, indicating there was no sustained increase. In addition, the red cell and platelet counts continued to fall by the day, which is nothing new. This simply means I still need blood transfusions and the time for my miracle has not yet arrived.

On June 4th I wanted to conduct my own little test and told my doctor to skip the scheduled platelet transfusion that day so I could see if my body would produce platelets if in dire need. Surprised at my request, he warned against this since my platelet count had already fallen to 17,000—a level which clearly warranted a transfusion. I told him it was only for three days and since he could not force me to get the platelet transfusion, he reluctantly agreed to my experiment.

I knew it was in my best interest to get as few transfusions as possible because my body could be building a resistance to transfused blood. If this were the case, my body could reject additional transfusions at any point and leave me with little time to live. Since fewer transfusions are better, and since I wanted to see if my body would produce more platelets if they were seriously needed, I proceeded to skip this one scheduled transfusion and recheck my platelet count in three days.

On June 7th my platelet count had fallen sharply to 3000! It was not only disappointing that the platelets had not held at all, but it was very dangerous and could have resulted in internal bleeding. An immediate platelet transfusion was ordered. Because the platelet level had fallen so low, the doctors ordered some additional blood tests that day to ensure I had not brought on any new complications. They drew a total of 4 tubes of blood, bringing the total to 153 since I began this journey.

Doctor Update

I spent a great deal of time over the past few weeks seeking out doctors and medical advice. I want to work with professionals with whom I am comfortable, who take an interest in me, and who I feel know what they are doing. Below are the results of my findings based on the various professional groups:

- **Western**

I have seen four doctors/specialists from the western medical profession, and all completely agree with the current diagnosis and prognosis. None of these doctors have offered any new ideas or suggestions for a different treatment. All have recommended that I submit to another ATG treatment to be followed up with more Cyclosporine. They tell me that if the 2nd ATG attempt does not work I will need a bone marrow transplant, providing a suitable donor is located. The odds of surviving a marrow transplant are very low; without one I will die from the disease. Although I have been placed on national and worldwide marrow search databases, no match has been found. This group of medical doctors is the least optimistic of my survival.

- **Naturopathic**

Naturopathy is "a system of treatment of diseases that avoids drugs and surgery and emphasizes the use of natural agents (such as air, water and herbs) and physical means (such as tissue manipulation and electrotherapy)." I have been to two naturopaths since being discharged from the hospital.

I have written to you about the first one, with whom I opted not to continue. He was neutral, neither optimistic nor pessimistic. He seemed less educated than I had hoped and I feared I might become an experiment in an area in which he was perhaps unfamiliar.

I met with the second naturopath this week. Two individuals I know personally recommended him. He seemed laid back, tired and somewhat disinterested, although he had extensive knowledge. Both my wife and I were concerned about his office; it was a melting pot of religious books and figurines from Hinduism to Taoism, New Age to Buddhism and more. They sold herbs, tonics and incense—it reminded me of the "head shops" of the 1970's. It was here, however, that I learned of Dr. Peter D'Adamo.

Both of the naturopaths I visited seemed indifferent to my diagnosed illness. I felt like a number, a non-issue. I would love to find a person that would consider my diagnosis as a challenge, one who would take a personal interest in helping me. Neither of these gentlemen fit the bill.

- **Herbal**

I visited a Chinese herbal and acupuncture doctor this week who is familiar with aplastic anemia, as it is much more common in China. She asked some of the same questions as the Western medical doctors to try to determine how I might have contracted it. She also carefully examined my blood reports and tests.

She gave me some herbs to boost my blood and energy levels, but did not seem optimistic about my recovery. She repeatedly cautioned me to take care of myself and to avoid illness. She was more concerned than all of the other doctors I have seen, even worried about me, saying, "This is a very difficult illness." She showed great empathy, but lacked optimism. I was looking for both.

- **Spiritual**

Marjorie Cole has a different perspective than any of the others. Both my wife and I are interested in hearing more about what she has to say. She feels that a "crack in my spiritual armor may have occurred" resulting in the release of a "generational curse". She felt I may be in need of deliverance from a spirit that has attacked and oppressed me and my health.

Our society does not talk much about things like this these days, but this happened over and over in the Bible. Sickness was due to an evil spirit that oppressed a man, woman or child. There are spiritual laws and spiritual weapons that are used for the purpose of spiritual battles. Even though we cannot see them or fully understand them, I believe they do exist.

The Apostle Paul said, *"For though we walk in the flesh, we do not war according to the flesh, for the weapons of our warfare are not of the flesh, but divinely powerful for the destruction of fortresses."* (2 Corinthians 10:3-4) Paul is pointing out that even though we are physical beings (walking in the flesh), we do not battle according to the physical realm, but rather the spiritual realm.

He elaborates on spiritual warfare in the 6th chapter of Ephesians when he states that our battle is not against flesh and blood (physical realm), but against powers and principalities in the heavens (spiritual realm). The weapons used in such battles are faith, God's Word, prayer and action—acting out what one says they believe. When these spiritual weapons are used effectively they become "divinely powerful for the destruction (demonic) of fortresses," resulting in healings, miracles and various "breakthroughs" as they are called.

Knowledgeable in the area of spiritual warfare and deliverance, Marjorie also showed concern for me and optimism for healing through prayer and deliverance. Her services are in great demand, so I will not be able to see her again until later this month.

Prophetic Messages

I have had several pastors and prophetic ministers deliver messages "from God" that are anywhere from interesting to bizarre. In each case, it was important for me to discern the message.

One such "bizarre" message came in the form of a letter addressed to me, written by a so-called prophetess. In the long letter the woman told me that God would only heal me if I helped her and her family financially; failing to do so would result in my death.

This was difficult for me to process and I tried to understand *why* I received such a letter. I wondered repeatedly what God wanted me to do. After I discussed it with my wife and close friends, I prayed about it, and ended up throwing the letter out! I chose not to believe these words, since they brought only fear. *"God has not given me a spirit of fear, but of love, power and a sound mind,"* so her letter was inconsistent with God's word.

The message from Pastor Steve Munsey, *"There is someone here tonight who the doctors have told does not have long to live; God is going to remove that sickness; and add 15 years to your life"* has proven to be one of my most interesting messages. Unlike the one from the "prophetess," this message was consistent with God's Word and produced joy in me, not fear.

Quiet Time with God

What does God want to tell me? I need to be quiet before God on a regular basis and just listen. In my time with Him this week, I was given peace by His Spirit that I will be healed. That is all I really need isn't it? So I simply need to step out of the busyness of the day and be quiet and listen. He loves it when His children do that.

Blood Numbers

June 7th	My Blood Counts	Notes	Normal Range
Red	8.4*	Last Transfusion: 14 Days	13.5 – 17.5
White	1,400	Count 3 Days Ago: 1,000	3,500 – 10,800
Platelets	3,000*	Last Transfusion: 9 Days	130,000 – 430,000
Neutrophils	0.4	Most abundant white cell	1.9 – 8.0

* 1 bag of Platelets was transfused June 7th (dangerous level)
* 2 bags of Red Cells were transfused June 8th
* Tubes of Blood Drawn since Illness: 153

Weight Numbers

Daily range 154-156 lbs. Feeling very well.

Eyes

I might be noticing some slight improvement; but it is hard to measure the change. Scar tissue from the retinal hemorrhaging is still evident, causing blind spots, but the "roaring lion" image has become faint.

Closing Verses

"For this is the love of God, that we keep His commandments and His commandments are not burdensome." (1 John 5:3)

"Let us not love with word or with tongue, but in deed and truth. We will know by this that we are of the truth, and will assure our heart before Him, in whatever our heart condemns us; for God is greater than our heart and

knows all things. If our heart does not condemn us, we have confidence before God; and whatever we ask we receive from Him, because we keep His commandments and do the things which are pleasing in His sight." (1 John 3:18-22)

"How will we escape if we neglect so great a salvation?" (Hebrews 2:3)

Blessings!

Jeff Scislow

P.S. I am way behind on email responses. I still have several hundred to read and send replies. I will respond!

July 6, 2001

Greetings!

The past month has really flown. We've been getting some terrific weather here in Minneapolis and I am more comfortable being outside, especially at the soccer games of my seven and nine year-old boys. All the nice weather has actually kept me from giving you an update on my progress. Please excuse the long delay in writing.

Each day I am more comfortable with "normal" living. I am going to church again (as of two weeks ago), eating at restaurants occasionally (as of nearly three weeks ago), and of course, going on real estate appointments (as of nearly one month ago). I praise God for His protection and the peace He gives me in my heart.

Soon I will share in detail some new record-setting blood numbers that just came in this week. I am beginning to see the manifestation!

Remember the promise: *"After you have suffered for a little while, the God of all grace, who called you to His eternal glory in Christ, shall Himself, restore, strengthen, perfect, establish and confirm you."* I have never forgotten it!

A Tornado or a Flood?

I have long pondered the question of whether the diagnosis of aplastic anemia was the result of a "tornado" or a "flood" hitting my body. A tornado comes unexpectedly and swiftly does major damage. Then is suddenly gone, nowhere to be found. The damage is done, the attacker gone.

In contrast, a flood rises slowly and hangs around for a while, continuing to damage and put pressure on the area. (In this case, my bone marrow.)

I shared this metaphor with my doctors, and asked whether the disease is a tornado or a flood. I have yet to get an answer from any of them. The doctors do not know, the naturopaths do not know, none of the professionals I have spoken to know. The way I see it, treating a disease of a "tornado" nature would be quite different than treating the same disease of the "flood" nature. How can any treatment be prescribed if the prescribing doctors do not know the answer to the question—tornado or flood?

If my marrow was hit by a "flood," and if this flood is still present and still putting pressure on my bone marrow, then immune system boosters—like Echinacea, MGN-3 and Goldenseal—would only add to the weight on the marrow by enhancing white "fighter cells" to kill any marrow. Instead of helping the immune system and marrow, taking such immune system boosters would *damage* it further. Remember, aplastic anemia is an Auto-Immune disease whereby one's own immune system detects the bone marrow as a foreign invader and kills it. I must conclude, if the disease is still present in the form of a flood, taking immune system boosters could be quite dangerous.

On the other hand, if my marrow was hit hard and damaged by a tornado, resulting in a greatly reduced white cell count, then those same immune system boosters would *benefit* me by strengthening and protecting me from germs, infections and their associated ramifications.

MGN-3 is not well-known by many, including the medical doctors caring for me. It is a relatively new immune system enhancer that boosts the effectiveness of white fighter cells by 300% (not in numbers, but in activity levels). It also modulates and regulates the immune system and has proven to be a wonderful supplement for fighting cancers, since many cancers develop as the result of a weakened immune system.

In my research about MGN-3, I have repeatedly attempted to reach the research scientist who developed the product. I left several detailed messages for him, but have yet to receive a call back. I hope to ask him what he knows about aplastic anemia and whether he believes MGN-3 would be beneficial or detrimental for someone who has been diagnosed with the disease.

I did successfully reach two different product managers at Lane Labs, the company that manufactures MGN-3. I presented my flood and tornado scenarios to them, but neither had an idea as to whether their product might be helpful for a person having been diagnosed with aplastic anemia. They advised that I do more homework before trying the supplement. I agreed, since I still feel the risk of taking MGN-3 outweighs the potential benefit at this point.

Heavy Metal (no not Rock)

In late June I met for a second time with one of the naturopaths I met earlier in the month. We discussed heavy metal toxicity and the chance that aplastic anemia could be the result of exposure to some type of heavy metal or other toxin. We decided to find out.

We sent hair samples from the back of my neck to a laboratory in Chicago for analysis. A few days later, the naturopath called to tell me that my levels of aluminum and tin were *very high*. The aluminum build-up most likely occurred from standard antiperspirant usage over the years. We have no idea why the tin levels are so high. In either case, there was no immediate cause for alarm based on this preliminary report. A full report with recommendations should arrive next week sometime.

While studying toxicity, I learned that Benzene is the only substance listed on the Centers for Disease Control's *most dangerous substance list* that attacks bone marrow. I'm not aware of any possible exposure to Benzene, but I found it interesting that it attacks bone marrow in particular. For those interested in the top 20 most dangerous substances list, you can find it here: www.atsdr.cdc.gov/cxcx3.html

Back Pain Healed

Three weeks ago a friend felt directed by the Lord to tell me to take my family out of town for a day or two, just to get away. I considered this a great idea, and my family and I made plans to drive about an hour south to Lake City for the day. We planned to leave around 10:00 a.m.

An hour before departure time, I ran to Rainbow Foods to pick up not two, not four, but ten forty-pound bags of salt for the water softener. Although I had been feeling very good, I had not exercised in quite some time. I loaded all ten bags into the shopping cart, wheeled them out to my truck and proceeded home. From the truck, I carried the bags one at a time down to the basement of my home and into the utility room.

Feeling good and with only two bags to go, I jerked them out of the back of the truck in one motion, one in each hand. As I caught the weight of those last two bags, the middle of my back nearly gave out. I continued into the house, carrying them down the steps into the basement. Half-way across the basement floor I suddenly froze and dropped the bags as a sharp pain exploded in my back. I could not take another step.

Forgetting about the salt bags lying on the floor, I eventually managed to get up the steps to the main floor where I carefully sat down in a chair. The pain was awful. I grabbed an ice pack and rested on the couch. I could barely move.

Before long, my kids said, "Come on, Dad! Let's go!" Unable to acknowledge their request, I just laid there immobile and in pain. My wife told the kids that Dad had hurt his back. "We'll just stay home today and go another time." The kids were quite disappointed.

185

I prayed right there on the couch saying, *"Lord, I am sorry. I really messed up. I have felt so good lately that I was not thinking. I was not in shape to haul all that salt and then manhandle two bags at a time. It was stupid! I am sorry. I know that You wanted me to take this trip with the family today—to have fun and get away. I need Your help now. In Jesus' name I ask that you loosen the muscles in my back so that I can get up and go with the family. I trust You and thank You! Praise Thy name! Amen!"*

I have thrown my back out several times in the past; I know how painful it is, I know it can take several days to several weeks to get back to normal. I tell you this most truly: ten minutes after praying, I slowly got up from the couch. I carefully walked around, praising God. I walked outside. I gently took steps so that I did not pull any more back muscles. The looser I felt the more I praised God! I was ready to try to get up into the truck; I pulled myself up, I got out of the truck, I got in it again, I got out again. My back was tender, but the contracted muscles had loosened! "Praise God, I am ready to go!" We loaded the kids in the truck and hit the road!

My family had a blast spending the whole day together! This is my God at work! It was not only special to get away with the family, but also to be reminded that God was there, listening to me and caring for me.

I am reminded each and every day that some bizarre thing has attacked my health and is threatening my life. Like many people, I want quick results. I want the answers to my prayers manifested *now* for healing. The waiting is hard, but God's promise is true. I need to be faithful to His promise. If I do not waver in my belief, God will perform His promise as a result.

In the case of my back, God moved on the spot because it was important to have a quick answer. In the case of my aplastic anemia diagnosis, I must continue to trust God that His timing will be perfect and that healing will come, just as I trusted the Lord to loosen my back muscles when the healing was needed!

Healing Rooms

While in the hospital I read a book about John G. Lake, an incredible man who was born in Canada in 1870. Among other significant accomplishments, he founded the Healing Rooms of Spokane in Washington. The Healing Rooms were a special place where people could go to receive prayer. The anointed prayer warriors, "technicians," saw and prayed for 200 people per day on average!

Spokane hospitals began closing down because so many people around Spokane were being healed. God was moving powerfully through Lake's ministry. As a result, Spokane was officially named the "healthiest" city in the USA!

After Lake passed away, the healing rooms soon went by the wayside, until recently when they reopened in Spokane. Since the reopening, other ministries have gone to Spokane and have had their prayer ministers trained under the guidelines and principles that John G. Lake developed in the mid-twentieth century. One such ministry is *Healing Center International*, located here in the Twin Cities.

My wife and I have visited this Healing Room three times in the past three weeks. Each time we have been blessed to have intelligent, well-trained Christian counselors listen to us, ask lots of questions and then pray for exactly what we need. There is a genuine desire to get to the root of problems and to come against them in Jesus' name, expecting the Lord to move and heal (whether physical, emotional, spiritual or financial).

If there is anyone in the Twin Cities area wishing to receive prayer from the same counselors that I have been seeing, have them contact the Healing Center International at (763) 503-4693. They are located at 1710 Douglas Dr. #260, Golden Valley, MN 55422. The web address is: www.healingcenterintl.org/ss/live/

Blood Numbers—A Closer Look

Now for some exciting news! Yesterday, July 5th, my blood numbers reached new heights in three major categories—white count, platelets and neutrophils! In addition to seeing these new highs, I noticed something extremely interesting in my blood test results which date back to when I began taking herbs and received the Word from the Lord about "tilling, readying and taking care of the field." Allow me to elaborate a bit more than I have in the past on these blood numbers, as I believe something is about to break me free from this disease!

Since this journey began, whenever my white count hit a new high, it always fell back again, usually on the next test. Now, for the first time my white count has stayed steady. It did not fall back after hitting a new high. In fact, on July 2nd my white count hit 1700 and remained 1700 for my July 5th test. These are the highest white counts produced since I was diagnosed with aplastic anemia.

My average white count was just 500 during the month of April. In May the average increased to 925. In June it inched up to 1,250. So far in July the average has been 1,700! The normal white count range is 3,500-10,800. I am half way to reaching the normal range!

Three days ago I had a platelet transfusion and today my platelet count was 51,000! I either received some incredible platelets, or my counts are holding very well. Perhaps a combination!

Neutrophils are the most abundant type of white blood cells in humans and form an integral part of the immune system. My average neutrophil count was 0.0 during the month of April. In May the average increased slightly to 0.15. In June the average was 0.385. On July 5th the count hit 0.60—a new high! The normal neutrophil count range is 1.9 to 8.0. This new count puts me a third of the way to normal levels! Remember, I had a count of 0.0 when the doctors said I had NO bone marrow!

While at my oncologist's clinic to receive my latest blood transfusion, I noticed that a set of blood numbers in my CBC tests dating back to early May had been significantly changing!

The blood numbers I have been describing are "quantity" numbers, or blood "counts." Mine of course are well below normal. The significant change I have noticed is not in the "counts", but in the balance of the overall immune system. The percentages of neutrophils and lymphocytes as part of all white cells (the immune system) have been improving!

The few white blood cells that I have in my body are being produced in the lymph nodes, tonsils and spleen. These organs only produce about 5 percent of what is needed for a healthy immune system, while bone marrow (if present) produces 95 percent. Even though a very small "quantity" of white cells exist, the percentage "quality" of these cells within my overall immune system is improving!

The immune system is made up of a several different types of white cells. The three most predominant types are neutrophils, lymphocytes and monocytes. These three white cell types comprise nearly the entire white cell allocation (immune system). In a healthy immune system the neutrophil white cells comprise approximately 65 percent of all white cells, the lymphocyte white cells comprise approximately 25 percent of all white cells and the monocyte white cells comprise up to 10 percent of all white cells.

At the time I was admitted into the hospital, my CBC test results clearly indicated that my neutrophil percentage was nowhere near the normal range. It continued to get worse and worse, that is, until I stopped the Cyclosporine, began taking herbs and received a confirmation from the Lord on May 13th. My neutrophil percentage had fallen all the way to 7.4% on May 10th, but then turned 180 degrees and began rising, posting a percentage of 11.9% on May 14th and 15.0% on May 17th! It has continued to *rise* slowly back toward normal levels, as evidenced by each new CBC. On July 5th the percentage climbed to 35.7%! The normal range is 45.0 to 76.0%. This is amazing!

Similarly, the lymphocyte percentage was sick and out of balance when I arrived at the hospital. It continued to worsen until I stopped the Cyclosporine, began taking herbs and received a confirmation from the Lord on May 13th. My lymphocyte percentage soared all the way to 83.4% on May 10th and then turned 180 degrees and began falling, posting a percentage of 75.5% on May 14th and 64.3% on May 17th! It has continued to *fall* slowly back toward normal levels, as evidenced by each new CBC test. On July 5th the percentage is down to 50.6%! The normal range is 15.0 to 43.0%. I am getting close!

I feel very excited over this discovery! Something good is happening and I believe it is due to the herbs the Lord directed me to take. Once the soil (of my body) is tilled, readied and taken care of, the Lord will plant the seed of marrow and it will grow 100-fold!

After my blood transfusion, I located my oncologist and enthusiastically showed him the changes I noticed from my CBC test results dating back to May. With a mundane voice he said, "That does not matter. You don't have any bone marrow." I said, "No, it *does* matter; something is happening here!" He responded, "I am sorry. You don't have any marrow," and continued walking down the hall.

Disappointed that my doctor was not excited, I felt a bit discouraged during my drive home from the clinic. Before long, however, I gathered my thoughts and chose to believe that the change in the *quality* of my white cell composition was a BIG deal, even if the *quantity* was not there yet. I knew it was coming!

The following chart indicates a substantial improvement in the percentages of my primary white blood cells:

White Cell Percentages	May 10	July 5	Normal Range
Neutrophils	7.4%	35.7%	45.0 – 76.0%
Lymphocytes	83.4%	50.6%	15.0 – 43.0%
Monocytes	19.6%	12.0%	0.0 – 10.0%

There are only two known medical ways to beat aplastic anemia. One is a successful ATG treatment and the other is a successful bone marrow transplant. In my case, the ATG failed and no known marrow donor exists. As a result, the doctors say it is only a matter of time before I die from this disease. I have been unable to find an account of anyone recovering from aplastic anemia without success from one of these two procedures. I am anxious to learn of such a case and how the individual survived.

For the time being, I continue to seek the *Great Physician,* the Lord Jesus Christ, as my final authority on this healing. He said He would plant marrow in my bones again! He is the One in whom I place my trust!

Blood Numbers

July 5th	My Blood Counts	Notes	Normal Range
Red	10.2	Last Transfusion: 9 Days	13.5 – 17.5
White	1,700	Count 3 Days Ago: 1,700	3,500 – 10,800
Platelets	51,000	Last Transfusion: 3 Days	130,000 – 430,000
Neutrophils	0.6	Count 3 Days Ago: 0.5	1.9 – 8.0

* Tubes of Blood Drawn since Illness: 167

I have not had a face-to-face appointment with my doctor for over a month. Instead I simply go to his clinic to obtain blood tests and transfusions. I am familiar with the routine and have been working with the nurses.

Weight Numbers

Daily range 155-156 lbs. Steady with virtually no fluctuation. I feel very good.

Eyes

Scar tissue from the retinal hemorrhaging is still evident, causing some blind spots, but the "roaring lion" image is gone.

Closing Verses

"Heal me, O Lord, and I will be healed; save me and I will be saved, for You are my praise." (Jeremiah 17:14)

"Come to Me, all who are weary and heavy-laden, and I will give you rest. Take My yoke upon you, and learn from Me, for I am gentle and humble in heart; and you will find rest for your souls. For My yoke is easy, and My burden is light." (Matthew 11:28-30)

"How will we escape if we neglect so great a salvation?" (Hebrews 2:3)

Blessings!

Jeff Scislow

P.S. Keep praying! A big thanks to you all! Together we will see the love, power and purpose of God at work—for His awesome glory!

July 16, 2001

Great News!

On Thursday July 12th my blood numbers hit five new records. Four in the white count category, and one in the red count category! More on this awesome news later in this update!

Overall I have been feeling wonderful with no problems whatsoever. I keep my little bottle of liquid antibacterial hand sanitizer with me so that I can quickly cleanse my hands after shaking hands with someone. Although not a bad practice for anyone to incorporate into their daily life, it is an essential one for me; I don't need to land in the hospital (or possibly worse) because of a cold or flu.

Since I have been getting out of the house more and more, I have been able to spend a lot of time with the kids the past couple of weeks. Work has been "business as usual" with no self-imposed restrictions. We have been incredibly blessed in this area of our lives during the incredible challenge we've been facing. My wife has been wonderful throughout this time, doing everything that needs to be done—billing, various appointments, four children, school, meals, shopping, etc. She is awesome!

At this time, my wife is primarily helping with phones and client files in the office and I am back out on appointments. The doctor disagrees with this, but I sense the branch is strong, so I keep stepping out further and further with the faith that I am protected. Although my blood numbers are inching upward, I do not have an immune system capable of fighting off an invading germ—yet!

Thanks again for all of your prayers! All who have read my email and said a prayer for me and my family are so special. Each of your prayers has been heard and each of you plays a role in the movement of God in the lives of me and my family. Thank you so very much!

I have farther to go, but I will get there exactly as the Word of God stated! For that I thank Him and praise Him! I simply cannot put into words the joy and excitement I am experiencing as I see the manifestation of the miraculous healing begin.

Heavy Metal Chelation Scheduled

On July 13th I consulted with my naturopathic doctor about the heavy metals present in my hair analysis. Aluminum and tin levels were high and while the high aluminum levels may be due to antiperspirant use, we still had no idea why my levels of tin were so high. Speculating it could be from our house water, we've arranged to have my wife's hair analyzed as well.

In our efforts to provide a healthy environment at home, we've purchased a whole house water filtration system. Although we have a good municipal water system, toxins may still be present. Since toxins can be absorbed through skin, the body's largest organ, we opted for the water filtration system. We now enjoy bottle-quality water from every faucet and shower in the house!

Chelation therapy is defined in part as a process that "binds metals (such as lead or iron) in the body to form a chelation so that the metal loses its toxic effect or physiological activity and is eventually passed through and out of the body." The naturopathic doctor and I discussed the various chelation options at my appointment. While the intravenous method is quicker and more complete than the oral (supplemental) method, its cost is much higher and the chelation sessions must be administered at the naturopathic doctor's office. I chose the oral method and ordered my first supply of chelation supplements.

The oral chelation process can take up to six months to complete. The process, which I am starting this week, begins with liver and bladder cleansing. These organs need to be strong, healthy and cleaned out so they can begin receiving the heavy metal toxins that will pass through them as they are eliminated from my body.

There are no major side effects expected, since I will begin the supplements gradually, taking the chelating supplements every other day, working up to three times per day. This will help avoid overloading my liver or bladder with heavy metals. In three months I will have another hair analysis to determine the efficiency of the chelation up to that point.

Back to Church

Yesterday, July 15th, I attended a regular church service for the third time since early April when I was admitted to the hospital. The past two visits to church, I left just before the service ended, because I was not supposed to be in large crowds due to the chance of infection. Today I felt more comfortable, so I talked with anyone who wanted to say hello and get a firsthand update on my health progress. This was a very special time for me, and I felt blessed to be able to visit with so many of my friends.

Sunday's Sermon: The Principle of the Seed

During yesterday's church service, Pastor Dave Housholder, one of the Hosanna Church pastors, discussed Genesis 26:12. This verse says, *"Now Isaac sowed in that land and reaped in the same year a hundredfold. And the Lord blessed him."* I immediately felt the parallel of this verse with what the Lord spoke to my heart during my prayers on May 13th. The Lord had said that if I tilled the soil (of my body) by eating right and taking care of it, He Himself would plant the seed of marrow and it would grow a hundredfold! That meant no drugs, no medications and no transplants—hallelujah! With the blood counts on the rise, I believe the Lord has already planted the seed of marrow and that it is growing.

195

I have always believed my healing was a given, but I did not know *when*. Over the past couple of weeks there has been a marked increase in the blood numbers, especially those crucial white counts. I have not heard anything from the doctor about my improving test results, but the nurses are beginning to unofficially acknowledge them. As the numbers rise, I remind the nurses that this is the miracle that I have been expecting. Praise God!

Testing the Body's Endurance

Although I feel excellent and look much better, my true physical condition has been weakened as a result of 1) not exercising regularly, 2) being sick with hepatitis during February and March, 3) being confined in a hospital room for 28 days in April, and 4) being instructed by my doctor to refrain from any physical activity after being released from the hospital (in May).

For the past couple of weeks I have been doing simple exercises such as sit-ups and light dumbbell curls. While doing these I pay close attention to my need for oxygen (anemic responses). My breathing feels good, but my muscles tire quickly, either from lack of exercise, lack of oxygen to the muscles or both.

Since the oxygen to my lungs felt adequate, I pushed myself a bit more to see how my body would react to exercise. I took my mountain bike down from the ceiling hooks in the garage, pumped up the tires and went on an eight mile bike ride (on pavement) in 90 degree-heat last week. Although I had not biked since last year, I did not feel anemic. I praised God, because I knew that my hemoglobin was finally strong enough to produce the oxygen needed for such a ride!

Knowing that I had the energy to ride a bike, I wanted to test my ability to jog. I quickly learned that jogging is more demanding than riding a bike, I tired quickly and experienced both shortness of breath and a rapid depletion of leg muscle strength. My calves, shins and thighs seemed to fall asleep from a lack of oxygen after only a block, at best. If I had continued, I might have fallen since my legs had no more energy for additional steps. I had my work cut out for me and planned to keep exercising and believing in higher and higher blood counts.

Blood Numbers—Another Close Look

Now for some MORE exciting news! On July 12th my blood numbers hit five new records! As I mentioned earlier in this email, four of these numbers deal with my white counts and one with my red count.

Both my red blood cells and platelet cells continue to deplete slowly, and I receive both red and platelet cells through transfusions from donors. However, white cells cannot be transfused and are primarily manufactured in the bone marrow. My average white count was 500 in April, 925 in May, and 1250 in June. On July 2nd the white count reached 1700, on July 5th it held at 1700, and on July 12th the white count reached a new high of 1800! So far in July, my average white count is 1733! With the normal range being 3500 – 10,800, I'm half way to "normal" levels! Since my white cell count is increasing, something must be happening in the bone marrow!

In addition, the neutrophils—the predominant white cells within the immune system—hit a new high on July 12th! My average count was 0.0 in April, 0.15 in May, 0.385 in June, and a whopping 0.70 by July 12th! With normal range being 1.9 – 8.0, I'm more than 1/3 the way to "normal" levels! My neutrophil counts started at 0.0 when the doctors confirmed I had no bone marrow or stem cells. Still today, they are telling me I have no bone marrow. But I know that God is putting it back—all of it; and it will grow 100-fold!

I continue to see healthier percentages (quality) of the three primary types of white cells—neutrophils, lymphocytes and monocytes. They are all moving toward the normal range. The change is depicted in the chart below:

White Cell Percentages	May 10	July 5	July 12	Normal Range
Neutrophils	7.4%	35.7%	41.0%	45.0 – 76.0%
Lymphocytes	83.4%	50.6%	44.1%	15.0 – 43.0%
Monocytes	19.6%	12.0%	13.4%	0.0 – 10.0%

My hemoglobin number also set a record on July 12th. After my last red transfusion on June 26th my count rose to 10.9 and dropped to 10.2 by July 5th. One week later on July 12th, the count had dropped only fractionally to 10.0. In 16 days my red count has only dropped 0.9! Something is holding the numbers up and I say it is bone marrow!

Blood Numbers

July 12th	My Blood Counts	Notes	Normal Range
Red	10.0	Last Transfusion: 16 Days	13.5 – 17.5
White	1,800	Count 7 Days Ago: 1,700	3,500 – 10,800
Platelets	20,000*	Last Transfusion: 7 Days	130,000 – 430,000
Neutrophils	0.7	Count 7 Days Ago: 0.6	1.9 – 8.0

* 1 bag of Platelets was transfused July 12th
* Tubes of Blood Drawn since Illness: 169

Weight Numbers

Daily range 155-156 lbs. Steady with virtually no fluctuation. I am feeling very well.

Eyes

I had an appointment with the ophthalmologist on July 12th and was told that my eyes look wonderful. The retinal scarring from the hemorrhages are dissolving and getting thinner. He expects them to be gone soon. The surface area of the scar tissue has not changed, but the depth of the scarring is decreasing. Once the scar tissue completely dissolves, light will pass perfectly through the retina and my vision will be completely restored. Since some of the scar tissue still remains, I have some minor blind spots, but I have not seen the image of the roaring lion for several weeks now. He is in the process of being totally defeated!

Closing Verses

"Do not be deceived... EVERY good thing given and EVERY perfect gift is from above, coming down from the Father of lights, with whom there is no variation, or shifting shadow." (James 1:16-17) [Emphasis added]

"For all flesh is like grass, and all its glory like the flower of grass. The grass withers, and the flower falls off, but the Word of the Lord endures forever...." (1 Peter 1:24-25)

"How will we escape if we neglect so great a salvation?" (Hebrews 2:3)

Blessings!

Jeff Scislow

P.S. Thanks for your continued prayers! They are working!

August 15, 2001

So much has happened since I emailed a month ago, which is the only reason you have not heard from me. When this journey began, I promised to keep you all posted with every detail, so you can count on that! I am ready now to update you with a number of awesome experiences, as well as a significant scare that just occurred.

The DOs and DO NOTs

I often think back on what it was like in the hospital, especially the week prior to my release. That week the doctor visited almost daily. I was constantly reminded of my body's critical and susceptible state and told what to do to protect myself since I had virtually no immune system.

During my 28-day stay as a resident of United Hospital, my white blood cell count ranged from 200 to 800. Since the risk of viral, bacterial or fungal infection was critically high, many precautions were necessary. I was required to wear a mask whenever I had a visitor. Visitors had to wash their hands before entering the room and either wear a gown or keep their distance from me. I could not shake hands or hug anyone. All flowers or fruits I received from loved ones were confiscated due to the risk of an airborne infection.

Then the warnings became even more bizarre and detailed. Instructions on the bathroom wall provided advice on which direction to wipe myself after a bowel movement to lessen the chances of bleeding. Other bathroom instructions detailed how to rinse my mouth after meals with a baking soda and salt formula they prepared for me. I was instructed to brush my teeth gently with a "feather-like" toothbrush to prevent my gums from bleeding.

The doctor informed me that most aplastic anemia patients have died from complications (colds, flu, pneumonia, etc) from being in what others consider a normal environment, "so *you* best be careful."

That last week before my discharge, I received even more "survival" instructions since I was about to enter the real world of "germs." In addition to the aforementioned procedures, they told me to avoid malls and other crowded areas. I was to stay around the house, but avoid the garden, plants and my dogs! "Better yet, get rid of them." When I asked if I could kiss my children, I was advised "not to take the risk." Tears welled up every time I thought of this.

When I inquired about the possibility of going out on real estate appointments, I was advised not to because of "differing" germs and not knowing whether someone in a particular house was sick. When I asked about attending church, they recommended against it since there were too many people around.

In addition I needed to always keep a thermometer nearby to frequently check my temperature. If my temperature hit 101, I needed to immediately return to the hospital for attention and hospitalization.

Are you getting the picture? It did not end there.

I wondered if there was any hope for a successful ATG treatment. According to the doctor, there was only a slim chance of it working because no marrow was detected in the biopsy. If it did work, the blood numbers would never reach normal levels, but they might reach levels that could allow me to survive and live a normal life, with limitations. However, even if the ATG were successful, there would be a 50/50 chance of relapse—my bone marrow would again come under attack, fail to produce the required blood cells, and I'd be right back in the hospital again.

The ATG treatment failed.

There was one last possibility—a bone marrow transplant. This could be done, providing there was a matching marrow donor. However, even with a *perfect* matching donor, there would be only a 25 to 30%

chance of surviving the procedure. If I survived the procedure and the transplant was successful, there would still be the possibility of marrow rejection for years to come.

It was easy to get depressed by all this information. At times I thought, "Why would I want to go home? I might as well just stay in the hospital. Is there any hope in battling this long line of seemingly impossible hurdles?" Clearly, this was a true challenge for me. How I responded to all this was totally up to me and I thank God I had a choice. Each of us has a choice as to how we will respond to adverse situations.

I meditated often on the first chapter of James, verses 2-3: *"Consider it all joy, my brethren, when you encounter various trials, knowing that the testing of your faith produces endurance."* This was the biggest trial I had ever faced and the Bible said I should be *"joyful"* during this time. In 1 Peter 4 it says that I should rejoice in the midst of my fiery ordeals and trials. This is a far cry from a natural response, but I made the choice to trust in God, not my natural response.

1 Corinthians 2:14 says, *"But a natural man does not accept the things of the Spirit of God, for they are foolishness to him, and he cannot understand them, because they are spiritually appraised."* I believe the "natural" response to my situation would be to wallow in the circumstances and ultimately succumb to them, but this is not what God wants *anyone* to do. God asks us all to call on Him in our time of need, to *"... draw near with confidence to the throne of grace, so that we may receive mercy and find grace to help in time of need,"* (Hebrews 4:16) and to *"walk by faith* (in His promises*) and not by sight* (in all circumstances)." (2 Corinthians 5:7) [Emphasis added]

When one chooses to completely trust God and His Word, and is not moved away from that hope as a result of challenging circumstances, then God *will* respond. Why? Because He loves us and because He honors His Word! Remember, *"If you abide in Me, and My words abide in you, ask whatever you wish, and it will be done for you."* (John 15:7)

So what issues are getting you down? Are you willing to come boldly to that same throne of grace where the Living God awaits your cry? He loves you and desires to have a wonderful relationship with you. We only need to humble ourselves and become like children in our hearts. *"...God is opposed to the proud, but gives grace to the humble."* (James 4:6)

My trust in God is a living testimony of an awesome miracle in progress—God fulfilling His Word because I believed Him all along. I cannot express in words how truly blessed I am! Whosoever trusts in the Lord will not be disappointed.

Where are the Doctors?

Surprisingly, I have not had an appointment with my oncologist since May 14th, a week and a half after being discharged from the hospital and about the time I stopped taking the drug Cyclosporine. He has not asked to see me since. I had been to his clinic for regular blood transfusions, of course, but that was based on *my* scheduling the appointment for the transfusions.

None of the specialists at the University of Minnesota have made an attempt to follow up with me either. We spoke only once when I met with them back in mid-May, and I expected to hear back from them by June 1st, the time they had set for me to decide if I was comfortable in having the team at the U of M perform my bone marrow transplant. I was not particularly eager for their call, but I found their lack of follow-up interesting, especially when a marrow transplant fetches $450,000 per procedure.

Once in June, I attempted to get an appointment with an oncologist's office to obtain additional opinions, but his office never got back to me. I found it interesting and concluded that our meeting was simply not meant to be.

I have an appointment with an oncologist at the Mayo Clinic later this month, but I think I will cancel it. I feel strongly that my miracle is at hand.

All along my spirit has shown me that I will be miraculously healed, without a bone marrow transplant. If I were contacted today and told that a perfect marrow match had been found, I would decline the procedure.

Chelation Started

On July 22nd I started the six-month oral chelation program to clear heavy metal toxins from my body. Although tin and aluminum are unlikely to have been related to the destruction of my bone marrow, I felt chelation would not only lower these high metal levels, but would also promote a healthier state for my body.

Losing it FAST!

On July 23rd, the day after starting chelation, I received both a platelet and hemoglobin transfusion. Everything seemed fine until the morning of July 26th when I felt very tired and a bit lethargic. I asked my wife to drive me to my 2:00 p.m. appointment at Healing Center International. When we arrived I did not feel well at all. Something was wrong.

Elaine Bonn, prayer counselor and founder of HCI, met us as we arrived and noticed immediately that I did not look well. She directed me to rest in one of the rooms until she and another prayer minister could come in and pray for me; I sat down in a chair and immediately fell asleep! Ten minutes later Elaine returned and woke me up.

She asked me when I had received my last transfusion and I told her that it was three days ago on the 23rd. She asked, "Did you pray over the blood as you were receiving it?" Although I had always prayed in the past when I received blood, I could not remember doing so this last time. Elaine began praying and instantly sensed something was wrong with the blood I received from the last transfusion. She thought that something spiritual in nature might have transferred with the blood.

While she shared this with me, I became more lethargic, very dizzy, and felt my veins grow cold. My physical state declined rapidly and I had no idea why. I envisioned being rushed back to the hospital in an ambulance to get this blood out of me before it was too late. I felt like I would lose consciousness. I did all I could to maintain a state of awareness and not freak out; "Lord, help me!" I kept saying to myself.

Elaine, knowing something was definitely wrong, said to me, "Let's go back mentally to when you got the transfusion three days ago. Let's pray through this as you receive the blood." She prayed for the blood as I received it, asking the Lord to make it pure with His blood and to filter anything not of Him from flowing into my body. She and the other prayer minister prayed for 10-15 minutes and as they did, I began to feel better and my racing thoughts slowed. On the drive home I gained more strength and clarity of mind. By evening I was completely refreshed and have felt wonderful ever since.

Once again, God protected me! Whatever was going on with my body and blood that day, God intervened and turned a possible disaster into another miracle. I was truly at the right place at the right time that day! Amen!

Chelation Aborted

At the end of my visit to the HCI on July 26th, Elaine inquired about the chelation program I had started on July 22nd. We prayed about it and Elaine felt led by the Lord to ask me to stop the program. Interestingly, when I began taking the chelation tablets I was confused about the schedule. The more I studied about how I was supposed to take the tablets, the more questions I had and the more confusing the schedule became. Somewhat bizarre I know, but *"God is not the author of confusion..."* As a result, I took Elaine's suggestion as if it were the Lord's and aborted the chelation program that day.

Blood Numbers Fall, then Rise

Confirmation that chelation was wrong for me showed up in my next blood test. Just prior to beginning the chelation program, my percentage allocation of the white cells were within the NORMAL range! The neutrophil percentage of white cells had risen to 45.2 (normal 45-76%) and the lymphocyte percentage had dropped to 39.5 (normal 15-43%)! This was awesome!!!

Once the chelation began, however, the percentages quickly reversed and fell out of the "normal" ranges. The white cell count also declined after I started the chelation program.

The Lord spoke to Elaine while I was at the HCI, and urged her to have me stop the chelation *before* the blood test results indicated that it was damaging to me. Without the Lord speaking to Elaine, I could have continued to take the chelation tablets and my condition could have grown even worse. Praise God for His servants who hear His voice!

Since stopping the chelation, the declining white cell numbers have reversed and are now improving again. Those four days of chelation erased three to four weeks of white count progress!

A Word of Healing

On July 19th, I received the following prophetic word from a fellow believer whom I do not know, nor have I ever spoken with. This woman, a RE/MAX real estate agent from South Carolina who had been receiving my email updates, blessed me with the following email note:

Date: Thursday, July 19, 2001 13:41:05
Importance: High

Jeff,

Sometimes I hear from God very clearly. Today, while I was playing a computer game, I heard God say this to me:

> *"Tell Jeff he has endeared himself to Me. I have healed many of disease, including aplastic anemia, and very few have expressed such high levels of gratitude and praise to Me."*

It reminded me of when Jesus healed the 10 lepers and only one returned to thank Him.

Webster's definition:

    endear: 1. To make higher in cost, value or estimation
                    2. To cause to become beloved or admired

Jeff, you are His beloved.

Ginger Stolp
REMAX Realty Professionals
Greenville, SC

A Curse is Broken!

On August 3rd, after a scheduled platelet transfusion, I headed north to the northern suburb of Arden Hills to attend part of the annual Holy Spirit Conference held at the North Heights Church. I was particularly interested in an afternoon session featuring a woman named Marlene who was scheduled to speak about how the Lord had healed her 20 years ago. She had suffered all her life with cerebral palsy and was miraculously healed by the Lord!

Her story was incredible and I felt blessed to hear it. At the end of her talk, an older gentleman took the microphone and invited anyone who wanted prayer for healing to come forward and Marlene would pray for them. Half the room of over 200 went forward. Since I believed in my heart that my healing was already manifesting day by day, I did not feel pulled to ask for a healing prayer. I asked God, "Do you want me to go forward and pray with Marlene?" After a minute or two, the Lord said, "No, go and pray with the man." The Lord referred to the man who had invited people to pray with Marlene.

I immediately walked from the back of the room to this man who was packing his briefcase and preparing to leave the room. His hand-written name badge read "John". I asked John if I could pray with him and he said, "Sure, have a seat. What would you like to pray about?"

I said, "Well, I was in the hospital back in April. In fact, I was there for a month and the doctors diagnosed me with a blood disease they said is going to kill me."

"STOP!" he interrupted. He reached out, put his hand on my head and said, "The Lord has a Word for you," and delivered this powerful message from the Lord:

> *"A curse has come against your bone marrow from four generations ago, and I'm breaking it now, and filling your bones with fresh, clean, healthy marrow!"*

I could not believe what he said! We had not discussed the diagnosis or prognosis! With tears of joy and laughter I exclaimed, "How did you know that?"

"The Lord has used me this way for years," he responded as he walked away.

I immediately called home to my wife and said, "IT'S DONE! My miracle has arrived in the physical!" I began running around the church telling several of my friends that were at the conference— "It is done! My healing miracle has come! A curse has been broken! The manifestation has arrived!"

Marlene never spoke about generational curses; it was not the topic of the day at the conference. John (who I later learned was an evangelist) knew nothing about me or my condition, yet he shared a Word from the Lord about a generational curse and restoring my bone marrow! His prophetic words aligned with what the Lord told me on May 13th when He said He would *"plant the seed of marrow and it will "grow" 100-fold!"* I believe that 100-fold means "perfect" or "full". Now, God just said He is "filling" my bones with marrow! Amen!!!

John's words, "fresh, clean, healthy marrow" were nearly identical to the very words I have spoken out loud each day since I wrote them on a post-it note and stuck them on the wall! My post-it reads, "Thank you, Father, for the fresh, powerful and healthy bone marrow!" In addition, John's prophetic words confirmed Marjorie Cole's idea of a possible generational curse that needed to be broken. God chose to personally break it!

Some of this is heavy, even for me. But I am sharing this incredible journey with you as it happens. Sometimes I cannot even believe it myself! God is really GOOD!

Jogging Resumed

In my last email I shared that I had begun jogging. After about ten days, I pulled a calf muscle, perhaps as a reminder to take it a bit easier. In any case, the muscle is better and the walking and jogging have resumed.

Hemoglobin Lasting Longer

Great news about my hemoglobin! My previous transfusion of red blood cells lasted 27 days—the best ever! The one prior to that lasted 18 days. Now, my current transfusion appears to be doing even better yet; the red count is holding steady between 10.4 and 10.6 with barely any change in 3 ½ weeks!

"We Can't Keep Giving You Blood!"

When I was at the clinic on August 10th to receive a scheduled platelet transfusion, the nurse asked me, "What is your plan?" I said, "To be 100% healed." She said, "I mean with getting blood, what is your doctor saying?" I said, "I haven't talked with him for quite a while." She then told me, "We can't keep giving you blood without an order from the doctor." I said, "I understand, but the doctor has not asked to see me. I will meet with him if he likes."

Our dialogue continued along that vein and the nurse shared her concern over the fact that I had not seen the doctor since May 14th. The office phoned later that day and scheduled an appointment to "see the doctor" on August 16th. I believe this appointment will be interesting. I know that I am seeing a *positive* rise in my blood numbers and I hope the doctor sees them too. It will be good for him!

The Significance of May 13th

Over the past couple of weeks I have often pondered the Word I received from the Lord back on May 13th. God told me that night that *"a farmer does not plant seed in the field until he has readied and tilled the soil. Likewise, you till the soil of your body (by taking care of it) and I will plant the seed of marrow and it will grow 100-fold."*

This Word has come alive. I have learned that to "grow" is a process and this is exactly what I am seeing happen in my life. The seed has been planted and it is growing. If I "take care of the field" and don't do anything foolish to dampen that growth (such as chelation), the seed will grow and produce 100-fold.

Hundred-fold, as I mentioned earlier, is "perfection," or "fullness" and I trust it will happen. How long will it take? I don't know. But I know that God will not do half of a job. Each time I get blood numbers that are a bit better, I am so excited! It is a new, refreshing blessing all over again!

My white blood cell percentages were the most out of balance on May 10th. On May 13th, the Lord spoke to me saying *"I will plant the seed of marrow."* This is precisely the date that these white count numbers turned around and began improving! Incredible!

The devil loves to throw doubt and fear into my mind on the way to the clinic each week. He loves saying, "The best is behind you. The numbers can't last. They'll be down today. No one survives this. It's not really marrow; it's just a bi-product of the transfusions you're getting."

But the Bible says, *"...greater is He who is in you than he who is in the world"* (1 John 4:4); ... *resist the devil and he will flee from you."* (James 4:7) Do you know something? It works! Therefore, *"put on the full armor of God that you may be able to stand firm against the schemes of the devil"* and all the invisible powers that we wrestle against. (Ephesians 6:10-17)

Blood Numbers—A Closer Look

As of August 10th the white count was at a high of 1900! This count is critical since it represents my immune system. Check out the increased blessing I am receiving: The *average* white count was 500 during the month of April, 925 in May, 1250 in June, 1683 in July and now it is 1900! With the normal range of 3500 – 10,800, I am more than half way to "normal!"

The neutrophils reached 0.8 as of August 10th, which is a new high. The *average* monthly counts have been 0.0 in April, 0.15 in May, 0.385 in June and 0.667 in July and they are now at 0.80! The normal ranges are 1.9 – 8.0 and I am now nearly one half of the way towards entering the normal range!

We continue to see healthier white cell percentages. Unfortunately, the chelation program set my progress back about three to four weeks. Since then however, the allocation percentages of the three primary white cell types—neutrophils, lymphocytes and monocytes—have continued to improve!

Below, you can see a table which depicts the significant turnaround in the health of my white cell percentages since I began taking herbs and receiving the Word from the Lord.

White Cell Percentages	May 10	July 12	Aug 10	Normal Range
Neutrophils	7.4%	41.0%	42.4%	45.0 – 76.0%
Lymphocytes	83.4%	44.1%	46.7%	15.0 – 43.0%
Monocytes	19.6%	13.4%	9.2%	0.0 – 10.0%

Blood Numbers

August 10th	My Blood Counts	Notes	Normal Range
Red	10.4	Last Transfusion: 18 Days	13.5 – 17.5
White	1,900	Count 11 Days Ago: 1,500	3,500 – 10,800
Platelets	26,000*	Last Transfusion: 7 Days	130,000 – 430,000
Neutrophils	0.8	Count 11 Days Ago: 0.6	1.9 – 8.0

* 1 bag of Platelets was transfused August 10th
* Tubes of Blood Drawn since Illness: 179

Weight Numbers

Daily range 157-158 lbs. Steady with virtually no fluctuation. Feeling very well.

Eyes

My vision continues to improve and is nearly normal! God is restoring me as He promised on late night TV back in April! (1 Peter 5:10)

Closing Verses

"... fixing your eyes on Jesus, the author and perfecter of faith...." (Hebrews 12:2)

"Therefore there is now no condemnation for those who are in Christ Jesus." (Romans 8:1)

"For I know the plans I have for you,' declares the Lord, 'plans for welfare and not for calamity to give you a future and a hope.'" (Jeremiah 29:11)

"How will we escape if we neglect so great a salvation?" (Hebrews 2:3)

==

Jeff Scislow

August 26, 2001

The excitement is building each day! With so much happening so quickly, I felt that I needed to provide you with another email update even though it has only been eleven days! Allow me to pick up where I left off; just prior to my long-awaited appointment with the oncologist.

What Medications are You On?

On the afternoon of August 16th, I had my first appointment in over 90 days with my primary oncologist—the one who saw me daily while I was in the hospital. Even though the oncologist had been following my blood test results, it was necessary to have an official appointment with him in order for me to continue to receive blood transfusions. Over these past three months, I often felt like I had been "written off" as a patient after I stopped taking Cyclosporine. That decision, along with my *positive* response to *negative* news, may have caused the doctor to keep his distance. Who knows for sure?

Shortly after I arrived at the doctor's office, I was brought into the examination room where the nurse asked me in the most generalized sense, "What medications are you taking?" I chuckled inside thinking, "Shouldn't you know a bit about your patient? I replied, "No medications—not since May."

When the doctor arrived and began looking over my steadily rising numbers, I was truly hoping he would express some optimism of his own. He acknowledged that "the numbers are improving some—they're certainly not going down." I felt like saying "brilliant observation," but of course, I did not. I was simply hoping he would acknowledge that a miracle was in progress; I just wanted him to be amazed at something he could not explain medically.

He acknowledged there had to be marrow present for these numbers to be rising like they were. In an attempt to justify why the blood counts had risen, he admitted there must have been marrow in the first place and that the ATG treatment, which was deemed a failure back in April, must now be working all of the sudden in August! He groveled to find an explanation; and I knew he was feeling uncomfortable. I did not debate his observations with him.

The facts had been noted all along. Six doctors, including oncologists, surgeons and pathologists, from United Hospital, the University of Minnesota, as well as two outside medical opinions, all concluded that there was no marrow or marrow stem cells present on April 9th of this year when the biopsy was done. The neutrophil count was 0.0 all throughout April of 2001, providing further evidence of the absence of bone marrow. The U. of M. team stated that I had an "unfortunate case of bad luck." Each of the doctors concluded that death was the likely outcome.

Our conversation continued with me asking, "What will it take…" the doctor interrupted and completed my sentence, "to make me happy?" "Yes," I replied, with a smile on my face. The doctor continued, "Well ultimately, your blood levels need to get to the point where you would no longer need *regular* transfusions. That means a *less than normal level*, but one in which you could be sustained." Knowing that he and I had totally different expectations, I asked, "What would prevent my blood levels from returning to normal?"

His response was, "When a person has aplastic anemia, the blood levels never go back to normal; the disease can become aggressive at any time causing the blood levels to fall again." With full assurance I stated, "But I don't have it anymore, it is gone and it is not coming back!" I affirmed that my blood counts *will* rise to normal levels again. He was quiet. Believe it or not, he then asked me if I wanted to repeat the ATG/Cyclosporine treatment again in the hospital. I politely said, "No thank you."

The blood chart the doctor was looking at during our appointment was from the previous week. I was not scheduled for a blood test until the following day, but since I was there, he suggested I have the test taken right then. I agreed.

I did not see the doctor again after the test. I was thrilled to see the increase in numbers again! My platelets jumped to 46,000! With great joy, I canceled my scheduled platelet transfusion for the next day, August 17th. My next blood test was scheduled for Thursday, August 23rd.

Like Deer in the Headlights

I have spoken to a number of people in the "medical field"—even Christian doctors and nurses who regularly attend church. Nearly everyone has had the same viewpoint—*medical science is your only answer.* In numerous instances I have had the opportunity to share with doctors and nurses, unrelated to my case, the facts of my aplastic anemia diagnosis. When I get to the "faith," "healing" and "miracle" portions of my story, nearly all become like deer caught in the headlights. They don't seem to get it—even some who say they have "the faith!"

The concept of supernatural healing has a tendency to be challenging for many in the medical field. Their training is based on facts and science, not on faith and invisible attributes.

I have been constantly told by persons in the medical profession, "God can heal you *through a bone marrow donor.*" I typically respond, "I agree," but then add, "But deep down in my spirit I don't believe I will need a marrow transplant because God has shown me differently." The common response, which appears as a challenge to my reply; "Well if the numbers fall back down, you would consider it would you not?" Again, I clearly state, "They are not going to fall back; God is not going to do a half-way job. He is going to do a wonderful, miraculous job, just as His Word and Spirit have promised me." Right about here I lose many, as my "faith" concept flies right over their heads.

I firmly believe that God *does* heal through medicine and through doctors, but *in my personal case,* I have come to believe something different has occurred—a total supernatural healing! I believe each person should search their heart, listen closely for the answers to their prayers and act accordingly. God promises that His Holy Spirit will lead us into all truth.

Daniel's Trial

God is the "same yesterday, today and forever." We all know the story of Daniel and the lion's den. Daniel was faithful to his God and stood firm, continuing to worship and pray even though a law was created against such acts. When those seeking to destroy Daniel reported to the king that Daniel was not observing the king's law and that, according to the king's decree, Daniel must be thrown to the lions, the king reluctantly concurred.

Daniel was thrown into the den of hungry lions. All night long Daniel remained among the lions. In the morning the guards were commanded to open the den and see whether Daniel's God had delivered him. There they found Daniel unharmed. The king ordered Daniel out and ordered Daniel's accusers to be thrown into the den. Scripture reports that before the accusers "hit the ground, they were torn apart by the lions."

God had sent an angel to shut the mouths of the lions while Daniel was in the den. He was under God's care and protection because Daniel trusted God. God heard Daniel's prayer and honored his faith and his cry in his time of need. This is a miracle. Wouldn't you agree? (Daniel 6:1-28)

In the same way, under the care and power of the same God, the one that Daniel served thousands of years ago; I too called on, trusted in and waited on God for a miracle. What's been the result?

With my being exposed to sick adults and children off and on during the time of a critically compromised immune system, God sent His power (His angels?) to shut the mouth of a killer disease called aplastic anemia, and to stand firm against any cold, flu or other germs that could kill me. Is there any difference between these two miraculous outcomes other than the details? There isn't. They are both miracles. I serve the same God that Daniel served. God is no respecter of persons. He can do the same for you as He did for me, and as He did for Daniel.

"And without faith it is impossible to please Him, for he that comes to God must believe that He is and that He is a rewarder of those who seek Him." (Hebrews 11:6)

Let There Be Neutrophils!

While meeting with the doctor on August 16th, before the blood test that day, he pointed out, as his nurse did on my previous visits to the clinic, that the most important number he was watching was the *neutrophil* number (the primary indicator of the strength of the immune system.) He kept telling me that any good news I might be "reading into my numbers" is *irrelevant* (i.e. the percentages of the white cells within my immune system). "The neutrophils are everything," he'd say. Praise God, I agree! "Let there be NEUTROPHILS!"

On August 23rd my neutrophil count had soared. It was double the count from just a week earlier and this latest number of 2.0 places my neutrophil count within the "normal range"! Yeah!

The white count, the red count and the platelets are all still low, but they are rising and will continue to rise to perfectly healthy ranges! Expect it! I do!

Blood Numbers

Blood Numbers	Aug 10	Aug 16	Aug 23	Normal Range
Red	10.4	10.4	10.6	13.5 – 17.5
White	1,900	2,100	3,000	3,500 – 10,800
Platelets	26,000*	46,000	31,000	130,000 – 430,000
Neutrophils	0.8	1.0	2.0*	1.9 – 8.0

* Platelets last transfused on August 10th
* Red Cells last transfused on July 23rd
* Neutrophils within Normal Range on August 23rd
* Tubes of Blood Draw since Illness: 179

The white cell percentages (quality) of my immune system, which I personally have been watching ever so closely, have dramatically improved as well over the past few visits. All are now normal! Check them out...

White Cell Percentages	Aug 10	Aug 16	Aug 23	Normal Range
Neutrophils	42.4%	46.9%	67.3%	45 – 76%
Lymphocytes	46.7%	42.4%	25.4%	15 – 43%
Monocytes	9.2%	9.4%	7.3%	0 – 10%

NOTE: It occurred to me this past week that the ATG/Cyclosporine treatment that I was prescribed was apparently doing the exact opposite of what it was supposed to. It was designed, in part, to suppress (kill) a part of the immune system—the part that was attacking my bone marrow. Lymphocytes, the white cells that are primarily made up of 'T' and 'B' and 'natural killer' cells, are the ones which were responsible for killing my bone marrow. What I learned, by careful examination of all my blood test numbers, is this: The more Cyclosporine that I took, the higher the percentage levels of (killer) lymphocytes that were produced. This was the exact opposite of what I thought the goal was—to cool down the immune system and stop the attacking cells! It was my understanding that the lymphocyte percentage should have dropped by using these drugs, but it continued to rise until I took myself off the treatment/drug on May 10th and began taking herbs. The percentage of lymphocytes as a part of my immune system reached 83.4% on May 10th. The normal range is 15-43%. This undoubtedly raises questions—I'm simply thankful!

Weight Numbers

Daily range 157-158 lbs. Steady with virtually no fluctuation.

Eyes

Almost perfect; very little blind spots remain. Vision tested at 20/20!

Closing Verses

"And there is salvation in no one else; for there is no other name under heaven that has been given among men by which we must be saved."
(Acts 4:12)

"'For I will restore you to health and I will heal you of your wounds,' declares the LORD...." (Jeremiah 30:17)

"How will we escape if we neglect so great a salvation?" (Hebrews 2:3)

Jeff Scislow

P.S. Remember *the letter* the Lord asked me to write the night before Easter, on April 14th? It was written for the doctors and nurses who took care of me at the hospital and at the clinic. I was to share this letter with each of them on the day I was miraculously healed. I am being reminded that the time has nearly arrived!

September 17, 2001

In my last update I began with the words, "With so much happening so quickly...." Perhaps I should have waited to use those words for this email. The terrible event that occurred in New York City six days ago is having a profound impact on our nation, as well as the entire world.

Terrorists Attack our Nation

Before I begin sharing the latest on my health, I want to encourage each of you reading this "email" update to *"Trust in the Lord with all your heart and do not lean unto your own understanding. In all your ways acknowledge Him, and He will make your paths straight."* (Proverbs 3:5-6) I also wish to encourage you to support and pray for the leaders of our land; the President, his Cabinet, Congress, the Senate and our military.

Right at this very moment our leaders are facing some very difficult decisions. How should we respond to this cowardly, barbaric attack on our nation's people and freedom? A natural response might be to flex our military muscle in an attempt to prevent any future terrorist attacks while convincing enemy nations not to mess with the USA. These actions run the risks of escalation and, of course, unnecessary bloodshed. What does the Bible teach us? What is the most intelligent and appropriate response?

From the book of Romans we read, *"Let love be without hypocrisy. Abhor what is evil; cling to what is good. Be devoted to one another in brotherly love... fervent in spirit, serving the Lord; rejoicing in hope, persevering in tribulation, devoted to prayer... practicing hospitality. Bless those who persecute you; bless and curse not. Rejoice with those who rejoice, and weep with those who weep... Do not be wise in your own estimation."*

"Never pay back evil for evil to anyone. Respect what is right in the sight of all men. If possible, so far as it depends on you, be at peace with all men. Never take your own revenge, beloved, but leave room for the wrath of God, for it is written, 'Vengeance is Mine, I will repay,' says the Lord."

"'But if your enemy is hungry, feed him, and if he is thirsty, give him a drink; for in so doing you will heap burning coals upon his head.' Do not be overcome by evil, but overcome evil with good." (Romans 12:9-21)

Is this a tall order? I would say yes. But is not God capable of all things? Remember, God"... *is able to do far more abundantly beyond all we ask or think....*" (Ephesians 3:20) At this critical time in our history, we need divine guidance and intervention. We have a choice as to how we will act. Will we earnestly turn to the Lord and ask for His help?

How many times in the Bible do we learn—when God's people trusted Him to fight the battle on their behalf—that He delivered the enemy over to His people? The answer—EVERY TIME!

Our nation has an opportunity to seek the Lord and watch His mighty strength move powerfully on our behalf. Listen to the prayer of David, the King over all of Israel, as he calls on the Lord for help in the 35th Psalm. It's as if this prayer was written for us today in light of the 9-11 terrorist attack! Can we pray this prayer as a nation today?

"Contend, O LORD, with those who contend with me; fight against those who fight against me... Let those be ashamed and dishonored who seek my life; let those be turned back and humiliated who devise evil against me. Let them be like chaff before the wind, with the angel of the LORD driving them on. Let their way be dark and slippery, with the angel of the LORD pursuing them."

"For without cause they hid their net for me; without cause they dug a pit for my soul. Let destruction come upon him unawares; and let the net which he hid catch himself; into that very destruction let him fall."

224

"And my soul shall rejoice in the LORD; it shall exult in His salvation. All my bones will say, 'LORD, who is like You, who delivers the afflicted from him who is too strong for him, and the afflicted and the needy from him who robs him?'"

"They repay me evil for good, to the bereavement of my soul... But at my stumbling they rejoiced... they slandered me without ceasing. Like godless jesters at a feast, they gnashed at me with their teeth...."

"Do not let those who are wrongfully my enemies rejoice over me; neither let those who hate me without cause wink maliciously. For they do not speak peace, but they devise deceitful words against those who are quiet in the land. They opened their mouth wide against me; they said, 'Aha, aha, our eyes have seen it!' You have seen it, O LORD, do not keep silent; O Lord, do not be far from me."

"Stir up Yourself, and awake to my right and to my cause, my God and my Lord. Judge me, O LORD my God, according to Your righteousness; and do not let them rejoice over me. Do not let them say in their heart, "Aha, our desire!" Do not let them say, 'We have swallowed him up!'"

"Let those be ashamed and humiliated altogether who rejoice at my distress; let those be clothed with shame and dishonor who magnify themselves over me. Let them shout for joy and rejoice, who favor my vindication; and let them say continually, "The LORD be magnified, who delights in the prosperity of His servant." And my tongue shall declare Your righteousness and Your praise all day long."

Numbers Retreating

August 23rd was my first visit back to the Apple Valley Clinic since I was there in March. After my scheduled appointment with the oncologist on August 16th, he prescribed a weekly CBC (complete blood count) at the clinic of my choice. So, of course, it was nice to be able to conduct weekly testing near my home instead of driving to downtown St. Paul.

Since my test results on August 23rd I had been very excited about the increasing blood numbers, especially the white counts (my immune system). The numbers however, were not destined to stay there. The following week, on August 30th, the white count fell from 3000 to 2600 and the neutrophils fell from 2.0 to 1.5. Both the red and platelets counts remained fairly steady without the need of a transfusion, but what was happening to the white cells? Why were they falling?

One week later, on September 6th, the blood numbers fell even further. Even the red cell counts sank to 10.1 from 11.0 a week earlier; representing the lowest level since my last red cell transfusion back on July 23rd. The last thing I wanted was another transfusion, especially now that I believed I would never need another one.

The white cell count had also declined from 2600 to 2100 and the neutrophils fell from 1.5 to 1.2. Just two weeks earlier these numbers had been 3000 and 2.0, respectively. I had no idea what was happening.

Another Test of Faith

The enemy took advantage of these lower numbers. Immediately he came in like a flood. I was bombarded with *thoughts* of more transfusions, failed healing and an unbroken curse (as prophesied at the Holy Spirit Conference). It was awful. This news seemed worse to me than the news of the initial diagnosis back in April! I was so excited and optimistic after seeing a fairly consistent rise in the blood numbers over the previous weeks. What was going on now all of a sudden?

Prior to going in for the blood test on September 6th, I told some friends that I was expecting a hemoglobin (red cell) count near 12.0 that day. I was really feeling alert and strong. I also told them that I felt the transfusions were behind me and that I expected all the blood numbers to be within normal ranges by the end of September. So what was happening now with the falling blood levels?

These poor blood reports produced a powerful negative *physical* effect on how I felt. I immediately began to feel weaker. The next day on September 7th, I was *"feeling"* like my hemoglobin had fallen further; somewhere in the 9's perhaps. Then I realized something. It was that old foe again, the devil, trying to steal, to kill and to destroy! I cannot be blind to his schemes! I made the choice right then and there of *"…taking up the shield of faith with which you will be able to extinguish all the flaming arrows of the evil one"* (Ephesians 6:16), and to stand on the same exact verses I did from the beginning. This victory was mine, not the enemy's! It was not time for me to feel defeated or to become complacent; I needed to continue fighting this spiritual battle all the way through.

I am walking by faith, not by sight! Greater is He who is in me than he who is in the world! Jesus came to give life and to give it more abundantly! When the enemy comes in like a flood, the Spirit of the Lord will raise up a standard against him! I prayed, got prayer and confessed my healing out loud during the days ahead. My strength and faith increased. I was not going to allow the enemy to thwart the healing and incredible blessing that belonged to me! This is my victory! I'm going all the way across the goal line to score that touchdown!

I was reminded of the verse in James that has been my strength from the beginning of this battle: *"Consider it all joy my brethren when you encounter various trials, knowing that the testing of your faith produces endurance."* (James 1:2-3) I sensed I was being tested once again. I needed to keep focused on Jesus, the author and perfecter of my faith. I would not quit or be emotionally or spiritually overcome!

Immune System Moves to NORMAL Range

The next week's visit to the clinic, on September 13th, brought wonderful results—the best ever! By standing on God's Word and not the poor numbers or circumstances from the previous week, I once again saw the power of God manifested in faith! It is absolutely amazing, because it works!

The white count (immune system) which had been beaten down for two weeks straight now soared to a new high and entered the boundary of the "normal range!" It jumped all the way up from 2100 to 3500 and the neutrophil count increased from 1.2 to 2.0!

Not only did the white count soar, but so did the red count and the platelets! The red count rose from 10.1 to 11.4 and the platelets jumped from 35,000 to 54,000! All of these increased WITHOUT TRANSFUSIONS! Tears of joy are filling my eyes as I write you with this good news!

No More Blood for You

Just a few days before writing this update I recalled what transpired at the St. Paul clinic on August 10th. On that visit, one of the nurses asked me, "What's your plan?" My reply was, "To be healed 100 percent." She said, "I mean with getting blood; *we can't keep giving you blood.*"

> *"We can't keep giving you blood."*

The nurse's words were somewhat prophetic, as that was the last day I received a blood transfusion. It was a bag of platelets—my 41st blood transfusion since this journey began.

A Book?

About a month ago, as the blood counts began showing signs of a miraculous turnaround, several people began asking me about writing a book and sharing this incredible story with others. I must admit the thought had entered my mind, but I did not have any interest in doing this without the leading of the Holy Spirit. I prayed and asked the Lord to give me confirmation if this was what He wanted me to do. It was not long before I did, in fact, receive a prodding to write a book.

I am not an author. I do not know how to go about putting a "book" together. I don't know any editors or publishers. I have no idea where to start.

Since I have received various confirmations about moving ahead, I am asking for the Lord to provide me with the right person(s) to launch such a project. I simply said, "Lord, I am willing to do all I can, but I will need the right people to help. I will patiently wait on You. If you send the right people, I will know and we can proceed at that time."

If you feel the Lord leading you to help with any aspect regarding a possible book, please email me back.

Web Site Coming

Once all the blood numbers are normal and I am described as being "in perfect health," I intend to deliver the verse (Acts 3:16) to the world. This is the verse that the Lord gave me on April 11th while in the hospital. He told me, *"This is the verse that you will share with everyone on the day you're made whole."* I know that day is rapidly approaching. I will use a web site to boldly announce the miracle the Lord has done in my life; the miracle He promised to do, just as I believed He would do!

Once this verse is fulfilled in my life, *"being given this perfect health in the presence of you all,"* the new site will be brought online for the entire world to see. The site will have the name of this very special verse - www.Acts316.org

I would encourage you to share the web address with anyone who is sick. Forward these emails to anyone and everyone so they can see that God is, in fact, *"showing Himself strong through me before the eyes of many people,"* just like He said He would!

I have already seen and heard that these emails are inspiring and leading others, both to salvation and healing. That is their intent, to the glory of God.

Blood Numbers

Blood Numbers	Aug 30	Sept 6	Sept 13	Normal Range
Red	11.0	10.1	11.4	13.5 – 17.5
White	2,600	2,100	3,500	3,500 – 10,800
Platelets	33,000	35,000	54,000	130,000 – 430,000
Neutrophils	1.5	1.2	2.0	1.9 – 8.0

* Red Cells rising; last transfusion was July 23rd (56 days ago)!
* White Cells just entered Normal Range!
* Platelets rising; last transfusion was August 10th (38 days ago)!
* Neutrophils within Normal Range!
* Tubes of Blood Drawn since Illness: 185

The percentages (quality) of my primary white cells are very stable— right in the middle of the normal range!

White Cell Percentages	Aug 23	Aug 30	Sept 6	Sept 13	Normal Range
Neutrophils	67.3%	58.5%	59.0%	58.1%	45 – 76%
Lymphocytes	25.4%	33.2%	38.0%	33.3%	15 – 43%
Monocytes	7.3%	8.3%	3.0%	8.6%	0 – 10%

Weight Numbers

Daily range of 156-158 lbs - Steady with virtually no fluctuation.

Eyes

Almost perfect; very little blind spots remain. Vision tested at 20/20!

Closing Verses

"[If] *My people who are called by My name, humble themselves and pray and seek My face and turn from their wicked ways, then I will hear from heaven, will forgive their sin, and will heal their land.*" (2 Chronicles 7:14) [Emphasis added]

"*Jesus said to him, 'I am the Way, the Truth and the Life; no one comes to the Father but through Me.'*" (John 14:6)

"*So faith comes from hearing, and hearing by the word of Christ.*" (Romans 10:17)

"*How will we escape if we neglect so great a salvation?*" (Hebrews 2:3)

==

Jeff Scislow

P.S. Pray for divine wisdom for our nation's leaders; so they know how to respond in light of the terrorist attack on New York City. Keep praying for the complete manifestation of my healing! Thank you and God bless you!

October 4, 2001

May you have an awesome day! I plan to, as I share more exciting news with you!

If you have not yet shared these emails with others, I hope that you will, especially if you know someone who is sick.

We all need to encourage others when they are sick. The reason I send these emails to thousands is so others will be blessed with God's truth, particularly His truth concerning healing, as I am a living example!

If you believe that the words I have shared in my emails will impact another's life, by all means share them with someone who is hurting! You would be surprised how people react when you reach out to help. Don't take it for granted that they don't want help; people DO want help, especially if they are sick or in need. They will appreciate it more than you could ever imagine. Not only will you bless them, but you, too, will be blessed for taking the time to reach out. Remember, *"Faith without works is dead."*

The Doorstep of Normal

As I write this update the various blood components have somewhat stabilized, just outside the gates of normal. I feel excellent. For all practical purposes, I feel completely normal. My blood numbers, however, are still short of "perfectly normal." Before I share what I intend to do, allow me to brief you on the numbers.

- **Red Cells**

After retreating to a level of 10.1 nearly a month ago, the weekly hemoglobin numbers have been 11.4, 12.4 and 12.4, respectively. I cannot express how good the 12.4 level feels. I have more energy, but more importantly, I have more oxygen going to my brain which enables me to think clearer and quicker.

For nearly five months, my hemoglobin readings of 7.5 to 10.5 affected the clarity and crispness of thought that I otherwise enjoyed at my pre-hospitalized hemoglobin count of 15.4. Anyone who has dealt with low levels of hemoglobin knows what I am talking about.

- **White Cells**

Every third week it seems as though the white counts jump upward to new highs followed by two weeks of lower numbers. Now, I know that is not scientifically explainable, but over the past couple months we've seen a similar pattern. The past seven weeks have produced readings of 1900, 3000, 2600, 2100, 3500, 3200 and 3000, respectively.

Once again, the enemy took advantage of the lower numbers. Every time the numbers drop, I get barraged with thoughts that I will sustain these low levels, that I will get sick again or that the aplastic anemia is still there putting downward pressure on the bone marrow. All kinds of nonsense from the enemy!

The Bible tells us to *"resist him (the devil), firm in your faith"* (1 Peter 5:9); to *"Put on the full armor of God so that you will be able to stand firm against the schemes of the devil."* (Ephesians 6:11) Amen and Amen— this is what I choose to do.

- **Platelets**

The platelets, too, have followed an interesting pattern, although it is too early to believe this specific pattern will continue. For the past two periods of three consecutive weeks, the platelets hung in a tight range of 31,000, 33,000 and 35,000. From there they jumped to 54,000, 52,000 and 59,000. They are definitely getting better and I expect them to keep climbing to fully normal and perfect levels—above 130,000.

Press on to Perfection

It has become increasingly more comfortable to sit back and enjoy the life-sustaining blood numbers that I currently have. They are so much better than what I had been dealing with earlier in the year. The tendency is to thank the Lord for what He has done and leave it at that. But that is <u>not</u> what the Lord said.

On FOUR specific occasions, the Lord spoke to me about *full* restoration—to perfection! And I believe that. I cannot settle for acceptability, but for the fullness of the promise. The enemy would have me bask in my partially restored health, even though it is not perfect. But God has a bigger plan and somehow I am part of it. I am nearly over the goal line, the enemy is making his last stand, his last attempt to foil the promise of perfection! He will not prevail! The Lord is about to carry me over the goal line for that prized touchdown!

The *first* promise of perfection came on April 5th, two days prior to being admitted to the hospital. It was 4:00 a.m. in the morning. I awoke coughing up blood and went downstairs for a snack. I turned on the television only to find a channel that had a Bible verse displayed on the screen. It was 1 Peter 5:10. This verse was for me. God was foretelling me what was to come.

"After you have suffered a little while, the God of all grace, who called you to His eternal glory in Christ, shall Himself, <u>restore</u>, <u>strengthen</u>, <u>perfect</u>, establish and confirm you." [Emphasis added]

I received this by faith that night, just as I hold firm to it today. I have been restored and strengthened. I am soon to be perfected (with perfect blood numbers). I don't know what the Lord plans to do to *establish* and *confirm* me, but He will reveal it.

The *second* promise came on April 11th, the fifth day in the hospital; the day after I was diagnosed with aplastic anemia. The Lord spoke again through His Word as I was reading the book of Acts 3:16:

"On the basis of faith in His name, it is the name of Jesus which has strengthened *this man whom you see and know; and the faith which comes through Him has given him* [me] *this* perfect *health in the presence of you all."* [Emphasis added]

This verse not only jumped off the page of my Bible, but the Lord spoke to my heart and said, "This is you—you are to share this verse with everyone on the day you are made whole." Again we see key words match up with the first promise: strengthen and perfect!

The *third* promise came on May 13th, nine days after coming home from the hospital with no sign of marrow in my bones. As I was praying prior to going to bed, the Lord spoke to my spirit saying, *"A farmer does not plant a seed in the field until he tills it, readies it and then takes care of the field. You do likewise with your body and I will plant the seed of marrow and it will grow 100-fold."* Once again, we see God's words match up with what He spoke through His word previously in the first two promises. This time He was very specific and personal. God said He would plant the seed of marrow and that it would grow "100-fold."

Hundred-fold is perfection! In the parable of the sower (Matthew 13:18-23), seed fell on the road, the rocks, the thorns and the good soil. The seed that fell on the good soil was described as producing 30, 60 and 100-fold. The "good soil" was me taking care of my body (the tilling) and the promise was that the seed of marrow which the Lord promised to plant would grow 100-fold—and that is as good as it gets! It shall be perfect!

The *fourth* promise of perfection came on August 3rd, while at North Heights Church, an evangelist named John received a prophetic Word from the Lord which said, *"A curse has come against your bone marrow* *from four generations ago; I'm breaking it now, and <u>filling</u> your bones with fresh, clean, healthy marrow."* Filling means the process of making full—and full means 100%!

Isn't it awesome to see how God speaks to us and how His Word is flawless? I will be the first to say that it is not always easy to hear His voice. As I look back at each of these promises, I did not see how they would come together in the way that they did. I simply believed His Word and acted on what I heard from Him at that time. Only now, months later, do I see how these promises have all lined up! *"For I am confident of this very thing, that He who began a good work in you* [me] *will <u>perfect</u> it until the day of Christ Jesus."* (Philippians 1:6) [Emphasis added]

Speak it Into Existence

I have learned that we have authority over many things as believers, including our body—especially when it pertains to sickness. I have noted on several occasions that my blood levels rise when I speak openly to the marrow, the immune system and the blood cells. Below is a prayer of authority that I have been praying over my body.

"In the name of Jesus, I speak to you marrow, my friend, ordained by the Lord God to sustain life in my body, to grow according to the Word of the Lord and produce the fullness of hemoglobin, the fullness of platelets, the fullness of white cells and the fullness of a healthy immune system! I speak to you hemoglobin, platelets, white cells and immune system to grow to your fullness in accordance with your production from the marrow, to strengthen and protect my body to which the Lord has given abundant life. I rejoice in what the Lord has done; for He has squashed the plans of the enemy, which were to steal, to kill and to destroy. For the Lord Jesus has come to give life and to give it abundantly, not half way, not an unfinished work, but one that will bring about completion and perfection to that which He has started! Be all the glory to God our Father and to His Son, the Lord Jesus Christ, by whose stripes I am healed! Amen!"

The Doctor Called Me!

On September 25th my doctor called me to say, "You're certainly doing very well." I can't express how much that meant coming from the doctor who had been so negative about my health for so long. During our ten-minute conversation he suggested that I have my blood tested every two weeks instead of every week. But more importantly, I told him I had to share a couple of things with him.

I informed him that my blood tests seemed to indicate that the percentages of my primary white cells persistently worsened while I was taking the Cyclosporine and when I chose to stop taking the drug, the white cell percentages began improving almost immediately. He said that there was no correlation.

I went on to say, "But let me tell you what else happened within those same few days.... " I proceeded to share what the Lord told me about tilling the soil of my body and that He would plant the seed of marrow and that it would grow 100-fold. I told him that is why my blood counts are rising, and that "grow" means 'over time' and "100-fold" means 'perfection', and *that* is why I know that my counts will return all the way back to normal. The doctor was utterly speechless.

I told him that I had bought a gift for him and that I would drop it off the next time I was at the clinic. I told him that it was an excellent book, written by a medical doctor who describes how he combined his faith with his medical knowledge to treat and heal his patients. He seemed very happy about it.

Please pray that the Lord will use my life and testimony, as well as the book, to touch this doctor's heart; to ensure him a place in the kingdom of God.

Immune System Being Tested

As I write this email update to you, I should tell you that I have lost my voice. I have laryngitis! It began two days ago with a very sore and scratchy throat. It appears to be following the course of a viral strain that has hit many people in the Twin Cities over the past few weeks.

Six family members at my home have been suffering with this same viral bug. It starts with a scratchy throat. Then it proceeds to the loss of voice and then to a cough. With all my family sick, this thing caught up with me this time.

As of last week my white count was 3000 (normal range is 3500 – 10,800). The neutrophils were 2.0 (normal range is 1.9 – 8.0). So from these numbers, one would assume I am able to successfully fight off this virus. Will it take a bit longer to get over? I really don't know. What I do know is that I am thankful my blood counts are where they are today and not where they were a few months back!

I have not called the doctor because I believe all I have is a simple cold and a case of laryngitis. I don't want to take antibiotics unless it is absolutely necessary. My *new* immune system is simply going to be tested! It is going to have its first workout and get the chance to build up some new antibodies. My body is ready to fight the good fight!

Nutritional Update

I continue taking Dr. Richard Schulze's SUPERFOOD breakfast drink of herbs, vitamins and minerals each morning. I subscribe to Dr. Peter D'Adamo's advice in his book, "Live Right 4 Your Type," and eat and drink as much as possible according to my blood type. I know this too, has had a positive impact on my body as I continue to "till the field."

I have begun taking a few other basic nutritional supplements manufactured by Mannatech. These products are designed to enable/enhance cellular communication on eight cellular levels. The average "American" diet only engages cellular communication on approximately two levels, resulting in a weaker immune system.

Blood Numbers

Blood Numbers	Sept 13	Sept 20	Sept 28	Normal Range
Red	11.4	12.4	12.4	13.5 – 17.5
White	3,500	3,200	3,000	3,500 – 10,800
Platelets	54,000	52,000	59,000	130,000 – 430,000
Neutrophils	2.0	2.0	2.0	1.9 – 8.0

* Red Cells rising; last transfusion was July 23rd (73 days ago)!
* White Cells slightly under Normal Range
* Platelets rising; last transfusion was August 10th (55 days ago)!
* Neutrophils within Normal Range!
* Tubes of Blood Drawn since Illness: 187

The percentages (quality) of my primary white cells have stabilized nicely and are right in the middle of the normal range!

Date	Sept 13	Sept 20	Sept 28	Normal Range
Neutrophils	58.1%	61.0%	66.1%	45 – 76%
Lymphocytes	33.3%	32.0%	25.4%	15 – 43%
Monocytes	8.6%	7.0%	8.5%	0 – 10%

I will never forget the numbers in May! The neutrophils percentage was 7.4% and the lymphocyte percentage was 83.4%. What a miraculous turnaround! No treatment! No transplant! Just a miracle!

Weight Numbers

Daily range 156-158 lbs. Steady. No fluctuation.

Eyes

Almost perfect; very little blind spots remain. Vision 20/20!

Closing Verses

"Whosoever will call on the name of the Lord will be saved."
(Romans 10:13)

"And we know that God causes all things to work together for good to those who love God, and to those who are called according to His purpose."
(Romans 8:28)

"For there is one God, and one mediator also between God and men, the man Christ Jesus." (1 Timothy 2:5)

"How will we escape if we neglect so great a salvation?" (Hebrews 2:3)

==

Jeff Scislow

October 20, 2001

"This is the day which the Lord has made. Let us rejoice and be glad in it!" (Psalm 118:24)

I am confident that my full, complete and miraculous restoration to health will soon arrive. It's almost here! In this update I will share with you what I believe is the missing component to receiving *"perfect health in the presence of you all."*

I am getting somewhat anxious to return to the doctors and nurses who took care of me while in the hospital and clinics to show myself as a perfectly healed man! I look forward to handing each of them a copy of the letter I wrote back in April while in the hospital which explains how, on the basis of faith, the Lord healed me. Along with this letter, I will provide them with a perfect CBC blood test to prove my perfect health and as a testimony that God heals today!

I feel as if I could go today since I feel perfect, but the numbers need to be perfect for my visit to have the proper impact. The time is near—hallelujah!

A Powerful Cold Attacks

In my previous email I shared with you that my body was under attack from the common cold. It began with a raw, scratchy throat for a couple days and then the virus lodged itself in my vocal cords causing laryngitis for a few more days. From there, the cold expanded into my head and upper chest area. This particular strain of cold ran its course through my body in just over a week. I have heard from others that they have been battling this same viral strain for well over a month!

On the third day after the onset of this cold, I had a scheduled blood test at the clinic. My white count had risen to 6000, exactly double from the previous week. The neutrophils more than doubled to a

241

count of 4.1! This rapid increase in the numbers proves that once my body came under pressure, the marrow went to work and kicked out white cells to fight and kill off the cold virus! Many of us would take something as automatic as this for granted, but having been without an immune system, I can assure you just how precious these numbers are.

I took no medication or antibiotics. My system worked efficiently and effectively all on its own! Although a cough developed in my chest area, I made two separate trips to the clinic to ensure that pneumonia was not developing. On both visits the doctor indicated that my lungs sounded clear. Today the cough is gone and I feel great!

Without the Lord's protection (cocoon/bubble) over the past six months—such as those times when all my children were home sick—this type of viral attack could have killed me. The low white counts not only made me more susceptible to contracting a cold or flu, but would not have been sufficient to fight off any viral attack were I to have encountered one. Amazing isn't it? God is perfectly awesome!

How the Marrow Works

Bone marrow is an amazing component of the human body. It represents the inner most part of human physiology. It is the factory of "life blood." It produces the three major components of blood which are essential for life.

The hemoglobin (red cells) carries oxygen to the various parts of the body. Without oxygen, no bodily functions can operate. The platelets enable the blood to stay where it is supposed to stay—inside the blood vessels. Without platelets, one would bleed to death—not only as a result of an external cut, but also internally, as the blood would seep out of the vessels as a result of any type of bump or bruise.

The white cells are the defenders of the human system. They protect us from foreign invaders that would attack and kill off cells in our body—cells that are necessary to function and sustain life. They also protect us from the growth of unhealthy cells, such as cancer, which can overcome healthy cells and cause death.

When functioning properly, the marrow produces the appropriate amounts of each of these three major blood components. The moment a person is exposed to a virus or bacteria, the marrow receives a signal and immediately begins producing increased amounts of white cells to fight against the invading germs. Likewise, when a person gets an external cut or an internal bump or bruise, the marrow immediately begins producing additional platelets which are dispatched to the damaged area of the body to stop the bleeding.

White cells and platelets can be produced very quickly when the body comes under attack from a germ or in response to a cut or damaged blood vessel. This in turn can result in a rapid increase to the white cell or platelet counts. This additional "production" is on top of the regular production, which is ongoing for the replacement of dying blood cells in the body. The life span for white cells is typically just a few days, while the platelets live 4 to 9 days and hemoglobin cells live up to 120 days.

While the changes to the "counts" of white cells and platelets can occur rapidly, the same is not typically true for red, or hemoglobin cells. The counts of these cells change more gradually, primarily due to the fact that they last so much longer in the system once they have been produced.

Where am I going with this explanation?

In an attempt to understand why my platelet and hemoglobin counts have stabilized *below* the normal levels, I needed to understand more about how the marrow worked. Marrow works in response to the demand, or "tax" on the body. When white cells are needed to fight a foreign invader, the marrow produces more white cells. When platelets are needed to repair a cut or bruise, the marrow produces more platelets. Likewise, when hemoglobin is needed to supply more oxygen to the body, the marrow produces more hemoglobin.

Since the Lord has put "fresh healthy marrow" back in my bones, my body has only had one "fire call"—the viral cold I just experienced. This event caused the marrow to do its job perfectly! On the other hand, there has *not* been a "tax" on my body with respect to a cut or bruise (platelets), or for additional oxygen (hemoglobin). As a result, my body has not told the marrow to produce more than what is necessary. This was my hunch as to why my levels had stopped rising and stabilized a bit short of normal ranges. But now I needed to confirm my hunch by performing a little test.

My Part—His Part

Once again, I recalled what the Lord told me back on May 13th, and I continue to be amazed at the significance of it: *"A farmer does not plant a seed in the field until he tills it, readies it and takes care of the field. You do likewise with your body, and I will plant the seed of marrow and it will grow 100-fold."*

As I thought more about this, I realized that the farmer does not simply ready the soil, he also takes care of it until harvest time! He tills, plants, waters, fertilizes and continues to tend to the field until the crop grows to its fullness. I thought I had already done all the right stuff, but I began to sense that I was missing a very important component of this process. I was eating properly, getting plenty of rest, but I was not exercising!

Exercise, of course! This made perfect sense now. If I were to exercise, I would be "taxing" my body and putting a demand on my marrow to produce more hemoglobin to carry the needed oxygen to my muscles and organs.

I was anxious to run this "idea" past any of the doctors at the clinic. On my next visit, I found one and asked whether exercise would increase the hemoglobin levels in my blood. After acting surprised and saying, "You don't exercise?" he went on to say, "Not only will exercise increase your hemoglobin levels, but it will also increase your platelet levels." I felt like informing this doctor how I was previously instructed not to exercise, but felt it did not matter now. What I just heard was awesome news! There it was! The missing component!

Then this dawned on me: What have we heard since childhood? To be healthy we need to eat right, get plenty of rest and exercise regularly! This is exactly what the Lord was saying when He said to "take care of your body like the farmer takes care of the field...." In other words, *"You do the part that only you can do, and I will do the part that only I can do!"*

At the Y-M-C-A!

Still enthused by what the doctor said about exercise being able to boost my stagnant blood levels, I went down and purchased a family membership at the YMCA. I have been going regularly over the past week. I cannot tell you how "out of shape" my muscles had become, not having exercised at all this year. My body had felt fine sitting in a chair at the office, talking on the phone or getting in and out of the car. But lifting weights and jogging again—wow! My body was definitely being "taxed!"

I am excited to tell you that I jogged *one mile* without stopping yesterday! This was a great accomplishment for me, even though it took over 9 minutes. I plan to gradually increase the frequency and intensity of the workouts. It has been painful, but I need to press on and push my blood levels to "perfectly normal" so that I can go forth and share this incredible miracle with the doctors and nurses and, of course, each of you! God has a plan for my perfect health and it shall be fulfilled according to Acts 3:16. I must continue to do my part and not give up or settle for less!

Blood Numbers

Blood Numbers	Sept 20	Sept 28	Oct 5	Oct 12	Normal Range
Red	12.4	12.4	12.4	12.2	13.5 – 17.5
White	3,200	3,000	6,000	4,500	3,500 – 10,800
Platelets	52,000	59,000	56,000	65,000	130,000 – 430,000
Neutrophils	2.0	2.0	4.1	3.4	1.9 – 8.0

* Red Cells stable; last transfusion July 23rd (almost 3 months ago)!
* White Cells within Normal Range!
* Platelets stable; last transfusion August 10th (over 2 months ago)!
* Neutrophils within Normal Range!
* Tubes of Blood Drawn since Illness: 189

Below are the percentages (quality) of my primary white cells. All are in the normal range, with the neutrophils on the high end of normal as they increased to fight the recent viral cold. All look great!

White Cell Percentages	Sept 20	Sept 28	Oct 5	Oct 12	Normal Range
Neutrophils	61.0%	66.1%	68.0%	75.7%	45 – 76%
Lymphocytes	32.0%	25.4%	28.0%	17.2%	15 – 43%
Monocytes	7.0%	8.5%	4.0%	7.1%	0 – 10%

Weight & Eyes

Weight: 156-158 lbs.
Eyes: Almost perfect. Vision 20/20.

Closing Verses

"For God so loved the world, that He gave His only begotten Son, that whoever believes in Him shall not perish, but have eternal life." (John 3:16)

"Jesus said to her, 'I am the resurrection and the life; he who believes in Me shall live even if he dies.'" (John 11:25)

"How will we escape if we neglect so great a salvation?" (Hebrews 2:3)

==

Blessings!

Jeff Scislow

November 21, 2001

Happy Thanksgiving! Time has sure flown by since my last email to you one month ago. Here in Minnesota we have been enjoying the most spectacular November in history, with temperatures in the 60's and 70's for most of the month so far. Normally, during this time of year our highs are in the lower 40's.

More great news will follow in this email update as I continually thank the Lord for what He has done and for what He is planning to do!

Pump it Up!

In the last email update I described how my white blood count had doubled as a result of my body needing to fight off a cold virus. I explained that when my body was being tested, the marrow rose to the occasion by producing more white cells to combat the attacking virus. The new marrow proved to work just fine.

I also commented on the fact that my platelet and hemoglobin counts had stopped rising and stabilized below normal levels. I went on to say I had a hunch that my body needed to be "taxed" in order for the marrow to produce higher levels of platelets and hemoglobin. I can now report that my hunch proved to be correct!

By moderately exercising a few times per week, I have seen a dramatic rise in the hemoglobin count! The count, which had stabilized around 12.2, jumped to 13.9 after two weeks of exercise and then to 14.2 after another two weeks! The normal range for an adult male is 13.5 to 17.5. So the hemoglobin has reached NORMAL!

Likewise, the platelets began moving upward as a result of the exercise. They rose from 65,000 to 80,000 over a four-week period. I fully expect them to continue to rise to the normal range of 130,000-430,000. They are currently at their highest level since the marrow was destroyed back in April!

I still recall some of the interesting comments my doctor made during our August 16th appointment: "When you have aplastic anemia, you will need a bone marrow transplant to rid yourself of the disease, otherwise you will always have the disease and your blood numbers will never go back to normal." My response to him was, "I don't have it anymore; I have been healed and my numbers are going back to normal!"

On that day when I spoke those words to him, my hemoglobin was 10.4, my white count was 1900, and my platelet count was 26,000. Today, those numbers have risen to 14.2, 5200 and 80,000, respectively!

Although I have not spoken to my doctor since late September, he has to be amazed at my blood tests! I know he sees them, as each test result is faxed to his clinic in St. Paul. The counts keep increasing; how can he explain that? I know he can't. That might be the reason I have not heard from him. I wonder if he ever asks himself, "Who is that guy who says, 'I don't have it anymore; I have been healed and my numbers are going back to normal?'"

Restoring and Strengthening

Two days before I was admitted to the hospital, the Lord showed me 1 Peter 5:10 by way of a television program at 4:00 a.m. in the morning. The verse says, *"After you have suffered a little while, the God of all grace, who called you to His eternal glory in Christ, shall Himself, restore, strengthen, perfect, establish and confirm you."*

I've continued to ponder this verse. I believe that God is going to fulfill this verse in my life—point by point. There are five specific things that the Lord says He will do. I truly see the first two happening today and the other three just around the corner.

The first is *restoration*. God is restoring my health! Day by day the evidence is appearing in my blood tests. I am being restored from the man who was given no hope. I was described as, "The man who got hit by lightning," the one "who had an unfortunate case of bad luck," and was told, "we're sorry; there is nothing we can do, there is no cure and you will likely die." In the midst of those dark days, God protected me and has now restored me!

Secondly, He promised to *strengthen* me. A good example of this deals with exercise. Three months ago, I could not jog a single block due to excruciating pain in my legs from the lack of oxygen available to my muscles. Earlier this week I ran a 6:40 mile!

> Three months ago, I could not jog a
> single block due to excruciating pain in my
> legs from lack of oxygen getting to my muscles.
> Earlier this week I ran a 6:40 mile!

I feel S-T-R-O-N-G-E-R by the day and again, I thank God for His promise to strengthen me!

Thirdly, He will *perfect* me. In Acts 3:16 God promised to give me perfect health in the presence of you all. He even told me to write a letter to the hospital staff while I was "without hope", as a testimony and explanation of the miracle they would witness in me. In addition, back in May He told me to tell everyone everything; that He would show Himself strong through me before the eyes of many people. Once again, God is acting on His Word!

Fourth, He will *establish* me. I believe that God is preparing a ministry for me and He will establish me in it. This will occur at the right time and place.

Fifth, God plans to *confirm* me. I will be the confirmation of what God can and will do in the lives of those who believe! No one will be able to refute what God miraculously did in my life; as I am a confirmation, proof and testament to His love and power.

An Onslaught of Fear

It's quite amazing how the enemy constantly seeks out ways to attack us. He looks for any weak spot or circumstance to make inroads into our lives—with one purpose: to steal, kill and destroy.

Allow me to share five circumstances which the devil used as weapons to mount an all-out attack on me just a couple of weeks ago, and what I did to maintain victory over him. The attack had been building, but came altogether in full force on a particular Monday evening.

Circumstance one: Three nights earlier I had received a call from a person in one of my small groups who informed me that a close friend was not expected to live through the night. He had been diagnosed with aplastic anemia and it was about to overcome him. I was told that this man was seemingly doing alright, but then all of a sudden his white blood counts fell. He then contracted pneumonia and has been unable to fight it off. On Sunday, I learned from my small group friend that this person had, in fact, died over the weekend.

Circumstance two: A few days earlier (prior to Monday evening) I ran across one of my neighbors who happens to be in the medical field. I had previous discussions with him about my health, faith and miraculous progress. And even though I presented a convincing case, he remained somewhat skeptical. This day was no different. After I mentioned that all my blood levels were rising, he stated that "the hemoglobin and platelets really don't matter; it is the white count that is most critical to your health. That is usually what falls and causes those with aplastic anemia to die." This is exactly how the man in circumstance one died.

Circumstance three: After my bout with a cold in October, my white count dropped back down to 3000 after rising to 6000. I was not only discouraged that the count had fallen all the way down to 3000, but that it was no longer in the normal range. The enemy continues to bombard me with fearful thoughts of my "white count falling to dangerously low levels again, at any time and without warning."

Circumstance four: I had been watching and waiting for a small scab on my body to heal while these other things were going on. Instead of healing in five to seven days (what I would consider normal), it was taking a couple weeks. Did the white count of 3000 result in the scab's longer healing process? Possibly. As minor as this may seem, it was just another issue that the enemy was using as he launched his assault, telling me my white count was not good enough to keep me healthy.

Circumstance five: In the early afternoon on this particular Monday, I began to develop a runny nose and a very raspy throat. By the time evening arrived I was finding it harder and harder to swallow. I knew it was the onset of a nasty cold.

By bedtime I was physically uncomfortable. I felt terrible. More importantly however, I was extremely discouraged that I was being hit by another cold, as I just got over one a few weeks earlier. This too, became a weapon of the enemy—taunting me that my immune system could not even protect me from getting another cold! I tried to sleep, but could not.

The assault mounted! The devil was throwing every spiritual weapon of fear and doubt at me! Those little voices would not let up, as they hammered and hammered on me: "There is no cure for aplastic anemia!" "Didn't the doctors tell you that!" "You're going to die, just like that person last Friday night!" "Your immune system is not working!" "Your nose is running from an infection in your throat." "Your white counts are falling, that's why that little scab won't heal!" "It's not a cold, you have pneumonia!" "Your body cannot fight it, it's too weak!" "The signs are clear all around you—why don't you accept it?" "Give up, you've lost the battle!" "You're going to die!"

Just before midnight my wife and I prayed for protection from all this negative chatter. I then tried to sleep, but the attack continued and began to escalate. I countered the attack by speaking Scripture verses out loud, over and over again; for *the sword of the Spirit is the Word of God.* I was in a major spiritual battle. I would not succumb to fear. I stood my ground by using God's Word, and then concluded by saying, "Greater is He who is in me that *you* who are in the world. Satan, you're the loser; you have lost this battle from the beginning; and you're even more of a loser because you don't see it; take your lies and leave in Jesus' name!"

I remember this battle going on until at least 3:30 a.m. From there I slept restlessly off and on for a few hours, but was up again around 6:30 a.m. Needless to say, I got very little sleep that night.

By morning things were much better. The onslaught of fear that tried to overpower me had subsided and the attack was over. Victory was mine! Even now it is hard to explain it all. I can say this for sure— Satan used a number of specific and related circumstances and threw them at me like flaming missiles, one after another, for hours while I was tired, weak and trying to sleep.

Perhaps that was part of the enemy's goal line defense that I needed to break through in order to score my touchdown. I never had an attack like that while in the hospital—and I was there for 28 days! But the victory was mine in the end, through the Word of God, which *is* the Sword of the Spirit!

253

Another Cold Put to Rest

This particular cold that came rushing on Monday night, along with all the flaming missiles of the evil one, did not last as long as the previous one. It hung around for about five days. Whether it was a weaker viral strain than the one I dealt with a few weeks earlier, or whether my immune system simply worked better and quicker, I really don't know. Since I have a choice, I will believe the latter—that my immune system is better than ever!

Group Testimony

I was blessed on November 18th to be able to share some of the miraculous details of what the Lord has done in front of a group of over 500 at Hosanna, my church in Lakeville, Minnesota. This was the first time I had the opportunity to give this marvelous testimony in front of such a large group. I am always willing to share this story, so if your church or organization wishes to hear it, I will do all I can to accommodate your invitation.

So Very Close

I know that I am about to see my blood numbers reach the point where I will return to the hospital to visit the doctors and nurses who initially cared for me. I look forward to giving them the letter I wrote in April and showing them the evidence of my "perfect health" in the presence of them all!

Blood Numbers

Blood Numbers	Oct 5	Oct 12	Oct 26	Nov 9	Normal Range
Red	12.4	12.2	13.9	14.2	13.5 – 17.5
White	6,000	4,500	3,000	5,200	3,500 – 10,800
Platelets	56,000	65,000	75,000	80,000	130,000 – 430,000
Neutrophils	4.1	3.4	1.7	3.5	1.9 – 8.0

* Red Cells stable; last transfusion was July 23rd (3 ½ months ago)!
* White Cells within Normal Range!
* Platelets rising; last transfusion was August 10th (3 months ago)!
* Neutrophils within Normal Range!
* Tubes of Blood Drawn since Illness: 191

Below are the primary white cell percentages (quality) of my immune system. All are within the normal range!

White Cell Percentages	Oct 5	Oct 12	Oct 26	Nov 9	Normal Range
Neutrophils	68.0%	75.7%	56.0%	68.0%	45 – 76%
Lymphocytes	28.0%	17.2%	31.0%	23.0%	15 – 43%
Monocytes	4.0%	7.1%	9.0%	2.0%	0 – 10%

Weight & Eyes

Weight: 155 – 156 lbs.
Eyes: Perfect 20/20 vision.

Closing Verses

"...God is opposed to the proud, but gives grace to the humble. Submit therefore to God. Resist the devil and he will flee from you. Draw near to God and He will draw near to you... Humble yourselves in the presence of the Lord, and He will exalt you." (James 4:6-10)

"You search the Scriptures, because you think that in them you have eternal life; it is these that testify about Me; and you are unwilling to come to Me so that you may have life." (John 5:39-40)

"Trust in the Lord with all your heart and do not lean on your own understanding. In all your ways acknowledge Him, and He will make your paths straight." (Proverbs 3:5-6)

"How will we escape if we neglect so great a salvation?" (Hebrews 2:3)

==

Be Blessed!

Jeff Scislow

December 12, 2001

As 2001 comes to a close in just a couple weeks, it will go down as a spectacular year; perhaps my best ever! Oddly enough, it began with a long string of unfortunate circumstances that never seemed to end. But looking back now, it is clear to see why I needed those experiences. Not only was my faith being tested, but my spiritual strength was being built up, so that I had the "endurance" to get through the most challenging battle ever—the one for my life!

If you've stuck with me this far through my journey—all those blood numbers, percentages and various reports from the doctors—I commend you; there is a lot to it. Each test and set of numbers was critically important to me, as I watched, waited and expected a miraculous improvement. Over the past year I have learned more about blood, health, herbs and healing than I could have ever imagined. Maybe after reading all my email updates you feel the same too!

Before I update you on some more exciting news and on my trip back to the hospital to deliver "the letter" to the doctors and nurses, I want to take a moment to thank each of you. Over these past months you have allowed me to share my life with you and to open up and let you know what was going on in my mind and my heart. It was not always easy to do, especially at first, but I always knew you were there; listening to me, encouraging me and praying for me.

Although I have never told you this before, I don't believe I could have made it without you. Just knowing you were out there, thousands of you, most of whom I have never met, gave me additional strength to forge ahead in my darkest hour. Yes, the Lord my God performed the miracle. He gave me the strength I needed and built me up when I was down, but you too were there for me each step along the way.

Your letters, cards and emails always showed your support, concern and love. Every time I heard one of you say you loved getting my emails, you were praying for me, or you had added me to a prayer chain, it touched my heart, fueled me and empowered me to cross over that goal line. Even though I was the one carrying the ball; the one who scored this time, we did it as a team. We scored the touchdown together! We are all winners and we all get to celebrate the victory!

Never forget the significance of encouragement. The impact it can have in another person's life is incredible. A kind word here and a supportive comment there will inspire others to reach beyond all their preconceived limitations. Keep believing in others and make sure they know you believe in them. Don't think these things don't matter, they do. I am living proof of that. From the bottom of my heart, thank you.

The Letter was Delivered!

I have waited a long time to deliver the letter that I wrote in the late hours of the night on April 14, 2001, from my hospital bed. This letter entitled, *"I've Been Miraculously Healed,"* was written for the doctors and nurses who cared for me while I was in the hospital. The Lord impressed upon me to write it at that time, explaining how I was miraculously healed and to deliver it when my health was restored. Being that "medical science" may have a difficult time explaining how an aplastic anemia patient returned to perfect health without a bone marrow transplant and without having any marrow or stem cells in their body, a letter explaining how the Lord did it miraculously was appropriate.

As a result of my platelet counts soaring to 110,000 on the December 7th test, I felt now was the time to deliver the letter and show myself to the doctors and nurses as the restored and strengthened man who has been granted "this perfect health in the presence of you all!"

"I've Been Miraculously Healed!"

On December 10th, with a stack of "letters" in hand, I made my way first to United Hospital. I experienced the most incredible emotions as I walked into the oncology ward, past the nurses' stand and toward Room 4526; the room that had been my home for much of the month of April. I stopped outside the door to the room and, in my mind, briefly returned to this most interesting chapter in my life.

I saw the layout of the room and in it the faces of many visitors. I saw all those "get well" cards and balloons that lined the ledge in front of the window. In the bathroom, next to the sink was my "feather-like" toothbrush carefully sitting in the disinfected cup. I saw the walk-in shower that I waddled into each day as I pulled that silly apparatus-on-wheels alongside of me. It had held the bags of blood, saline and antibiotics that were connected to my right arm through needles and IVs twenty-four hours a day. I remembered wrapping my arm each day in plastic cellophane before making my way to the shower in order to protect all those needles.

I saw the bed, the lights—both on and off—and the ink marker board with all my Bible verses on it. How could I forget the blood cart alongside my bed, I saw it quite vividly. I even caught a glimpse of me doing a market evaluation on my laptop while sitting up in bed.

All this took just a few seconds, but the memories will last a lifetime. I realized then, more than ever, just how blessed I was not to be in that room any longer and that I was, in fact, a walking miracle.

I returned to the nurse's stand and recognized two of the nurses who had cared for me. At first they did not recognize me, being that they had not seen me since early May. After informing them of who I was, they responded, "Oh my gosh! You look great! Did you get a bone marrow transplant?" "No," I replied, "do you remember what I said—that the Lord was going to heal me miraculously? Well, He did it! No transplant! No medical explanation!" They were amazed and somewhat puzzled at the same time, but shared in my excitement.

I began to tell them about the letter I had for them; how I had written it back in April from Room 4526. At this point these two nurses became speechless. I left them a number of copies of the letter and asked them to circulate it among the staff, the patients and especially the doctors. They agreed. I trust this most interesting letter will impact them all in a very positive way.

I had really hoped to see my doctor, the oncologist who cared for me while I was at United. My last visit with him face-to-face was back on August 16th. I knew it would be good for him to see me, but it was not meant to be. I left him the book, "Healing Prayer," by Dr. Reginald Cherry, M.D. that I had purchased for him. I trust that book will be a blessing in his life.

From the hospital I headed to the clinic where I had been an outpatient for over three months. It was there that I had received all my blood transfusions since being sent home from the hospital. In like fashion, I visited with a couple of the nurses that had cared for me. They, too, were surprised, even thrilled. After visiting for at least an hour, I once again left a large stack of "letters" as a testimony of the miracle that God had performed in me.

A Final Word

Before beginning my email communication with you, the Lord told me to tell everyone, everything. I was told to open up and share the detailed events as they happened, as well as describe certain events that had not yet occurred. I have done that.

At the time I began writing to you, the Lord spoke something very profound to me. In fact those words are more profound today than they were back then. I shared those words with you then, and in conclusion, with joy in my heart and tears in my eyes, I wish to share them with you once again:

> *"I am going to show Myself strong through you before the eyes of many people."*

Blessings,

Jeff Scislow

Where Am I Now?

Epilogue

It has been seven years since my encounter and victory over aplastic anemia. Outside of a minor cold once a year, I have remained in perfect health. The disease was defeated and shall never return. This is a continual and on-going promise for me. As a result, I do not think or worry about it coming back, as some medical professionals would have me think. Do you remember what we are supposed to do with those kinds of negative thoughts? *"Take them captive to the obedience of Christ,"* and speak God's Word, His promises out loud!

As I look back over those critical months of my life, I appreciate the significance of recognizing those very special messages that the Lord gave me. The promises of my being healed. He always gave me what I needed; at the time I needed it, so that I remained strong no matter what the circumstances. Allow me to review these significant moments of importance and promise.

Personal Promises of Healing

"The Lord is preparing you for difficult times that lie ahead." These are the words the Lord spoke to me through Pastor Dave Housholder in November of 2000. Although these words were not very encouraging at the time, they were the answer to my question: "Why are so many strange and unusual things continuing to happen to me?" The answer itself was powerful. If the Lord is preparing me for difficult times, then He not only intended for me to be prepared for them, but to endure and have victory over them as well. Once I understood this, my faith and determination were taken to a whole new level.

"After you have suffered a little while, the God of all grace, who called you to His eternal glory in Christ, shall Himself restore, strengthen, perfect, establish and confirm you." This was the verse I saw at 4:00 a.m. just two days before being admitted to the hospital. This verse carries a very personal message in regards to what I was about to go through;

265

a challenging time, but with a promise of victory at the end. The Lord made sure I saw this verse by having me up in the early morning, at the exact time, on the exact day, on just the right channel!

When Pastor Pat Moe expressed to me how she had seen Gabriel the angel standing outside my hospital room door, I was ecstatic! I immediately responded to her by quoting Psalm 34:7 out loud, *"The angel of the Lord encamps around those who fear Him, and rescues them,"* and continued, "I am going to be rescued!" Again, the Lord gave me a sign of His hand being upon me in the midst of a terrible time. I did not blow this off as some imaginary vision that someone had seen, but received it for exactly what it was; a promise that the Lord would rescue me from whatever I was about to encounter.

The day after receiving the deadly diagnosis, I happened to read Acts 3:16 which says, *"On the basis of faith in His name, it is the name of Jesus which has strengthened this man whom you see and know; and the faith which comes through Him has given him this perfect health in the presence of you all."* I immediately received this verse into my heart, taking ownership of it as I spoke out, "That's going to be me; that verse is talking about me!" Instantly the Lord responded to my spirit saying, *"That's the verse you're going to share with everyone on the day you're made whole."* Once again, God was telling me I would be restored to perfect health as a result of my faith in Jesus.

From here God began to educate me more with His Word and through the use of other believers in order that I gain a greater understanding of His principles of healing. He used a past client, who led me to Pastor Holmes who prayed for me; resulting in a healing from internal bleeding. The principle of sowing and reaping was put to the test. Upon passing that test a message was delivered to me by a man named Paul; *"tell Jeff he is healed."* When I failed to understand the significance of those words, God sent my friend with a taped message from Chip Brim that opened my eyes to what those words meant. In the midst of these events the Lord told me to *"write a letter"* to the hospital staff; telling them in advance of my physical healing and how it was that it came about.

Next God began to work on my heart so that nothing would hinder my prayers, nor impede the miracle that I sought. He helped me to see things in my life that I was unaware of, but things that needed to be taken care of in order to receive the miracle I so desperately needed.

As I received all these signs and words of promise, I continued to gain strength in the midst of the most bizarre time of my life; not physical strength, but spiritual strength. I maintained a child-like faith, knowing that God was with me and would never leave me or forsake me. (Hebrews 13:5)

When released from the hospital, I was sent home with no hope. I was told to stay away from my kids, not to kiss my wife, to get rid of my pets and not to go out in public. During the first week out of the hospital the Lord sent one of my rental tenants to me. That visit resulted in me changing my diet. I also began to take herbal supplements. The Lord then confirmed my actions by saying, *"A farmer does not plant a seed in the field until he tills it, readies it and takes care of the field. You do likewise with your body, and I will plant the seed of marrow and it will grow 100-fold."* Here again, God was promising to perfectly restore my health as He continued to *"supply all my needs according to His riches in glory in Christ Jesus."* (Philippians 4:19)

The final promise of a complete healing came from my incredible encounter with evangelist John Kittleson on August 3, 2001. Through John, the Lord delivered this powerful message to me: *"A curse has come against your bone marrow from four generations ago, and I am breaking it now, and filling your bones with fresh, clean, healthy marrow!"* Once again, I received the promise of complete healing; *filling* my bones meant "100 percent complete"!

I know as a fact, through both faith and experience, that no matter what our challenges in life may be, God wants to see us through; He wants us to have a successful outcome. In Joshua 1:7 we are told, *"...be strong and very courageous; be careful to do according to all the law which Moses My servant commanded you; do not turn from it to the right or to the left, so that you may have success wherever you go."*

The Word makes it clear that it's all up to us. We're given a choice. IF we do all He has asked of us in His Word, THEN we can expect to receive from Him those things He has promised from His Word. It is really that simple. Nothing is impossible for God. We need to know what He says (the Bible), believe in what He says (faith), act upon what He says and be patient for the answer to arrive. It will!

Business Restored

While going through the challenges of 2001 the Lord provided for me and my family. We actually did more real estate business while I was in the hospital and over the few months that followed, than was done the last half of 2000! As I walked out on that branch of faith, going on listing appointments without an immune system, God continued to bless us with fruit from that labor.

The latter half of 2001 yielded a harvest of business. Sales began to roll in one after the other. The Lord restored all that which was lost in 2000 and then some. When I was going through the tsunami of challenges, there was a moment of time when I compared myself to Job. From the actual story of Job, we know the Lord restored him with much more than he had lost. Now, in some respects, I once again felt like Job; as the Lord has restored me bountifully as well.

In February of 2002, I was honored by RE/MAX North Central, with something called the "Spirit Award". It was given to honor me for not only finishing 2001 as the #2 sales agent in Minnesota, but also for the conditions under which I accomplished those results. David Linger, Regional Director, put it this way, "This award is not just an award about 'sales', but about 'attitude'; an attitude of faith, determination and spirit; and in this special case, one that has resulted in a miraculous recovery from an incurable situation." At first, I was not aware he was speaking about me! My name was called and I stepped up to receive the award. Perhaps this was God's way of "confirming" me. Nevertheless, it was a very special time; one that I will never forget.

Jeff Scislow being presented with the 2001 'Spirit Award' by RE/MAX Regional Director, David Linger - February 2002 at the RE/MAX Regional Awards Banquet in Minneapolis, Minnesota

Real estate continues to be a blessing for me and my family. Each year since 2001 has been an excellent one; with 2006 being my best ever, when I completed 283 sales transactions and placed #1 in Minnesota and #10 in the United States.

Ministry

Over the past few years I have regularly taught classes at Celebration, the church I am now attending in Lakeville, Minnesota. The primary objective of my classes has been to strengthen believers in their faith walk and to encourage them to utilize their gifts and talents. I challenge my class attendees to examine themselves by asking if they are fulfilling the two primary responsibilities they have as Christians: 1) *Works* as a believer; as we are His workmanship created in Christ for good works; and 2) *Obedience*.

I have regular opportunities to speak and to share my testimony of God's healing power and my "Journey to a Miracle". I enjoy encouraging others and challenging them in their faith. I teach on healing and how God is no respecter of persons. He is able and willing to heal all—and He does so today!

Who was that Man named "John"?

I have often been asked, "Who was that man who prayed for you to break the generational curse?" Interestingly enough, I did not know who he was for over 3 years after the encounter I had with him on August 3, 2001 at North Heights Lutheran Church.

One day I got a "lead" on who he might be. I followed up on it and learned he lived in a small town in Iowa. I found his phone number, called him and had to leave the following message: "Hi John, you don't know me, not really anyway. We've only met very briefly, but I need to tell you something that will bless your socks off! So call me as soon as you can."

When John called me back later that day, I reminded him of what had taken place on that very special day in August of 2001 and the amazing results that followed. After hearing the outcome, John stated that, "Your healing is one of the top three miracles the Lord has worked through me." When I asked him what the others were, he commented the Lord once used him to raise up a man who had been dead several minutes. Nothing is impossible for those who believe!

Over the past few years, John and I have done several healing services together. We would individually teach, and then pray for those that were sick at the end of the service. He is an amazing man.

John Kittleson, known as the 'UPS' Man for the Lord, has been an evangelist for many years. I've asked my friend to comment on the incredible event that took place at North Heights on August 3, 2001. Here are John's comments:

"I've been involved in the 'healing and deliverance' ministry for over 30 years. During this time I have witnessed Jesus' miraculous touch many times. One of the most remarkable miracles that God has done was the deliverance and healing of Jeff Scislow from a fatal bone marrow disease. The Holy Spirit gave me a supernatural revelation of Jeff's condition and I simply obeyed by breaking a genetic curse and commanding the disease to leave in Jesus name and to give Jeff new bone marrow. The Lord honored Jeff's faith and ministry and healed Jeff. All the glory and praise to Jesus, the Healer!"

Why the Delay in Finishing the Book?

I have some thoughts as to why the book has not gotten out until now. The primary reason has to do with the many spiritual attacks that have thwarted various efforts on my part to sit down and complete the last 10% of the book, as 90% of it was written while I was sick! It does take time; and time in many cases is something my own lifestyle tends to use up quickly. It is not that I did not want to take the time, but on numerous occasions there have been events and circumstances that would pop up just as I was preparing to complete the book which truly prevented me from progressing.

An example of this took place as recently as December of 2007, when I traveled to Cancun, Mexico by myself to spend the necessary time to

271

"finish the book". In a fluke accident in the resort's gym, I herniated a disc in my lower back. The pain prevented me from doing any work at all on the book while in Mexico. Upon my return back home I began taking herbs specifically designed for lower back pain/problems and within a month the pain was completely gone! I was once again determined to finish the book.

During the last week of January 2008, I traveled to Hawaii where I was speaking at an annual real estate event. I arrived a day early in order to spend time "finishing this book".

While in the hotel room that overlooked the ocean, I opened up my slider door to the balcony, the fresh air and the sound of the waves below. I began to write some of my final thoughts in this book. Within minutes and to my amazement, a beautiful white dove landed on the railing of my balcony. He watched me as I worked for a moment, and then hopped down onto the balcony floor. The dove then walked into my room and stood in front of me. I reached for my camera to take a picture of this most interesting occurrence, expecting the flash to scare him off, but it did not. In fact I continued to take flash photos of this dove as it watched me and walked around my hotel room! He stayed with me for over a half hour before making his way back to the balcony, up onto the railing and finally flying off again.

Was this some sort of "sign" from God (as the Holy Spirit is depicted as a dove in the New Testament)? I am not certain. It was very inspiring to say the least, not only to me, but to those I have shared the story and photos with. It was as if God inspired me to finish those last parts of the book and showed His approval by sending a dove.

Dove Photos

What's the Doctor Saying Now?

During 2002 I made 8 monthly visits to my local clinic for the purpose of follow up blood testing; January through August. I decided to discontinue the follow up visits after my August appointment and my 200th tube of drawn blood since the onset of these health challenges. My blood counts during this period of time were quite good. Hemoglobin was consistently strong; always well within the normal range. The white count consistently hovered around the low end of the normal range. The platelets on the other hand, after hitting 110,000 in December of 2001, retreated to a below normal range of 65,000 to 85,000. Even though I did not need any transfusions in 2002, I was not satisfied with the low platelet counts and continued to believe they would rise to normal again.

In October of 2003, I had an annual physical which included the standard CBC blood test. The red count was a strong 15.8, the white count was 4200 and the platelet count was 121,000, representing the highest to date. All other aspects of my health were excellent.

In December of 2004, I again had a physical indicating a clean bill of health. My platelets had *finally* reached the "normal" range with a count of 173,000! Persistent faith pays off! These stubborn platelets finally lined up with God's promise!

It took me three more years to get in for another physical. Once again my blood counts were all normal. In December of 2007 my red count was 15.5, the white count was 5300 and those platelets were now 209,000!

To my amazement, I have not seen my oncologist once since my last face-to-face with him on August 16, 2001, nor have I even spoken with him since late September 2001, when we talked on the phone. I have made several attempts to catch him at his clinic with no success. I left him a book entitled, "Healing Prayer" in December of 2001, my testimony on CD in June of 2002 and a nice business article on my success in the real estate industry in the fall of 2007. I have yet to hear from him.

On a positive note, I have visited with several other doctors who work in the local clinics near my home. They have been supportive and certainly surprised and enthused by the miraculous outcome I have had the joy of experiencing.

December 26, 2007 Blood Test Results

Order CBC W/ PLATELETES, DIFF [85025] Order #: 25851522 Spec #: W58662 Class: Normal

Patient Name	**Sex**	**DOB**
Scislow, Jeffrey Floyd (0000018953)	Male	8/1/1956

Results   CBC WITH PLATELETS, DIFF

Result Information

Result Date and Time	Status	Provider Status
12/26/2007 4:04 PM	In process	Ordered

Component Results

Component	Value	Flag	Low	High	Units	Stat
WBC	5.3		4.0	11.0	10e9/L	Fin
RBC	4.47		4.4	5.9	10e12/L	Fin
HGB	15.5		13.3	17.7	g/dL	Fin
Hct	43.6		40.0	53.0	%	Fin
MCV	98		78	100	fl	Fin
MCH	34.7	H	26.5	33.0	pg	Fin
MCHC	35.6		31.5	36.5	g/dL	Fin
RDW	12.7		10.0	15.0	%	Fin
PLT	209		150	450	10e9/L	Fin
Diff Method	Pending					Inc

Nutritional Update

I continue taking Dr. Richard Schulze's SUPERFOOD breakfast drink of herbs, vitamins and minerals each morning. I blend them up in a full pitcher of fruit and serve these outstanding smoothies to my entire family.

Ever since 2001, I have subscribed to the advice of Dr. Peter D'Adamo in his book, "Live Right 4 Your Type." I simply eat and drink according to my blood type (as much as possible). I know this too has had a positive impact on my body as I continue to "take care of the field."

I have begun taking a few other basic nutritional supplements for maintenance and overall health. One such supplement is called Ambrotose and is manufactured by Mannatech. This incredible product is designed to enable/enhance cellular communication on all eight known levels. The average "American" diet (of poor food) only enables (effective) cellular communication on two levels. This typically results in a weaker immune system. When the levels of cellular communication are fully utilized and functioning properly, the body does what it is supposed to do by way of protecting itself from germs and other invaders.

It is much easier to remain healthy by taking care of the body with a proper diet, restful sleep and exercise, than it is to nurse a sick body back to health. With that in mind, I ensure I do all I can to maintain this perfect health in the presence of you all!

For Jeff Scislow, maintaining good health includes training and running periodic races. In 2002 he was one of the top finishers for his age in a local community "2 mile run".

Closing Thoughts

Thank you so much for allowing me to share this chapter of my life with you. I encourage you to make the most of your life, your health and your relationships. Most of all, I encourage you to strengthen your relationship with God the Father, through His Son Jesus Christ. Without *that* relationship in place, nothing else matters at the end of the day.

His love for you is no different than His love for me, as He is not a respecter of persons. He plays no favorites. Jesus is the same yesterday, today, forever. If you abide in Him and His words abide in you, then you can ask anything, and He will do it for you! He is the Way, the Truth and the Life; no one comes to the Father, but through Him. How will we escape if we neglect so great a salvation?

Appendix

Beyond Belief

Secrets of Healing

Are you sick? Is there someone you know, someone you love, that is sick or battling a physical or emotional challenge at this time?

In this segment I wish to point out some of the important principles that will pave the way for you to be healed. I know that God is able and willing to heal you. If He healed one, He will heal all; for He is no respecter of persons.

There are "hindrances" however to receiving what God wants to bless us with. He is a sovereign God and the Bible is filled with "IF's" and "THEN's". If we do our part, God will do His part. I realize that volumes have been written on this topic and I will not be able to cover every possible "what if" or question that may arise out of my comments here, but I will give you enough information and Scripture to empower you to act and move toward receiving all that God has in store for you!

I share these 'Secrets of Healing' as one with experience. In April of 2001 I was diagnosed with aplastic anemia, an incurable disease whereby my body's own immune system had destroyed all my bone marrow and its related stem cells. My prognosis was death, since there was not a matching marrow donor in the world. Yet without medical explanation, bone marrow miraculously began growing in my body. It was through faith, prayer and persistence that I am fully healed today. See www.acts316.org

The Bible verses that follow prompted me to examine closely all areas of my life before the Lord, to trust Him completely, to stand 100 percent on His Word and to walk totally by faith and not by sight, as I expected a miracle. The Lord honored this and miraculously healed me!

A Fact

"The thief [devil] *comes only to steal and kill and destroy; I came that they may have life, and have it abundantly."* (John 10:10) [Explanation added]

On one hand the devil has a clear mission—one of destruction and of death. Jesus on the other hand offers us freedom, life and victory over our adversary the devil. Jesus is our source for healing.

Obedience

Obedience is an important part of healing, as well as a condition to getting your prayers answered. God cannot bless one who is living in or practicing sin. In 1 John 3:22 it says, *"and whatever we ask we receive from Him, because we keep His commandments and do the things that are pleasing in His sight."*

Another verse from the Old Testament carries the same principle of obedience, as a prerequisite: *"And He said, 'If you will give earnest heed to the voice of the Lord your God, and do what is right in His sight, and give ear to His commandments, and keep all His statutes, I will put none of the diseases on you which I have put on the Egyptians; for I, the Lord, am your healer.'"* (Exodus 15:26)

Unconfessed Sin

If your heart is revealing sin that needs to be confessed, then do it as a prerequisite to expecting your prayers to be answered. *"If we confess our sins, He is faithful and righteous to forgive us our sins and to cleanse us from all unrighteousness."* (1 John 1:9) King David made it quite clear in Psalm 66:18 when he wrote: *"If I regard wickedness in my heart, the Lord will not hear."*

An Unharmonious Relationship

An unharmonious relationship between a husband and a wife will hinder your prayers, as we read in 1 Peter 3:7: *"You husbands in the same way, live with your wives in an understanding way, as with someone weaker, since she is a woman; and show her honor as a fellow heir of the grace of life, so that your prayers will not be hindered."*

Selfishness

Another hindrance to prayer, as we learn from James 4:3: *"You ask and do not receive, because you ask with wrong motives, so that you may spend it on your pleasures."*

Unforgiveness

Unforgiveness is a major challenge for many; it is also a major hindrance to prayer. Many believers do not receive answers to their prayers because somewhere along the line they have wronged someone, or they have been wronged by someone and have failed to humble themselves and seek reconciliation. Jesus taught the Sermon on the Mount in part with these words: *"Therefore, if you are presenting your offering at the altar, and there remember that your brother has something against you, leave your offering there before the altar and go; first be reconciled to your brother, and then come and present your offering."* (Matt 5:23-24)

Again, later on in the same teaching Jesus states: *"For if you forgive others for their transgressions, your heavenly Father will also forgive you. But if you do not forgive others, then your Father will not forgive your transgressions."* (Matt 6:14-15) Unforgiveness in our hearts creates a division in our relationship with God.

Unbelief

Many are troubled by unbelief. Doubt, fear and worry seem to creep in and take over where faith should be abounding. Listen to the outcome of unbelief as written in James 1:6-7: *"But he must ask (God) in faith without any doubting, for the one who doubts is like the surf of the sea, driven and tossed by the wind. For that man ought not to expect that he will receive anything from the Lord."*

Self-Examination

The Apostle Paul wrote to the Corinthians pointing out that many of them were weak, sick, and had died because they had not judged themselves correctly. Many of these believers were *not* getting healed of their sickness and disease! They were praying, yet remained sick! God definitely wants to answer all our prayers, but He is bound by His Word. He is the Righteous Judge and is no respecter of persons. *"For there is no partiality with God,"* we're told in Romans 2:11. If we fail to know what God's Word says, so that we know how to live our lives, then we can miss out on some very important aspects of living; including healing. *"My people perish for lack of knowledge...."* (Hosea 4:6)

In Joshua 1:7 we are instructed to, *"Only be strong and very courageous; be careful to do according to all the law which Moses my servant commanded you; do not turn from it to the right or to the left, so that you may have success wherever you go."* By spending time in God's Word we get to know His Word; and through this knowledge of God's Word our *"...senses* [get] *trained to discern good and evil."* (Hebrews 5:14) [Explanation added] As a result, we are able to examine ourselves and our lives, and make corrections along the way. If the believing Corinthians had done this, they might have examined themselves, made adjustments in their lives, and received healing from their sicknesses. *"But if we judged ourselves rightly, we would not be judged."* (1 Corinthians 11:31)

When You Pray, Go to God in Complete Humility

Ask the Holy Spirit to reveal anything in your life that is not pleasing to God. Ask for forgiveness, turn from it (repent), and thank the Lord for His forgiveness. When your heart is pure before God, then you can approach the throne of grace with boldness and receive help from the Lord. Listen to the invitation from Hebrews 4:16: *"Therefore let us draw near with confidence to the throne of grace, so that we may receive mercy and find grace in time of need."* When your heart is pure and cleansed (by God) it is easy to approach the Lord with confidence and to find the help you seek!

Worshipping and Honoring God

Worshipping and honoring God for who He is brings with it many blessings, including healing: *"But you shall serve the Lord your God, and He will bless your bread and your water; and I will remove sickness from your midst... I will fulfill the number of your days."* (Exodus 23:25-26)

Having Faith and Trust in God

Having faith and trust in God will empower His promises to transform your life. One of the most powerful passages for protection comes from Psalm 91: *"A thousand may fall at your side, and ten thousand at your right hand, but it shall not approach you... For you have made the Lord, my refuge, even the Most High, your dwelling place. No evil will befall you, nor will any plague come near your tent... 'Because he has loved Me,' says the Lord, 'therefore I will deliver him; I will set him securely on high, because he has known My name. He will call upon Me, and I will answer him; I will be with him in trouble, I will rescue him and honor him. With a long life will I satisfy him and let him see My salvation'."*

Promises

"Bless the Lord, O my soul, and forget none of His benefits; who pardons all your iniquities, who heals all your diseases; who redeems your life from the pit, who crowns you with loving kindness and compassion." (Psalm 103:2-4) *"Then they cried to the Lord in their trouble, and He saved them from their distresses. He sent His Word and healed them, He delivered them from their destructions."* (Psalm 107:19-20) *"I will not die but live, and will tell of the works of the Lord."* (Psalm 118:17)

Knowing and Standing on God's Word

Knowing and standing on God's Word is not only powerful, it is life itself: *"My son, give attention to My words; incline your ear to My sayings... Do not let them depart from your sight; keep them in the midst of your heart. For they are life to those who find them and health to all their body."* (Proverbs 4:20-22)

It is finished!

Do you believe that health and restoration from your sickness has already occurred? Do you believe that you have been healed, but that the manifestation is all that you are waiting on? I believe our healing is *done*. If our hearts are right before God and we ask in faith, I believe we tap into that healing power; the healing that took place over 2000 years ago when Jesus paid the price for our sins and our sicknesses. What do *you* think?

From Isaiah we read: *"But He was pierced through for our transgressions, He was crushed for our iniquities; the chastening for our well-being fell upon Him, and by His scourging we are healed."* (Isaiah 53:5) We *are* healed! It is an absolute! The Word does not say we *will be* or *may be* healed. It is a finished work. Many may struggle with this, but if I am any testimony to your struggle, simply believe it by seeing what God has done in me and become *"... imitators of those who through faith and patience inherit the promises."* (Hebrews 6:12) Imitate Daniel as he prayed, fasted, expected, and persevered until he received! (Daniel 10) God cannot "not do" what His Word says "He will do." God says: *"...I am watching over My word to perform it."* (Jeremiah 1:12) When we believe in God's Word and don't give up He will bring it to pass!

Move Your Mountain

Jesus said: *"Truly I tell you, if you have faith and do not doubt... you can say to this mountain* [of sickness, or whatever], *'Be taken up and cast into the sea,' and it will happen."* (Matthew 21:21) [Emphasis added] In the book of Mark this same passage is told with more emphasis: *"And Jesus answered saying to them, 'Have faith in God. Truly I say to you, whoever* [you included] *says to this mountain, 'Be taken up and cast into the sea,' and does not doubt in his heart, but believes that what he says is going to happen, it will be granted him. Therefore I say to you, all things for which you pray and ask, believe that you have received them, and they will be granted you."* (Mark 11:22-24)

The readers of my book have had the privilege of seeing this same "mountain-moving" faith work within me from day one of that life-threatening condition. Not that I have something extra or different— as faith comes from the Lord—but having seen my mountain moved by faith, I want you to realize that this same faith *is available to you.*

"This is the confidence which we have before Him, that, if we ask anything according to His will, He hears us. And if we know that He hears us in whatever we ask, we know that we have the requests which we have asked from Him." (1 John 5:14-15)

Promise upon promise awaits you in the Bible. Remember: *"faith comes from hearing, and hearing by the word of Christ."* (Romans 10:17) The more of the Word we have in our hearts, the stronger our faith.

287

The stronger our faith, the more miracles we will experience. Keep in mind our battle is not against flesh and blood, but against powers, principalities and spiritual wickedness. When I was afflicted with this disease I knew the Word; I had it in my heart. I was armed and ready to do battle. Even so, I went to God's Word more and more and dug in for answers to new perplexing questions that arose out of this trial. I quoted Scripture daily, listened to healing tapes and always thanked the Lord for the expected result as if I had already received it! Even though my healing was not yet evident in the physical realm, I rejoiced, knowing that I was already healed in the spiritual realm. I patiently waited for the physical appearance (manifestation) of healing, knowing that it would come, and it did! God always has more for us, all of us! Take the time and get into the written Word of Him who created you. He is *"... able to do far more abundantly beyond all you ask or think...."* (Ephesians 3:20)

God's Endorsement

I believe that it is God's will to heal everyone. Everyone who came to Jesus for healing—expecting to be healed—was healed. 100% success! Jesus is the same yesterday, today, and forever. He is our Great Physician and can heal in a variety of ways, providing they are in accordance with what He has already declared in His Word.

I believe that we have Christian responsibilities. The choices we make with respect to those responsibilities pave the way for results we see in all areas of our lives, including healing and answered prayer. While I was sick, I personally examined myself and wanted to ensure I did everything I could to receive from the Lord; not wanting anything to hinder my prayers. I received a miracle! As a result, I have made it a point to teach and share with others exactly what I did to receive the miracle. Below, I would like to share a short story that will inspire you and encourage you to seek and believe in a miracle for yourself and for those you love.

In June of 2002, while on a listing appointment with a couple who were moving back to their hometown, Rebecca, the wife, became intrigued with the healing miracle that happened in my life. It was just a month earlier when she heard me speak at church and give the full account of my testimony. Knowing that my talk had been recorded, she asked me for a copy of the CD recording.

On two occasions, during the time it took me to list and sell her home, Rebecca and I spoke intently about what I went through and the supporting Bible verses that I followed during the period of the illness. In fact, we spent nearly three hours discussing God's promises, how I responded to the challenging events and the specific things I did that brought about the miraculous results. Rebecca absorbed all these details with great interest. The real estate market was good. I sold the house quickly, and Rebecca and her husband moved in short order.

In December of that same year, while on vacation, I picked up a voice mail message from Rebecca. When I called her back, she shared the following incredible story with me:

> "Amy is a friend of mine who I have known since childhood. She had been fighting liver and pancreatic cancer for a while. Back in August, the doctors stopped her treatment and she was sent to hospice care. She was given two weeks to live.

> "At that time, the Lord spoke to me audibly." I jumped in and asked, "Audibly?" "Yes, audibly; just like you're hearing me on the phone," Rebecca continued.

> "The Lord said to me, 'Rebecca, I want you to go to Amy and teach her what you learned about healing while you were in Minnesota and give her Jeff's CD.'" I was on the other end of the phone saying, "Oh my gosh, something great has happened!"

Rebecca continued, telling me that she had never experienced anything like this. She informed me she had never witnessed to her friend Amy about the Lord, but since she heard God's audible voice and the fact that Amy had perhaps days to live, she went on her assigned mission to speak to Amy.

Rebecca told me that Amy listened intently to what Rebecca shared with her. Amy listened to the CD. She then asked for a Bible and for healing tapes. She read and she listened. She asked for praise CD's and listened. She wrote out post-it-notes of Bible verses and affirmations of her healing and posted them on the walls. She spoke them out loud daily. She made changes to her diet. She basically duplicated all the activities that I had done while I was sick in 2001.

Rebecca continued on the phone with me saying, "And day by day she gained strength; and now, after four months, there is no more cancer in her body! The doctors cannot explain it, but she is perfectly healthy! I just thought you would like to know."

Beyond Belief? Not to me. I know and have experienced the same power of God's Word and His promises. He has encouraged me to share all that I have learned; and I believe He has endorsed my message of Him, as evidenced in Amy's healing. He is NO respecter of persons, therefore I encourage each of you who are in need of a miracle to, *"be an imitator of those who through faith and patience, inherit the promises."* (Hebrews 6:12)

> *"Be an imitator of those,*
> *who through faith and patience,*
> *inherit the promises"*

28 Verses from the Hospital

Each day while in the hospital from April 7, 2001 through May 4, 2001 (28 days), the Lord put a particular Bible verse in my heart. Each day, I made a point of writing down the verse on the ink marker board on the wall of my room. These verses not only gave *me* strength, but ministered to my visitors and the hospital staff as well. Allow me to share those 28 daily verses with you here, as well as their significance as it applied to me:

Day 1   **James 1:2-4, 9**

"Consider it all joy my brethren, when you encounter various trials, knowing that the testing of your faith produces endurance. And let endurance have its perfect result, that you may be perfect and complete, lacking in nothing... But the brother of humble circumstances is to glory in his high position."

This passage has always given me strength—before, during and after my hospital stay.

Day 2   **1 Peter 5:6-10**

"Therefore Humble yourselves under the mighty hand of God, that He may exalt you at the proper time, casting all your anxiety (cares) upon Him, because He cares for you."

"Be of sober spirit, be on the alert. Your adversary, the devil, prowls about like a roaring lion, seeking someone to devour. But resist him, firm in your faith, knowing that the same experiences of suffering are being accomplished by your brethren who are in the world."

"And after you have suffered for a little while, the God of all grace, who called you to His eternal glory in Christ, shall Himself, restore, strengthen, perfect, establish and confirm you!"

The last passage here—verse 10—is the passage I received while flipping channels on the television at 4 a.m., just two days before being admitted to the hospital. I stood on this promise all the way through my journey; knowing that I would be restored in the end!

Day 3   **Hebrews 4:12**

"For the Word of God is living and active and sharper than any two-edged sword, and piercing as far as the division of soul and spirit, of both joints and marrow, and able to judge the thoughts and intentions of the heart."

The third day in the hospital was the day they performed the bone marrow biopsy; I could not think of a more fitting verse!

Day 4   **Isaiah 54:17**

"No weapon that is formed against you shall prosper... "

No weapon or sickness from the enemy will prosper or be victorious over me! If God said it, then it's settled!

Day 5   **Psalm 34:7, 17, 19**

"The angel of the Lord encamps around those who fear Him, and rescues them."

"The righteous cry, and the Lord hears and delivers them out of all their troubles."

"Many are the afflictions of the righteous, but the Lord delivers him out of them all."

These powerful promises, especially the first one, seemed fitting in that our Prayer/Care Pastor from church had seen the angel Gabriel standing outside my hospital room door!

Day 6   **Jeremiah 29:11**

"'For I know the plans that I have for you,' declares the Lord, 'plans for welfare and not for calamity to give you a future and a hope.'"

At no time did I believe my life would end as a result of this ordeal! Although the doctors, the textbooks and all those Internet write-ups indicated the odds were greatly against me, I knew that if God was for me, WHO could be against me?

Day 7   **Proverbs 4:20-22**

"My son, give attention to My words; incline your ear to My sayings. Do not let them depart from your sight; keep them in the midst of your heart. For they are life to those who find them and health to all their whole body."

I received this promise unto myself! By having the Word of God in my heart, it would result in health to my entire body!

Day 8   **1 Peter 4:12-13**

"Beloved, do not be surprised at the fiery ordeal among you, which comes upon you for your testing, as though some strange thing were happening to you; but to the degree that you share the sufferings of Christ, keep on rejoicing; so that also at the revelation of His glory, you may rejoice with exultation."

I personally could not imagine anything more "strange" than what happened to me! I went from a perfect bill of health in 2000 to a death sentence in 2001. No doctor could explain how or where this killer disease came from, let alone provide any hope for overcoming it. That qualified as "strange" in my book. But through this strange and challenging time, I still rejoiced; knowing that, at the revelation of His glory (my perfect health report), I would rejoice with exultation!

Day 9   **John 15:7-11**

"If you abide in Me, and My words abide in you, ask whatever you wish, and it shall be done for you. My Father is glorified by this, that you bear much fruit, and so prove to be My disciples."

"Just as the Father has loved Me, I have also loved you. Abide in My love. If you keep My commandments, you will abide in My love; just as I have kept My Father's commandments, and abide in His love. These things I have spoken to you, that My joy may be in you, and that your joy may be made full."

If we abide in Christ, He will give us all things that we ask of Him. He does this for three reasons: First and foremost, that His Father be glorified, secondly, that we bear fruit for Him, and thirdly, that we prove to be His disciples (followers). Do we see responsibility here? I do. Only by bearing fruit for Him are we considered one of His disciples. As such, if we ask anything according to His will, He will give it to us, and the outcome is our being FILLED WITH JOY!

Day 10   **1 John 3:22**

"And whatever we ask we receive from Him, because we keep His commandments and do the things that are pleasing in His sight."

This promise is much like the previous one. If we abide in Him (do the things which are pleasing in His sight), then <u>whatever</u> we ask of Him, we will receive from Him. This is what is so incredible about having a relationship with the Creator of the Universe. Our biggest challenge comes from whether or not we desire to 'keep His commandments, and do the things which are pleasing in His sight.' When we make the choice to put our trust in Him and follow in His ways, then the awesome and unlimited promises from above become ours for the asking.

Day 11   **1 John 5:14-15**

"This is the confidence which we have before Him, that, if we ask anything according to His will, He hears us. And if we know that He hears us in whatever we ask, we know that we have the requests which we have asked from Him."

Although this promise is very much like the previous two, we see faith at work here. "If we know that He hears us (by faith), we know that we have the requests which we have asked from Him (by faith)." None of the passages indicate "when" we will receive the answers to our requests, but that we "have" received them when we ask! This is why it is critical when we ask, according to God's will, that we trust Him in delivering the answer *in His perfect timing!* This is where our faith is tested! Will we patiently trust God to answer in His timeframe? In Hebrews, chapter 6, verses 11-15, it says in part, *"show the same diligence so as to realize the full assurance of hope... that you will not be sluggish, but imitators of those who through faith and patience inherit the promises!"* God is rarely early, but He is never late! Wait on the Lord. Trust Him and He will fulfill His promises!

Day 12   **2 Timothy 1:7**

"For God has not given us a spirit of fear, but of love, power and a sound mind."

While in the hospital—as well as today—I have had plenty of opportunities to become fearful. But God empowers believers so that they will not be overcome by fear. He does not give us that kind of spirit. He gives us one of love, power and sound mind. The Bible tells us that the fruit of the Spirit is love, joy, peace, patience, kindness, goodness, faithfulness, gentleness and self-control. Fear is nowhere to be found in God's fruitful Spirit. The "power" part of what God gives us is His promises. When we call on and put our faith in God's promises—WOW! The "POWER" is released in our lives and 'miracles' happen!

Day 13   **Hebrews 6:11-12, 15**

"And we desire that each one of you show the same diligence so as to realize the full assurance of hope until the end, so that you may not be sluggish, but imitators of those who through faith and patience inherit the promises."

"And so, having patiently waited, he (Abraham) obtained the promises."

Several chapters in the book of Hebrews are dedicated to having a strong faith. One such example is chapter 10, beginning at verse 35: *"Therefore, do not throw away your confidence, which has great reward. For you have need of endurance, so that when you have done the will of God, you may receive what was promised... 'But My righteous one shall live by faith; and if he shrinks back, My soul has no pleasure in him.' "* Confidence and endurance of faith shall be rewarded. God actually expects this from us as believers. So I encourage each of you who are facing a challenging mountain in your life to stand firm in your faith, not to shrink back, knowing there is a great reward if you don't throw away your trust and confidence in the Lord. Remember, "If you have the faith of a mustard seed, you can say to any mountain, 'Be cast into the sea,' and nothing shall be impossible for you."

Day 14   **2 Corinthians 5:7**

"For we walk by faith, not by sight."

Each morning around 6:30 a.m., the nurse came in to draw two to five tubes of blood for testing. Each day, mid-morning, the results of these tests were written on a sheet of paper that was taped on the wall of my hospital room. Each day I expected my results to miraculously return to normal, but they never did, not while in the hospital. But I did not get discouraged. I repeatedly told myself, "I am not going to focus on what I can see, but on what I cannot see. I am going to believe in a miracle and not be disappointed in these posted results. I am going to *walk by faith, not by sight.*" I knew the blood numbers would change and be restored—to the glory of God!

Day 15   **Proverbs 3:5-8**

"Trust in the Lord with all your heart, and do not lean on your own understanding. In all your ways acknowledge Him, and He will make your paths straight. Do not be wise in your own eyes; fear the Lord and turn away from evil. It will be healing to your body and marrow to your bones."

I often catch myself not following the first part of this passage, as I am quite the "thinker." All too often I try to "figure things out" on my own. The Bible tells me not to do this however, but rather to trust in the Lord with ALL my *heart.* As a result of doing this, the Lord will direct my paths; meaning every area of my life! Psalm 37:4 says, *"Delight yourself in the Lord, and He will give you the desires of your heart!"* Think about that one for a moment! Pretty awesome, huh?

I especially like the latter half of the above passage about "not being wise in your own eyes and turning from evil, for it will be healing to the body and MARROW to the bones." From that, I think of the verse in Proverbs 26:12 which says, *"Do you see a man wise in his own eyes? There is more hope for a fool, than for him."* We can see from these verses that God rewards humility... *"God is opposed to the proud, but gives grace to the humble... therefore, humble yourselves under the mighty hand of God, and He <u>will</u> exalt you."* (1 Peter 5:5-6)

Day 16   **Ephesians 5:22-33**

"Wives, be subject to your own husbands, as to the Lord. For the husband is the head of the wife, as Christ also is the head of the church, He Himself being the Savior of the body. But as the church is subject to Christ, so also the wives ought to be to their husbands in everything."

"Husbands, love your wives, just as Christ also loved the Church and gave Himself up for her, that He might sanctify her, having cleansed her by the washing of water with the Word, that He might present to Himself the church in all her glory, having no spot or wrinkle or any such thing; but that she should be holy and blameless. So husbands ought also to love their own

wives as their own bodies. He who loves his own wife loves himself; for no one ever hated his own flesh, but nourishes and cherishes it, just as Christ also does the church, because we are members of His body."

"For this reason a man shall leave his father and mother, and shall be joined to his wife; and the two shall become one flesh. This mystery is great; but I am speaking with reference to Christ and the church. Nevertheless, each individual among you also is to love his own wife even as himself, and the wife must see to it that she respects her husband."

As a husband, I am to honor my wife; just as Christ honors the church. Christ gave Himself up for her—the church—that He might 'sanctify' her, that He might 'present her to Himself in all her glory;' spotless, blameless and holy! We husbands are to do the same with our wives! It does not end there. Husbands are to love their wives as they would love their own bodies; nourishing and cherishing them, just as Christ does the church. Through marriage, the husband and wife become ONE FLESH in the sight of God. Just thinking about that is awesome in itself. Paul describes it as a "great mystery." Wives too, are to honor and respect their husbands. Being "subject to" their husbands does not mean that the husband has the right to be "lording over" their wives. We can see from this passage that both are to love and cherish each other.

Day 17   **1 Chronicles 4:10**

"Now Jabez called on the God of Israel, saying, 'Oh that You would bless me indeed, and enlarge my border, and that Thy hand might be with me, and that You would keep me from harm, that it may not pain me!'"

This prayer was incorporated into a book entitled, "The Prayer of Jabez." It was one of the best sellers in the country as of mid-year 2001, with some eight million copies sold! The prayer begins with Jabez asking God to "bless me indeed." What Jabez is asking God to do is to provide the kind of blessing that only God, in His infinite wisdom, can provide. Unfortunately, this is NOT how many of us approach God in prayer. We ask for things we feel we need or want, but does not God truly know best? Jabez is simply allowing God to provide the best possible blessing! The word "indeed" was added to emphasize the urgency and is almost a demand on God for a prompt response.

Jabez also requested that God "enlarge" or expand his "border." He simply wanted the Lord to open more doors of opportunity in order that he could do bigger and better things for the Lord. The Bible tells us if we are "faithful with little, much will be given," but here we see Jabez already asking the Lord to give him "more."

It was also requested by Jabez that God's hand be upon him. In other words, Jabez was requesting God's favor in all his endeavors; that God would guide him through every twist and turn he encountered. Jabez then asked for God's protection; that God keep him from harm. He prayed that God would keep him out of danger's way, far from the wiles of the devil, in order that it might not pain him. "Pain him," meaning that Jabez might not fall into temptation and sin, resulting in guilt and shame, having let God down. This is a complete and powerful prayer, at the end of which, "God granted him what he requested!"

Day 18   1 Peter 2:24

"And He Himself bore our sins in His body on the cross, so that we might die to sin and live to righteousness; for by His wounds [stripes] you were healed." [Emphasis added]

The power in this verse is that our healing is a finished work! Praise God! Jesus paid the price for our sins and our diseases on the cross! In Isaiah 53:5 it says, *"He was pierced through for our transgressions [sin]; He was crushed for our iniquities; the chastening for our well-being fell upon Him, and by His wounds we are healed!"* Again, we see that we ARE healed by what has already occurred nearly 2000 years ago! That is the promise from God's Word. And if we endure, by remaining faithful to what was promised, we will receive what was promised! (Hebrews 6:12)

Day 19   1 Peter 3:7

"You husbands in the same way, live with your wives in an understanding way, as with someone weaker, since she is a woman; and show her honor as a fellow heir of the grace of life, so that your prayers may not be hindered."

This verse came to me and reinforced my responsibility of honoring my wife. If I did not, there was a consequence; my prayers could be hindered! That's a big WOW! Note that this verse is not directed to the wife, but to the husband. The last thing I (or any praying husband) would want is to have their prayers hindered. Husbands can clearly see that we are called to live with our wives in "an understanding way... and to show them honor." If we fail to do so, our prayers may be hindered.

Day 20   John 10:10

"The thief comes only to steal and kill and destroy; I came that they may life, and have it abundantly."

The thief is clearly Satan, the liar, the deceiver, the accuser of the brethren, the god of this world, the prince and power of the air, the destroyer, the one who walks about as a roaring lion seeking someone to devour. But Jesus says that He came to destroy the works of the devil—to give life and to give it abundantly! That is the good news that is available to all who believe! Jesus clearly pointed out that we will have trouble and tribulation in the world, but that we ought to take courage because *"He has overcome the world."* (John 16:33) Again, my strength comes from the Word which says, *"Resist the devil and he will flee from you."* (James 4:7) We are called to *"be strong in the Lord* and in the strength of His might. Put on the full armor of God, that you may be able to stand firm against the schemes of the devil." (Ephesians 6:10-11) The victory is ours through Christ who loves us!

Day 21   **Isaiah 40:31**

"Yet those who wait for the Lord will gain new strength; they will mount up with wings like eagles; they will run and not get tired; they will walk and not become weary."

Patience and trust are key to "waiting on the Lord." I will admit, it is not always easy to do, but the reward is the receiving of God's promise. He is faithful to always keep His Word. His timing is perfect—better than anything we could ever "plan out" on our own! This passage has special meaning to me due to my experience with an anemic condition. I was in need of physical strength since any attempt to run (or walk at length) would cause me to tire and grow weary. But God promised that if I trusted Him and waited on Him, that I would gain new strength; I would run and NOT get tired, I'd walk and NOT become weary!

Day 22   **Philippians 2:3-4**

"Do nothing from selfishness or empty conceit, but with humility of mind regard one another as more important than yourselves; do not merely look out for your own personal interests, but also for the interests of others."

Regarding others as more important than ourselves is virtually impossible to do on our own. In other words, without the love of God flowing though us, it would be very unlikely that we could truly feel this way toward anyone else. We may want to live this way and act this way toward others, but only when we allow God's perfect love to flow through us can we "die to self" and truly put the interests of others ahead of ours. I work on this all the time, and most of the time, find it difficult to successfully accomplish. I think of the passage that

301

says, "The spirit is willing, but the flesh is weak." While in the hospital, God pointed out that I was not any better than anyone else. Granted, I have been blessed so much, but that does not mean that I am better than a person who has not received the same measurable blessings. God loves us the same. He is no respecter of persons.

Day 23   **Ephesians 3:20-21**

"Now to him who is able to do far more abundantly beyond all that we ask or think, according to the power that works within us (to Him be the glory)."

This passage is awesome. God is able to do things that exceed abundance; beyond all that we ask or think! Ponder that for a moment. This reminds me of the first part of the Prayer of Jabez where he asks God to "bless me indeed." This is just an example of how we enable God to deliver a blessing beyond all we ask or think.

Note the last part of this passage: According to the power that works WITHIN US. This power is already there! In chapter 1 of the book of Ephesians, Paul elaborates on this for us: *"... who has blessed us with every spiritual blessing in the heavenly places in Christ, just as He chose us in Him before the foundation of the world... according to the kind intention of His will... according to the riches of His grace, which He lavished upon us in all wisdom and insight... having also believed, you were sealed in Him with the Holy Spirit of promise, who is given as a pledge of our inheritance... and what is the surpassing greatness of His POWER toward us who believe. These are in accordance with the working of the strength of His might which He brought about in Christ, when He raised Him from the dead, and seated Him at His right hand in the heavenly places."* (Ephesians 1:3-20) This power is already there for us who believe! It works within us through faith and according to God's kind intention of His will.

Day 24   **Psalm 6:2**

"Be gracious to me, O Lord, for I am pining away; heal me, O Lord, for my bones are dismayed."

This verse seemed fitting as it deals with the bones. In it I cried for the Lord's gracious mercy to rescue me with healing.

Day 25   **Jeremiah 30:17**

"For I will restore you to health and I will heal you of your wounds, declares the Lord...."

Short, sweet and direct. I received this verse as a promise from the Lord. As I read this verse, I am reminded of the 1 Peter 5:10 verse which states that God will "restore" me after I have suffered a little while.

Day 26   **Psalm 103:2-5**

"Bless the Lord, O my soul, and forget none of His benefits, who pardons all your iniquities, who heals all your diseases; who redeems your life from the pit, who crowns you with loving kindness and compassion; who satisfies your years with good things, so that your youth is renewed like the eagle."

Of the many wonderful things God does out of His unconditional loving kindness and compassion, He heals ALL of our diseases. He satisfies our lives with good things so that we gain strength—even to the degree that we feel younger! I actually chuckle when I read this verse, thinking of how many people run to and fro, paying dollars upon dollars to find products, programs, etc., to make them look younger. But here we see a simple solution to the proverbial fountain of youth: "Bless the Lord from your heart and soul, and don't forget any of His benefits!"

Day 27   **1 John 5:4**

"For whatever is born of God overcomes the world; and this is the victory that overcomes the world—our faith."

I love this verse. It speaks of the power within us, given by God and through our faith, to overcome anything that Satan can dish out! As one who has accepted Christ as Savior and Lord (born again), I already have the victory through faith! So do you if you have invited Christ into your life. Nowhere in the Bible does it say we will have an easy life if we accept Christ into our hearts. We will have challenges, trials and tribulations like anyone else (if not more), but we have Jesus, *"our high priest who sympathizes with our weaknesses, and promises us mercy and grace to help us in our time of need."* (Hebrews 4:15-16)

Day 28   **John 11:4**

"…this sickness is not to end in death, but for the glory of God, so that the Son of God may be glorified by it."

This passage was given to me as a Word from the Lord by a pastor from Nigeria who visited me on the last day I was in the hospital. This verse was initially spoken by Jesus when He was told to come and heal Lazarus after hearing he was sick. As the account goes, Jesus did not heal Lazarus at that moment. In fact, Jesus stayed on two more days before leaving to go to Lazarus. By the time He arrived, Lazarus had died and been in the tomb four days. Just before Jesus raised Lazarus from the dead, He said, "Did I not say to you, if you believe, you will see the glory of God?" I too chose to believe, to look beyond the circumstances, just like Jesus looked beyond the circumstances of Lazarus' physical death. A miracle resulted!

Acknowledgments

We all experience challenges in life. It is during those difficult times that we need others the most. I wish to sincerely thank every person that prayed and showed concern for me.

To my wife Susy: You not only supported me emotionally and through prayer, but managed the office, our household and our four children. On top of this, you went on listing appointments in my absence in order to keep the business rolling. Simply amazing! Thank you from the bottom of my heart.

To my children: Although you were all quite young at the time, I commend you for being strong in your faith, knowing and believing that your dad would come home again; live and not die!

To my parents, my brothers, my sister and my entire family: I thank you for being there for me and believing that this was just another challenge for Jeff; one that he'd overcome. I can assure you, I would never want to have faced it without Jesus. This I know; I *can* do all things through Christ who strengthens me!

To my doctors and my nurses: I really wish to thank you for being there on a daily basis for me. Taking care of sick people really takes a special talent and a special heart. You must be incredibly patient, very understanding and empathetic. You must be a "giver" – and each of you was more than that. In many ways, I may not have been your "normal" patient. I chose to be joyful in order to combat sorrow, and chose faith to overcome fear. At the end of the day, victory was granted to me by the Lord. I am glad you had the opportunity to see it firsthand!

To my special friends who played a direct role in my journey – Pastor Dave Housholder, Shirley, Pastor Holmes, Paul, Pastor Moe, Regan, Doug Stanton, Monique, Elaine Bonn and Marjorie Cole: I simply have to say WOW! Thank you so much for hearing the Word of the

Lord as He spoke to you and used you to play a part in my miracle! I pray blessings over you always!

To all of you who prayed for me and took time to encourage me in my darkest hour: Your calls, letters, cards and emails meant more than you can imagine. They inspired me to *"fight the good fight!"* The power of a word of encouragement is profound! Never forget that! You have seen it with your own eyes! Yes, God said He would show Himself strong through me before the eyes of many people, but He used each of you to bring it to pass. Never stop encouraging others. You now know the power that your words have!

Below are just a few of the wonderful words of encouragement that I received from so many of you during my time of need. Thank you so much!

I cannot believe you are doing full time ministry; you are you know! God is behind all this. Touching so many lives is what's giving you the strength needed to inspire so many.

You have a team out there that waits to hear. God is the head of the team, you my friend, are the outstanding coach!! Many on the team you are ministering to will come to know the very true meaning of faith by the example you are setting. What powerful messages.

Won't it be great when God heals you to just get out and minister in person to many? God sure is using you now in a way that could only be done due to your circumstances. He always has a plan.

By the way, the first prayers said Wednesday evening at church were for Jeff Scislow!! PLEASE keep sending your God given messages and also God led decisions regarding treatment.

Diane F.

Words can't describe how I am feeling right at this moment. I've been reading your email for over an hour now and crying the entire time.

God's timing is such an amazing one. Your experience is simply so amazing. I am so proud of your strength, attitude, and devotion to the Lord. You are such an inspiration to all you know and touch. I do want you to know that because of your awesome letter, many will become believers.

My team and I will be praying for you and your family on your road to recovery and miracles. I just want you to know that personally, this letter has hit me directly between the eyes. As I was sitting in my car at the airport last night, I had a personal and emotional moment that really took me by surprise. I felt the need to rededicate myself to the Lord in such a way that I never had before. This morning, feeling much better, but not entirely there, I opened my email to find 70 emails waiting to be read. I scanned the list to pick the ones I want to read first. I was drawn to read yours first. WOW!! You said things *to me* that I needed to hear so very much.

Thank you so much for sharing this experience with so many. I look forward to getting regular updates from you on your progress and miracles.

Bonnie Mullinax

I am so very happy to hear that you are feeling much better, and I am sure that the good Lord has plans for you, just as He does for all of His children. I pray that you will recover fully, and take the path that has been set for you.

God bless you and I am praying for you and your family. Give my love to Susy.

Bill K.

I just sat down and read your email Update. Your experiences are very moving and motivating. I want to reiterate that our limited experience with you on a business level is one of the top five "life experiences" that I have seen the Lord deliver to me. I'm eagerly awaiting number six (the news of your healing).

Let us know if there is anything we can do. Susy is doing a great job. She has risen to the challenges quite nicely.

Hope this finds you in great spirits and improving excellent health. My offer for bone marrow will always be open for you (even Jesus used mud to mix with His saliva to let the blind man see). God bless.

John Hanson

I've passed on your e-mails to my believer network (which includes my men's small group), and the response I've received has simply been amazing!! People really appreciated that I shared with them all that you've been experiencing. Your message of faith, hope and perseverance is having a deep impact on people.

I know Dan Johnson gave a copy of your story to a non-believer in his office, and he read the whole thing (all 21 pages) and was moved by it. Seeds planted. You are a model for us all. Your attitude and faith will allow God to heal you.

If you haven't already read it, please read "Secrets of the Vine", Bruce Wilkinson's follow-up to "The Prayer of Jabez" – it is very relevant to everything you are going through, and the message God is sending you.

You and your family will continue to be in my prayers.

Rick Millington

I just got your email update! I have been at The Cove in Asheville, NC, which is Billy Graham's Training Center. What a lovely place God has built there for a retreat.

Praise God for the incredible joy He has placed in you, for the healing, for waiting on His timing, for believing in Him through the trials... for the strength He has given you and the people He has placed in your path.

I had NO IDEA any of this was happening to you. Wow!

I'm so excited and encouraged to hear of your progress, but more importantly, your attitude! You are such an example, Jeff... thank you!

You are bringing such glory and honor to God because of the way you keep giving everything back to Him and allowing Him to work out His plan in you.

I will continue to pray for you and your family, Jeff!

Sandie

Tim and I were extremely inspired as we read through your entire e-mail! You have an incredible life. Have peace in knowing that your message has touched our hearts... I continue today to pray for guidance and to live my life as Jesus would (which is not always easy as I am sure you know).

Although I am a "novice", I will pray for your recovery. You must have the entire world praying for you by now! May God keep your spirits up and may that long awaited healing arrive shortly. You are truly an inspiration!!!!!!!

Jackie L.

I know you will get lots and lots of emails and I want you to know how much I appreciate knowing about your life at this time. You do know that I am one of many, many people that love you and respect you and what you have done for many of us.

I will pray for your needs you requested and I will also ask others to do the same. I also will pray that somehow I can find some ways to help you and your family in the future.

Nancy Argo

Just checking in to see how you are doing. I continue to keep you and your family in my prayers; that you will continue to stand firm on the healing promises of the Lord and in the victory Christ has already won for you. I pray that He will continue to carry you, comfort you, and give you strength to endure. He never forsakes those who seek Him!!!

Of course you are doing fine! The Holy Spirit, the very same power that raised Christ Jesus from the dead is within you and gives life! The prayer below was adapted from a book by William Bachus entitled, "The Healing Power of a Christian Mind."

"Lord, because we are members, by faith, of you Jesus Christ, we are heirs to the promises made in Your Word, which You said cannot be broken. We now, by faith, hear You saying to us personally, 'I am the Lord that healeth thee.' Help us to stand strong against thoughts that suggest Your Word is not true or does not apply to our situation. We firmly reject those thoughts and others like them, because they make You small instead of the great God that You are. Rather, we join with all the saints and exalt You and… we insist that You are on the side of our healing because Your unbreakable Word says so. Amen!"

Mary N.

I just received your May 2001 emails from Betty Hegner. Of course, I was stunned to find out what has been going on over these last several months. Your attitude is incredible, but Jeff, it does not surprise me... you have always been someone who believed strongly in whatever you decided to do. As those of us who know you well, and many who don't can see, when Jeff believes, Jeff does. It's your history... it's your record... you have always succeeded where others have failed. It's my belief that if anyone can do this, it will be you *again*! I will pray for you too and hope that it helps, if even just a little bit!

If I was there I'd give you a big hug right now, but I'm here, so I can't. Anyway pretend that I did because that hug is my attachment to you as a good friend, great person, great listener and sharer, and an all round great guy who is an inspiration to many! I'm on your team rooting and you're the coach ... go for another home run Jeff.

Allyson Hoffman

I am Char MacCallum's mother and I just want to encourage you to keep speaking the truth of God's Word. Jesus is the Life living through you and I love your faith. I do not believe in drugs and believe that Jesus is the Healer. I am waiting for your email that says, "I am healed!"

JoAnn Estebo

I read your story and it is amazing. It truly is an incredible journey for you. I did receive a great deal of positive messages for my own growth. Thanks also for your genuine concerns and love for your friends. You are in a hell of a fight and I, who does not pray very often, am praying for you, Susy and the kids.

Chip Neumann

Thanks for sharing what you have been going through the last couple of months. I was unaware that you had been so ill. I will pray that God will finish healing you and also continue to show you signs that He is listening and is there for you and your family. Your message was very inspirational and I feel fortunate that you shared this with me.

Beryl K.

I received your email & just finished reading the whole thing. I admire your strength & faith. I will pray for you & your family.

Last November I was diagnosed with Breast Cancer, but God has healed me of it! It is truly through His healing touch & all the prayers, that I am alive & well today.

Many people cannot understand how I went through everything I did & not "crash". I simply tell them that God held me up & I had faith that whatever God saw for me, I was ready on earth or heaven to follow His will.

Today however, I feel that I have not been listening & studying God's Word enough. He is speaking to me, but I either do not understand or Satan is trying to block the words.

Many of the scriptures that you shared; I am going to read and re-read.

Jeff, through your turmoil, you have no doubt helped many individuals and even though my faith is very strong, you have also helped me. God bless you.

Take care Jeff. I look forward to another update.

Linda McLean

Blessings to you, brother!

God is indeed blessing you, and Susy, and your entire family. Know that His love surrounds you and protects you. Know that the prayers of the righteous are flowing towards heaven on your behalf. Praise Him for the mighty works He is doing in your life! Thank you for sharing them with the world!

Pastor Janine Olson

Thank you so much for the update. I DID make it through the "book" email and I must tell you—I read without stopping! I am incredibly moved by your conviction and am convinced that the Lord has His hand on your shoulder.

I have wanted to pick up the phone on numerous occasions to call you just to say how often I think about you and your family. You are in my prayers and I appreciate your sharing God's Word as well as his Spirit.

It is truly inspirational to me and I am sure that others will be equally motivated by your ability to speak the Lord's word—and more importantly "His Love".

God bless you in your healing process.

Lisa

I will keep you in my prayers. You are such an inspiration. I have always respected the approach you take towards clients and other real estate agents.

Sandy J.

As you continue to grow in your strength and courage, we all are blessed to share this unfolding miracle. God bless you! I'll continue to pray for you and your family!

Amy Stoehr

I realize that God has His own plan and even though we may not like it, there is some good out of what He is doing with you.

The clarity you have, the ability to communicate and your refusal to be a victim, is a lesson for all of us. It is something I will learn from to make me a better father, husband, teacher and all-round better person.

I have added you to my prayer list and pray every day for a cure for you.

Although I have not been tested as a possible bone marrow donor, when back in Victoria next week I will commit to getting it done to possibly help you or help others.

You are an inspiration and I have huge respect for you,

Ron Kubek

You have me praying "differently" for you. I usually do not pray for physical healing. I always pray that a person would experience that "deep awareness of God's presence and power" which gives a huge release (calmness). You have expressed this in a wonderful way! It is a matter of praise! So I AM praying for continued healing for you, also that in this, your life would be a powerful witness and 'People of Faith' would be empowered and unsaved may come to Christ! PTL!

Sam

Quite a trial you are going through! Your strength, determination and faith are truly inspiring! I am with you! Keep me posted of your progress and I look forward to shaking your hand at the next RE/MAX Convention!

Kim Lund

All of our prayers are with you. "Ask and you shall receive"!

Bless you for asking and acknowledging that God is the One directing your life. My pastor reminded me recently that Salvation is not going to remove us from our tests, but it actually takes us through the fire so that we may turn them into Testimony.

So while going through the toughest moments of your trials, keep faith and allow God to take you through the burning fire as He did with Shadrack, Meshack and Abendigo; and allow Him to deliver you without even the smell of smoke!

Melanie B.

Dear Jeff,

I am sorry to hear about your health problems and I will pray for your recovery. I also wanted you to know that I am registered as a bone marrow donor. I have been on the registry for about 9 years and have been called twice as a possible match, most recently this past fall. Both times I gave more samples for further blood typing, but I was not needed to donate the marrow. I hope more people will choose to register as a potential donor. The more people in the registry, the more likely a match will be found for you. I am praying for you for a full recovery.

Helen Gunther

I read your e-mail regarding your health with disbelief.

I had not heard that you were ill and certainly did not know the severity of it. A person never knows how they will cope with such medical emergencies. You seem to be dealing with this as you have done with your real estate career—with nothing but your 100%+.

You have been in my prayers and in the prayers of everyone in my prayer group. With your strong faith in Jesus as your Savior and your Healer and your positive attitude, you will come out of this a stronger person.

If there is anything I can help you or Susy with do not hesitate to call. Keep us updated with your progress. I am grateful you let us know the situation. Best wishes for a speedy recovery.

Jo Ann Coplin

Jeff,

I was saddened to hear about your health. I know that attitude is a choice and you are a poster child for a positive mental attitude. GOD is with you and will see you through this. It is interesting how GOD uses us. He has a mission for you and it will unfold before you. I will be praying for you and wish you well.

Dennis Toomey

The testimony of the grace, mercy and love of God manifested during this time in your life is powerful. What a story you will have to tell! We praise God for your life and the future results of your witness. Blessings and as always, love to Susy and the children.

Bill & Liz Corwin

First and foremost, thank you! Thank God!

Praise to our Lord! You and I know the message of the joy and forgiveness that our Lord Jesus Christ has given us. I agree, it needs to be shared with others. People who do not know Him can have that same awesome happiness in their lives (if we tell them)!

Praise God! He so loves each and every one of us. Isn't it amazing?

I thought when my daughter was born a year and a half ago, "This is TRUE love, I have never felt love like this!" But now I know what TRUE love really is! He loves me so much, He sent me my daughter! She was the beginning of joy in my life! She brought me to Him to see how much I am loved!

Since reading your letters, you have simply inspired me to let others feel, and know of His love and forgiveness. And you have made it so simple!

Your testimony conveys this message in such a special way. Sometimes we hear Him, but we just don't listen. Thank you for listening to Him! Praise God!

Jessica Tietz

I have read and re-read both your extensive epistles about your life status, both physically and spiritually. I want you to know that I continue to pray for your complete recovery and for your achieving a successful mission of spreading the Word of God. I also want you to remember that God sends many messengers to us in the course of our lives, and we need a spiritual set of eyes and ears to receive the message. I am quite impressed with the number of messages you are receiving, and I am praying that they continue.

Mike

Jeff,

Do what you think is right and what you are most comfortable with. I know from my experience with an illness that you will get so many different opinions and sometimes you feel like you are playing Russian roulette with your life and that is very difficult. The choices I made during my illness were not exactly what my doctors had wanted, but what I thought was right for me. Trust your instincts and go with them. My prayers are with you and your family.

Jen

Are you seeing any signs of healing? We just wondered how you are doing. I bet it's nice to be home. I am still faithful that you will persevere.

When I talk about it, people look at me like I'm nuts. If you REALLY have no bone marrow, it sounds like you aren't supposed to be alive. I know God is working a wonder in you, and there is a reason we are witnesses to it, but I don't get it yet.

We are still praying in faith for your healing and restoration. If you guys need any help; meals, someone to watch your kids, anything... we would be honored to help. We love you too!

Deb Cliff

This is a wonderful adventure. I don't know you that well, but you always treated me fairly and honestly. Your letter opened my eyes a great deal. I loved reading it.

God bless you and your family and I will pray for both.

Mike Kangas

Your e-mail has really touched me for so many reasons. I've been really going through some trials lately too, and I know the giddy joy of seeing God work through tough trials. Mike continues to struggle with his health, as well as his walk with the Lord. He is, as I write this, reading your e-mail, and I know God will use that to bless him.

I have seen God at work, and my faith is being strengthened, refined, and made more pure. Only in weakness, can God make us strong.

I pledge to keep you and your family in my prayers. Please, please keep me posted as best you can on how you are doing. And, if I can donate blood or marrow for you, well, it would be an incredibly humbling privilege for me.

Cheryl

Diane and I paused for nearly an hour to read your "manuscript" email of a miracle in process. Thank you for your faith and for your courage. Please include us as you keep friends and family informed. We will pray for a miracle, delivered!

Dave and Diane

WOW!! Jeff -- what a note!! You inspired and motivated me as a Realtor and now, again—as a Christian. Bud and I were both "born again" in 1997 and were baptized in Lake Jordan here in North Carolina—it is wonderful the way God works.

Since the first note from Howard Brinton's team, we have been praying for you and your family. I will share this "note" with our ministers and our Bible study groups. Continue to keep us posted. If there is anything you need—just ask!! We're here for you!!

Beth McKinney

Tom from my men's group has been forwarding your e-mails to me. Jan and I and the kids have been praying for you. Our God is an awesome God!!!

Of course you are doing fine!!!!! God is in your heart!!!!! Even when you are not doing fine you truly are!!!!!   \o/   (this is the Praise the Lord e-mail sign).

God Bless & Keep the faith!

Michael Z.

Thanks for the email updates.

Thanks for including so much Scripture. Faith comes by hearing and hearing and hearing and hearing... so thanks for helping Janee & I grow in faith. We will continue to pray for you. I thank God for you and the incredible testimony He is building through your temporary circumstances. Thanks so much for providing a good example.

May the presence of God be especially real to you today and may you be blessed with the same blessing you've sown into others lives.

Steve & Janee' Wells

Hi Jeff,

We're praying that God will continue to comfort you and your family and that the Gentle Healer will heal you and give you hope and peace that passes all understanding. May the Lord give strength to your family and may the Holy Spirit place a fresh anointing on you so that those you encounter may know the reason for your hope.

Mike and Julie

I join you and your family in prayer for you in the name of Jesus, that you are cured of this disease. According to God's Word in Matthew 18:18-20, I join my faith with yours that you are healthy from the top of your head to the soles of your feet, and I praise God for his Word and his Healing of your body. Mark 5:34 Jesus said "thy faith hath made thee whole; go in peace, and be whole of thy plague."

Mark 16:15-18 is another Scripture that says you shall recover. Proverbs 12:18 says we need to "say" that we are healthy. I'm sure you are familiar with all these Scriptures, but my family and I read and say the Word just as you would take medicine. May God's blessings be upon you!

Carole M.

Jeff,

Thank you for sharing your testimony.

I have and will pray for your continued healing and that you'll be open to whatever the Lord has in His plan for you and your family. I am encouraged and strengthened by your story and most importantly how you are reacting to the adversities. Please keep me on your list to stay updated on your journey. Thank you and God Bless You.

Pat Zaby, CCIM, CRB, CRS

Jeff,

I can't wait to see what kind of ministry God is going to put you into!! All of us are just waiting for the miracle that has started to be complete!

Kristin Tonak

Dear Jeff,

I received your email! What an email that was!

You inspire me and I'm glad that you're getting better. You are in my thoughts & prayers every day & night!   If there is anything that I can do for you please let me know... just keep getting better and keep fighting!!

Susan

Hi Jeff,

I was shocked and saddened when I read your email, but most of all I admired your tremendous courage and outlook in life.

It sure sounds like you been through a very difficult period of time, but with your courage, determination and faith, I am sure you will be able to overcome this terrible illness.

I expect to hear some very good news about your health in the near future.

Lulu Sorbara

Jeff,

This is an awesome testimony! It helps us see life differently and an encouragement for us to get closer to the Almighty God. Praise the Lord that you feel better and we will keep praying for you & your family.

Elita Bald

Dear Jeff,

Thank you for blessing us by sharing your gifts from God!!! Gary & Nikki, Brittany and Ashley will continue to pray each and every night at bedtime for His grace to help you cross that goal line!!!!!

Gary & Nikki

Jeff,

Thanks for the updates. You are in my thoughts and prayers a lot. The word of God is pure truth!!!!

Kim Erickson

On Easter, Dan and I were going to see his family in St. Paul and as we were driving up 35-E, I had this overwhelming "feeling" to see and pray with you. My brother in Christ, our God is SO awesome and faithful. Your email has encouraged me and I praise Him for your obedience.

My continued prayers.

Sharon D.

Jeff,

Thanks for the update! God's timing is never late when we follow His rules. "Our rules" and our impatience cause us to think that He is late or maybe never coming. But when we look back on one of His miracles, we see the perfect timing. God IS awesome!

Geoff Barnabo

Dear Jeff,

First I want to say how moved I am by your letter. I am amazed by your faith and your strength with all you are going through. You are a strong believer and I know you will get through this. Please keep me informed as I pray for you and your family.

Rebecca

Jeff I need to share with you how much your email/letter touched both John and I. We re-read it together several times and feel extremely humbled to the power and might of our Lord. And yes, you are absolutely right in saying sending that letter out is indeed a form of ministry. I have been able to think of little else.

How in the world does Susy manage with the kids, work and keeping up at home? She gets a huge gold star! Happy Mother's Day to her! Let's keep praying & keep the faith!

Sandi

Jeff,

You have been in my thoughts, and my prayers are with you.

It encourages me to see you hold so strongly to your faith in God. As you quoted yourself, "If you abide in Me, and My Words abide in you, ask whatever you wish and it shall be done for you." (John 15:7).

God's blessing is on you!

Mark Allen

Jeff,

Thanks so much for your writing—I'm glad I'm on your list. You are an inspiration to me in so many ways.

Our family has run into several stumbling blocks in the past couple of weeks. None so serious, of course, but your words and experience really cause me to examine what's going on in my life and to re-examine my relationship with our Father.

Thank You!

Jeff Jones

Hi Jeff,

I'm so glad to see you've taken the time to write all this down. Your faith is an inspiration. I truly believe as you do; that the Lord is at work through all of this.

You and Susy and your family will continue to be in our prayers.

Kevin & Tammy Gilmore

Jeff,

I was so glad to hear that you DID get out of the hospital on Friday. You, Susy and your entire family are continuously in my prayers to help keep Satan at bay. Continue to seek God's will for your life and everything else will be taken care of. If you need anything, just ask.

Bob Corcoran, Corcoran Consulting

Dear Jeff and Susy:

My husband, Mark, forwarded your email to me because I, too, am a spirit-filled believer and he suspected I would be interested in reading your testimony.

It is amazing and a wonder to me how God moves and how precise his timing is. I make it a point, because I get so many emails, not to really read through many of them, but to either dismiss them or to just glance through them. Your email was lengthy to say the least, but I hung on to every word. I stand in agreement with you for your miracle; I see how God is moving in the midst of this.

I, along with many others, have believed God for Mark's salvation for at least 20 years. The portion of your letter that dealt with your salvation and how God met you at your place of need, I believe has touched my husband's heart and I will just allow the Holy Spirit to accomplish what needs to be done.

I wish to let you know you are surrounded by a company of like believers, who put their faith and trust in the most high God to do what He says He will do. Thank you for being a witness and a testimony to my husband and to me.

I then read with great interest your latest update. Every word is filled with the wonder of our Mighty God. Jeff, what you described (about going the natural way) and what God spoke into your heart bore great witness with me (for what it's worth). I am so cautious and careful when it comes to healing, because I <u>always</u> want to see the healing manifested. I'm saying that so you know as I stand in faith with you for the manifestation of your healing, I don't take it lightly; <u>I stand in faith with you!</u> I have witnessed so many miraculous touches from God's mighty hand—I learn so much about God from each and every one.

I can plainly see that God is doing a mighty work in your life and in Susy's. I call this the fine dining experience and I'm thrilled that you are taking the time to savor every bite. You will never be the same after this. As I read every word of your update, I was reminded that this is the hour for mighty demonstrations of God's power. He, Himself, has set this appointed time. I take great joy in the knowledge of this and I thank God for allowing me to be a partner with you in this particular mighty demonstration.

Please, do not hesitate to ask me for even the slightest thing and continue to be confident and assured that God has many people, unsaved and saved, cooperating with His Spirit every moment of every day to bring about the manifestation of His healing anointing in your body. Even as I write this, I'm getting the sense that it (His healing anointing) operates every moment at the fullest degree for that given moment in your spirit, your soul and your body to bring it to its perfect completion.

God bless! I hope that our paths will one day cross again in your new path of ministry. I will enjoy meeting the Realtor who became a minister!

Christine

Recommended Resources
Books, Web Sites and Ministries

Below are some of the valuable resources that I encountered on my *Journey to a Miracle*. I have read the books, visited the web sites and highly recommend these individuals, their products and their ministries. All have been blessings to me.

Books

1) *Healing Prayer* – by Reginald Cherry, M.D.

This book discusses God's divine intervention in medicine, faith, and prayer. I really enjoyed reading this book. The author, a medical doctor, is right on when it comes to healing and prayer. I have found his material scripturally accurate and a blessing to me. I especially liked chapter 6: *Six Biblical Foundations for Healing*

1. God Wants Us to be Healed
2. The Price for Our Healing has Already Been Paid
3. Be Persistent in Seeking to be Healed
4. Develop a "Feisty" Attitude
5. Find Your Unique Pathway to Healing
6. God Uses the Natural and Supernatural to Heal

www.DrCherry.org

2) *Live Right 4 Your Type* – by Dr. Peter D'Adamo

An excellent book that explores an individualized prescription for maximizing health, metabolism, and vitality in every stage of your life – based on one's "blood type".

The concept of this book is relatively new, but it has gained in popularity. Have you ever wondered why after eating certain meals you feel more "alert," while other times you feel "tired"?

Why sometimes you don't feel "full" and other times you feel "bloated"? Facts reveal that, based upon a person's blood type, their body will respond in one of three ways to whatever the person eats or drinks. The responses are beneficial, neutral or detrimental. In other words, based on your blood type, there are specific foods you should be eating and others you should be avoiding. Eating foods that do not interact well with your blood type can actually cause numerous health problems. Red meat, for example, should be avoided by those with blood type 'A,' but should be regularly eaten by those with type 'O.'

Additionally, the book explores life style and exercise programs that work best based on individual blood types. An incredible book that goes into great detail on how the human body works, and how it is all tied to our unique blood types!

In 1999, *Eat Right 4 Your Type*, Dr. D'Adamo's earlier book on this topic, was named one of the ten most influential health books ever written. Dr. D'Adamo was subsequently named the most intriguing health author of the year. He is the founder and editor emeritus of The Journal of Naturopathic Medicine.

www.dadamo.com

3) *A More Excellent Way* – by Pastor Henry Wright

A teaching on the spiritual roots of disease, the book provides detailed insight into:

1. Why mankind has disease
2. Spiritual roots of disease
3. Disease prevention
4. Blocks to healing
5. Specific diseases discussed

The author is rapidly being recognized for his understanding of healing and the prevention of disease from a spiritual perspective.

Pastor Henry Wright – Pleasant Valley Church, Inc.
4178 Crest Highway, Thomaston, GA 30286
(800) 453-5775
www.pleasantvalleychurch.net/index2.html

4) *God's Creative Power for Healing* – by Charles Capps

A wonderful 46-page "mini" book which has sold nearly 2.5 million copies! The lives of Christians around the world have been revolutionized by the powerful principles of confessing God's Word found within the pages of this book! You will learn how you can release the ability of God to heal by the words from your own mouth! Faith-filled words will put *you* over the goal line!

Charles Capps Ministries
P.O. Box 69, England, AR 72046
(501) 842-2576
www.charlescapps.com

Web Sites

1) Dr. Lorraine Day: www.drday.com

Dr. Lorraine Day, an internationally acclaimed orthopedic trauma surgeon and bestselling author, was for 15 years on the faculty of the University of California, San Francisco, School of Medicine as Associate Professor and Vice Chairman of the Department of Orthopedics. She was also Chief of Orthopedic Surgery at San Francisco General Hospital and is recognized world-wide as an AIDS expert.

She has been invited to lecture extensively throughout the U.S. and the world and has appeared on numerous radio and television shows including *60 minutes, Nightline, CNN Crossfire, Oprah Winfrey, Larry King Live, The 700 Club, John Ankerberg Show, USA Radio Network, Art Bell Radio Show, Three Angels Broadcasting Network,* and *Trinity Broadcasting Network.*

"You have cancer. You're going to die!" – the doctors told me. "But they were wrong!" says Lorraine Day, M.D. "I refused mutilating surgery, chemotherapy, and radiation, the treatment methods ALL physicians are taught, and got well by using God's natural remedies instead."

Dr. Day was diagnosed with invasive breast cancer but rejected standard therapies because of their destructive side effects which often lead to death. She chose instead to rebuild her immune system using the natural, simple, inexpensive therapies designed by God and outlined in the Bible, so her body could heal itself.

2) Dr. Richard Schulze: www.HerbDoc.com

"Learn how to take responsibility for your own health! The purpose of this web site is to inspire you to take responsibility for your own health and to cure yourself. All diseases are curable, but not all the people!" says Dr. Richard Schulze. *"It is all up to you. It is your choice whether you are going to be curable or not."*

"On this web site you can find hope, inspiration and guidelines how to cure yourself. Remember, real health is not a quick fix. You can read hundreds of testimonials from people who did 'the 'impossible' without help of their doctor, but what they really did was change their life. They survived Cancer, AIDS, Alzheimer's, and they beat Arthritis, Diabetes, Psoriasis, Eczema, PMS, Epilepsy, Multiple Sclerosis, Fibromyalgia..."

"Any healing method that does not incorporate working with deep reasons why someone is sick, will not give long term results. You may

cure one disease, or one part of your body, just to see disease appear on another part. Disease will be moving and transforming," Schulze writes on his site.

Ministries

1) Healing Center International

This is a wonderful place to go to have intelligent, well-trained Christian counselors listen to you, ask lots of questions, and then pray for exactly what you need. There is a genuine desire to get to the root of any issue or problem and to come against it in Jesus' name, expecting the Lord to move and heal (whether physical, emotional, spiritual, financial, whatever).

Healing Center International
1710 Douglas Dr. # 260, Golden Valley, MN 55422
(763) 503-4693
www.healingcenterintl.org/ss/live

2) Life Recovery – Marjorie Cole

Author of "Taking the Devil to Court," Marjorie Cole is an expert on generational curses and praying for deliverance. Her prayer and counseling sessions are helpful in understanding the potential cause of diseases.

Additionally, she maintains a wealth of knowledge with respect to spiritual warfare and clearly understands that *"our battle is against spiritual wickedness in the heavenly realm – not against flesh and blood."* (Ephesians 6:12) Since we wrestle against things we cannot see or fully understand. Marjorie is gifted in helping minister to people from this "spiritual warfare" perspective.

Life Recovery Ministries
7671 Old Central Av. NE, Suite 106; Fridley, MN 55432
(763) 785-4234
www.LifeRecovery.com

Submit Your Story!

Submit your story for the next Journey to a Miracle Book!

I am inviting and encouraging you to submit *your* story! We are collecting inspiring, TRUE stories related to God's miracles that have taken place in the lives of others. If you have such a story, we want to hear from you! The submissions will be compiled and distributed nationwide and worldwide. Our books will celebrate God, His Word and His people—our resilience, strength, laughter and tears—through your stories.

Who Do You Know With A Story?

Word of mouth will make these books a success, so please help us spread the word! If you know anyone who would be interested in contributing, or who has a story to tell, please pass on our contact information. We have all experienced miracles!

www.JourneyToAMiracle.com
editor@JourneyToAMiracle.com

Salvation Prayer

Heavenly Father,

In the name of Jesus, I present myself to You. I know that I am a sinner. I have messed up and done things that I am not proud of—things that are not pleasing to You. I have lived my life for myself. I ask You to forgive me.

I believe that Jesus died on the cross for my sins. I also believe that He rose again from the dead and lives forevermore. Lord Jesus, I need You. I want to turn away from my sins. I ask for Your help. Come into my heart and give me strength to live for You.

Thank you for forgiving my sins, saving me and giving me eternal life. Help me to become the person You want me to be. Thank you.

In Jesus' name I ask... Amen.

BEYOND BELIEF – Journey to a Miracle

Order Form

Book

____ 1 copy at $14.95 + S&H ($5 U.S.A., $8 Canada, $15 International)

____ 10 copies at $149 + S&H*

____ 100 copies at $1,120 + S&H*

____ 1,000 copies at $7,489 + S&H*

CD

____ 1 copy at $8 + S&H ($3 U.S.A., $4 Canada, $5 International)

____ 10 copies at $65 + S&H*

____ 100 copies at $500 + S&H*

Name: _____

Street: _____

City/State: _____ Zip: _____

Email: _____ Phone: _____

Bless a friend or loved one today with a gift of this book or Jeff's powerful Testimony on CD. You may order online, by fax or by mail. Please make checks payable to **Journey To A Miracle**. Please allow 1-2 weeks for delivery. * Bulk orders will be charged actual shipping and handling charges incurred.

Credit Card orders online at: www.JourneyToAMiracle.com

Journey To A Miracle
P.O. Box 240195
Apple Valley, MN 55124
Fax: (952) 953-0530